SOUTHWESTERN INDIANS

Arts & Crafts
Tribes
Ceremonials

SOUTHWESTERN INDIĀNS

ARTS
&
CRAFTS
—
TRIBES
—
CEREMONIALS

by Tom Bahti and Mark Bahti

KC Publications • Las Vegas • Nevada

Southwestern Indians

Edited by Cheri C. Madison
Designed by K. C. DenDooven

Copyright © 1997 by KC Publications, Inc.
3245 E. Patrick Lane, Suite A
Las Vegas, Nevada 89120

Original soft-cover edition authored by Tom Bahti
with revisions since 1982 by Mark Bahti.

1997 Edition, 1st Printing, hard-cover edition.
Contents of this book are drawn from the soft-cover editions, Revised 1997, of:
Southwestern Indian Arts & Crafts
Southwestern Indian Tribes
Southwestern Indian Ceremonials

LIBRARY OF CONGRESS: 97-070258 • ISBN: 0-88714-110-2

Created, Designed, and Published in the U.S.A.
Printed by Doosan Dong-A Co., Ltd., Seoul, Korea
Color Separations by Korea Kwang Yang Sa Co., Ltd.
Paper produced exclusively by Hankuk Paper Mfg. Co., Ltd.

KC Publications: Toll-Free: 1-888-KCBOOKS
Tel: 1-702-433-3415
FAX: 1-702-433-3420

This volume is dedicated to the belief that if we
understand and value the richness of other cultures
we will come to understand that, in the most
important and fundamental ways, we are all the same.

Acknowledgments

There are countless individuals and groups to be thanked for their valued help in providing information, insight, and inspiration to the author, photographer, and publisher. To all those people of good faith—faith in each other and in all of us—thank you. We gratefully acknowledge the use of original paintings from the following galleries and museums: Amerind Foundation, Inc.; James T. Bialac Collection; Elvis Torres Gallery; Simmons Collection; and Oliver Enjady's private collection. Arts and crafts items photographed came from numerous shops, museums, private collections, and individual Indian artisans. The work represents the broad range of items available at reputable Indian arts and crafts shops nationwide.

Contents

Chapter I

SOUTHWESTERN INDIAN ARTS & CRAFTS

The crafts and fine arts of the tribes of the Southwest present a dazzling array of style and variety. This section is designed to help the newcomer distinguish the craft traditions of the many tribes.

Art, way of life, and religion are inseparable parts of the whole for the Southwestern tribes. As the way of life among the tribes has changed, so have their crafts—art has always reflected changes in culture. The two succeeding sections will help the reader not only to better appreciate Indian arts and crafts, but to understand more fully the tribes themselves.

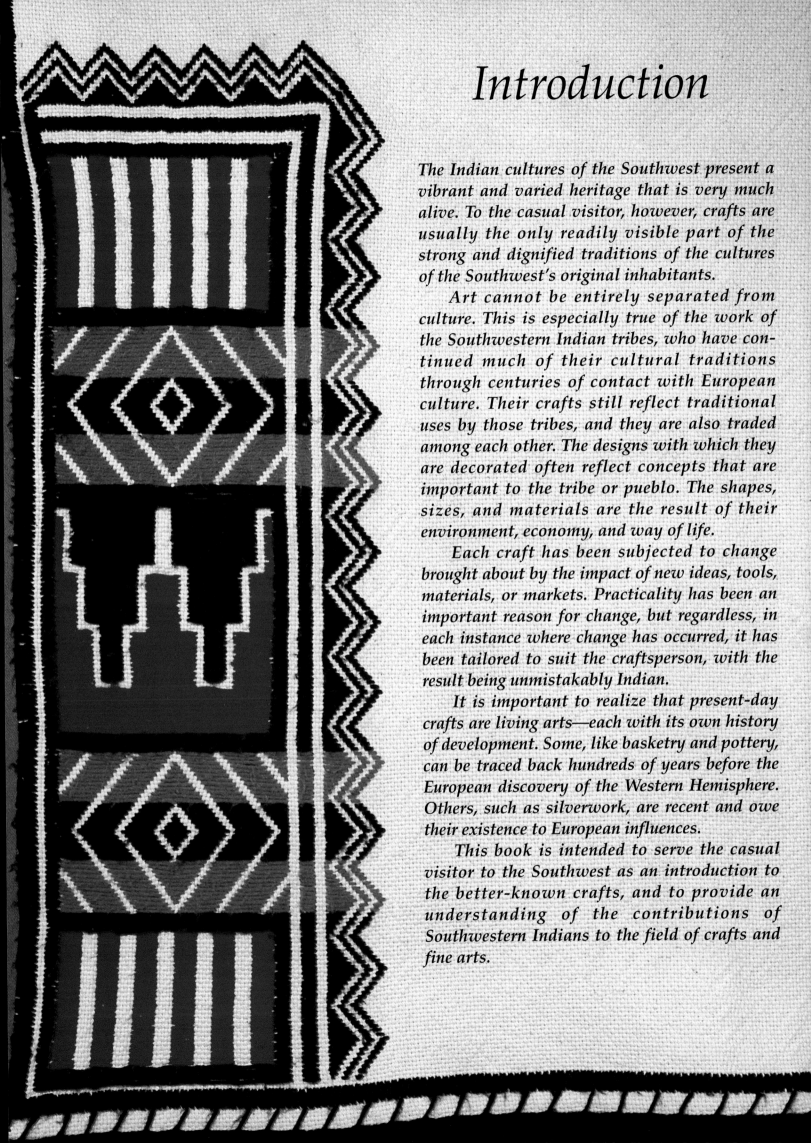

Introduction

The Indian cultures of the Southwest present a vibrant and varied heritage that is very much alive. To the casual visitor, however, crafts are usually the only readily visible part of the strong and dignified traditions of the cultures of the Southwest's original inhabitants.

Art cannot be entirely separated from culture. This is especially true of the work of the Southwestern Indian tribes, who have continued much of their cultural traditions through centuries of contact with European culture. Their crafts still reflect traditional uses by those tribes, and they are also traded among each other. The designs with which they are decorated often reflect concepts that are important to the tribe or pueblo. The shapes, sizes, and materials are the result of their environment, economy, and way of life.

Each craft has been subjected to change brought about by the impact of new ideas, tools, materials, or markets. Practicality has been an important reason for change, but regardless, in each instance where change has occurred, it has been tailored to suit the craftsperson, with the result being unmistakably Indian.

It is important to realize that present-day crafts are living arts—each with its own history of development. Some, like basketry and pottery, can be traced back hundreds of years before the European discovery of the Western Hemisphere. Others, such as silverwork, are recent and owe their existence to European influences.

This book is intended to serve the casual visitor to the Southwest as an introduction to the better-known crafts, and to provide an understanding of the contributions of Southwestern Indians to the field of crafts and fine arts.

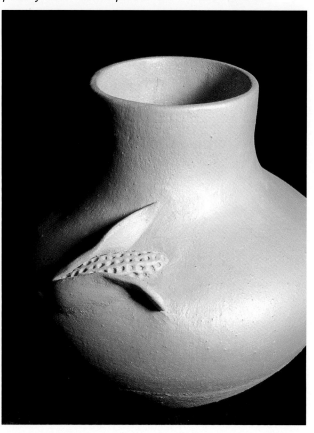

Acoma potters,
long famous for
their water jars,
storage vessels,
and serving bowls,
have also developed
art pottery such as this
plate—giving life to new design
forms which are based upon the old but reflect the individual artist more.

MARK BAHTI

This Hopi Masau'u katsina is an older style—complete with mineral and vegetal paints—that has been revived by younger Hopi artists who also use actual feathers. It is not only the artist and the collectors who affect what is produced. Federal regulations prohibiting the use of most types of bird feathers in items to be sold forced Hopi katsina carvers to make wooden feathers.

Corn is the most important crop of the Pueblo peoples. Its significance is seen even in contemporary pottery such as this piece from Picuris Pueblo.

Though machine-made copies and foreign imitations plague them, Indian artists take pride and satisfaction in continuing to create fine handmade work.

Aesthetics and Economics

"It's nice, but it isn't Indian" is a comment, usually made in reference to contemporary work, which reflects less the background of the work than it does the lack of knowledge of the speaker. Indian cultures are not, nor have they ever been, static or stagnant. They are alive and, as such, are continually growing and changing. "Traditional" does not mean better or more authentic—it refers simply to an earlier style or manner. Similarly, "contemporary" or "modern" is simply newer, not less authentic. The Navajo squash blossom necklace, an innovation of the 1870s, is now considered a typical piece of very traditional Indian jewelry. Many of the new design concepts, such as the setting of the turquoise on the underside of a bracelet or ring, are likely to be regarded in the future as traditional.

Some buyers of Indian art are of the opinion that commercialism is an evil that is ruining Indian art. Their concern whether a piece is "authentic or just made to sell" is one that fails to recognize that all crafts must have an economic basis or they will cease to exist. The craftsperson of any age or culture produces items to use, sell, or trade. When unable to barter labor as a craftsperson, the artisan must seek a livelihood at which a living can be earned. A craft with no market will cease to be created.

Concern whether an item was "made to sell" is often extended to whether it was made for sale to another Indian or to a non-Indian. It implies that if it is made for the non-Indian trade it is somehow less authentic. One would be hard-pressed to find an Indian craftsperson concerned over the cultural identity of the purchaser—the concern is that there *be* a purchaser. The integrity of the work has less to do with the viewer's analysis than the maker's intent.

Even today, comparatively few craftspeople derive most or all of their income from craftwork. Average annual income derived by Indian tribes from their crafts ranges from about 20 percent to less than 1 percent, depending upon the tribe. Economics plays an important role in the survival of a craft, but it would be a mistake to consider the true value of arts and crafts solely in terms of dollars and cents.

Designs used to decorate Indian crafts can sometimes be identified as representations of clouds, rain, lightning, birds, and the like. Rain obviously plays an important role in traditional Southwestern Indian life, but to assign it a simple meaning like "good luck" or "fertility" is to oversimplify. The pattern on a bracelet or in a rug

Hopi life has changed greatly in this century so it is only natural that those changes would be reflected in their artwork. The Hopi clown katsinas, like this Koshare, provide an opportunity for the Hopi to reflect on changes and satirize them.

"Traditional" is a relative term: much of what we think of as traditional Navajo jewelry was new and innovative barely a century ago. Much "modern" jewelry has its roots in the "traditional."

The sculptural form of traditional pottery and the sculptural quality of religious buildings known as kivas were merged in this work by an Acoma pottery artist.

does not "tell a story." The printed materials that purport to translate or interpret Indian designs are largely spurious. Some dealers in Indian art—Indian and non-Indian—will invent a story to go along with a craft item if they think it will encourage the buyer to make a purchase. (The so-called dream catchers are an example.) Poor craftsmanship cannot be improved by the addition of a colorful story—fine craftwork will stand on its own merits.

The Individual in Indian Art

Within the craft traditions of each Indian group there has always been room for individual artistic expression. The artisans were known within their small communities, and the notion of signing a piece was unknown. In the last 20 years, however, people buying Indian art and craftwork have become interested in knowing the identity of the artisan, with the result that, where possible, most works are now signed by the maker.

The emergence of the artist as an individual rather than simply as a member of the community has gone hand in hand with the increasing number and economic importance of Indian art exhibitions and competitions, as well as an emerging group of artists who have learned or furthered their art in an academic setting. The work of many of these artists reflects their personal perspectives and interpretations of their world, transcending craft and tribal boundaries. A few even consider their work to be less Indian art than art by Indian artists. Their blazing of new traditions makes it clear that the future of Indian art will be at least as rich and diverse as its past.

Feathers from the Eagle, most powerful of all birds, are revered by most tribes and used in many ways depending upon their beliefs. Indian painters, such as Oliver Enjady, use the feather to symbolize values, traditions, and the power or holiness of the subject matter. These dancers are the Apache Gaan who are the spirits of the mountains and protectors of the Apache and their homeland.

Styles and traditions that are revived can undergo an explosion of experimentation and innovation. A generation ago most pottery at Jemez Pueblo was limited to acrylic-painted sun-dried souvenirs. Since that time traditional pottery-making skills have revived and pottery artists are using those traditions to express their creativity.

K. C. DEN DOOVEN

Navajo artist Robert Sorrell incorporates designs inside this bracelet. A unique innovation, the technique was pioneered by the late Hopi artist Charles Loloma over 30 years ago.

Although inlay or mosaic work is primarily associated with Zuni Indians, a few Hopi as well as Navajo artists have begun to employ the technique. Spiny oyster shell, once the only source for a red or red-orange inlay material, was replaced by coral from the Mediterranean Sea (and now, the Sea of Japan). In recent years some artists have turned back to spiny oyster shell, as in these two buckles by Alex Beeshligaii. Hammered silver bracelets, an old tradition, have been updated with an ancient hand motif. They are meant to be worn so that the hands are visible atop the wrist.

The work of Indian artists, whether on or off the reservation, draws its strength and creativity from the land that shaped and nurtures their ancient cultures.
William Quotskuyva

New materials, new tools, new markets, and new techniques have helped shape Indian jewelry, but artists such as Alex Beeshligaii continue to draw upon the roots of their culture as a vital part of their vision and inspiration. With television, computers, and the growth of the West, Indian tribes are no longer as isolated as they once were. As the range of experiences of Indian artists expands, so does their range of expression, with some drawing more on ancient visions and others drawing on more modern experiences.

Indian art continues to change as Indian life changes. Artists experiment with new images, new perspectives, new techniques, and new materials. A stone Zuni Mountain Lion fetish was the inspiration for this sandcast glass sculpture by Navajo artist Conrad House.

THE INDIVIDUAL IN INDIAN ART

The importance of corn in the modern Indian diet may have diminished somewhat, but its place in Indian religion has not. Accordingly, even as innovation occurs, the corn motif remains strong. Randy Nahohai

In recent years Navajo folk art, itself a relatively new phenomenon, has become popular and encouraged many Navajo to produce pieces carved of sandstone as well as others of wood, metal, and dried, painted mud. Homer Warren

Sculpture is being used by a new generation to express personal creativity and traditional themes. In this alabaster sculpture by Jemez artist Clifford Fragua, the Pueblo dancer appears to be wearing an actual rain cloud instead of a headdress meant to symbolize rain clouds.

Navajo textile artist Isabelle John illustrates a weaver at work among the source of her wool with the weaver's view visible through the warp threads. Navajo weaving has long been a medium for expression of individual creativity. Trains appeared in Navajo rugs about the same time they began to cross Navajoland. Everything from landscapes and fairs to planes, zoo animals, semi-trucks, and cans of soda have appeared in Navajo weaving. Sometimes the expression of personal artistic vision has been as subtle as an unexplained variance in the pattern of asymmetrical use of color.

Indian pottery, whether for storage of food and water, daily use in cooking and serving, or religious uses, has always been created to be beautiful as well as functional. Collectors have prized it for its beauty alone. This bowl by ceramic artist Hubert Candelario from San Felipe illustrates the transition of Pueblo pottery from artistic utility vessel to pure art.

"Five Brothers," a painting by Tewa Indian artist Jordan Harvier, age 12, of Santa Clara Pueblo.

THE NEXT GENERATION OF ARTISTS

As with Indian culture itself, an important strength of Indian art is the teaching of new generations of artists and craftspeople by the older generation. In excavations of prehistoric pueblos archaeologists have not only uncovered some of the objects children played with, but objects they made as well. Works by those learning to perfect their skills have been found alongside those of more accomplished artisans.

Some artists have been trained by both Indian and non-Indian professionals at schools like the Institute of American Indian Art in Santa Fe, founded in 1962. Others have been taught and encouraged in elementary, middle, and high schools across the reservations, as well as in institutes of higher education on and off Indian lands. A number of accomplished Indian artists have made working with Indian children in the schools a priority.

But many still learn at home, usually from an immediate family member. Families take pride in continuing the tradition of artistic excellence, and children develop a sense of pride in themselves and their culture. Art often opens the door to learning more about one's culture. A grandmother instructing a child in the tedious and time-consuming art of basket weaving has time to talk of other things, including traditional stories and the value of keeping the language alive.

Young ceramic artists Brandon and Derek Gonzales learn a pottery tradition made famous by their great-great-grandmother Maria Martinez of San Ildefonso Pueblo.

Painting

Painting on paper is the most recent art expression to be adopted by Indians of the Southwest. Painting itself was practiced long before the Spaniards arrived. Hides, wood, pottery, stones, textiles, kiva walls, even canyon walls were decorated with paints from mineral and vegetal pigments. Artistic works ranged from simple geometrics to very complex, highly stylized, almost abstract designs and naturalistic animal portrayals.

Use of commercial watercolors began in the early 1900s. The pueblo of San Ildefonso produced the first artists in this new medium. Encouraged by painters, collectors, teachers, and anthropologists, many Pueblo Indians began to experiment with watercolor. The earliest depictions were usually ceremonial dancers or daily pueblo activities. In 1932 the U.S. Bureau of Indian Affairs established at the Santa Fe Indian School an experimental class designed to instruct young Native American students in the use of this medium. This led to the development of a popular group of artists whose style came to be known as the Santa Fe School. The program introduced Southwestern Indian painting as a successful new artistic expression in this country and abroad.

Nearly 40 years later the work of this group was criticized as being painted to suit non-Indian patrons. Contemporary artists, many of them graduates of the Institute of American Indian Art in Santa Fe, are now criticized for the same reason by those who prefer the earlier style. Critics on both sides of this controversy fail to recognize the importance of the artist-patron relationship that permits all art to exist. Both sides also fail to give the Indian artists credit for being both individuals and part of a culture that extends back over a thousand years.

Though many contemporary Southwestern Indian artists still use cultural themes in their works, an increasing number have developed personal interpretations and styles incorporating a wide range of media and techniques.

Many contemporary Indian artists attempt to portray the interrelatedness and levels of meaning in traditional Indian life through their paintings.
Oliver Enjady

This painting reflects both the personal artistic vision of the painter, Carl A. Vicenti, and the many aspects of the Jicarilla Apache religious Holiness Rite, a "long-life ritual" sometimes mistakenly referred to as a "Bear Dance."

Religious observances of the Pueblo Indians have long held an interest for the non-Indian, creating a demand for paintings that portray them. As photography and sketching are banned at most ceremonies, demand has increased for such work as this Zuni Shalako portrayal by the late Hopi-Tewa artist Ray Naha.

K. C. DEN DOOVEN

PAINTING

Silverwork

Silverwork, probably the best known of all Indian crafts, is often thought of as an ancient art. However, it is one of the most recent crafts to be adopted by the tribes in the Southwest. Prior to 1850, silver ornaments used by Southwestern Indians were obtained in trade or warfare with other tribes or Spanish settlers.

In the mid-1800s, it was the custom of Mexican *plateros* (silversmiths) from the Rio Grande Valley to roam through Navajo country producing silver trinkets in exchange for livestock. It was from one of these itinerant craftsmen that a Navajo blacksmith named Atsidi Sani, "Old Smith," is believed to have learned the rudiments of silverworking in the early 1850s. In the two decades prior to this time Indian metalworking

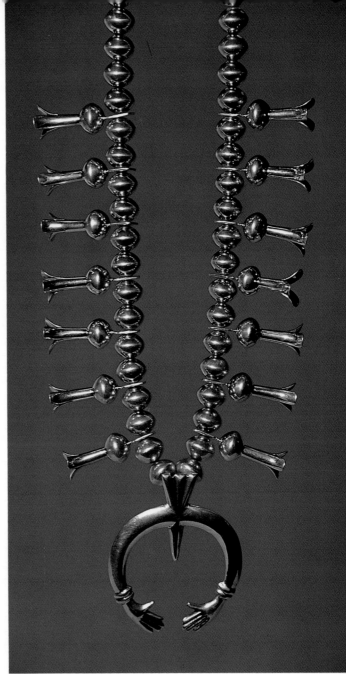

The squash blossom necklace evolved in the late 1800s, as Navajo smiths combined a new technology, silverwork, with Spanish- and Moorish-derived design elements to create a piece of jewelry that is uniquely Navajo.

Clusterwork—which we think of as typically Zuni—did not begin to evolve until the late 1920s even though the Zunis had been working silver in the late 1800s.

was limited to a few Zuni and Navajo blacksmiths who occasionally fashioned simple items of jewelry from odds and ends of copper and brass.

Frequent raiding by some Navajo bands and continual encroachment on Navajoland by Americans resulted in increased hostilities, which led to a military campaign against the Navajo by the U.S. Army. The Navajo were subjected to a brutal scorched earth policy that culminated in their imprisonment at Bosque Redondo, New

Mexico, far to the southeast of their homeland. During the years of their confinement (1864-68) it appears that more Navajos learned blacksmithing, but the development of silversmithing had halted. Disease and famine swept the tribe, killing one in four and finally forcing the government to admit failure in its attempt to relocate the Navajo. Within a few years of their return, a number of Navajo were working silver.

Hopi silversmithing began in 1892 but the technique of overlay work was not introduced until the 1930s and did not really take hold until after World War II. The Hopi Guild, established in 1949, used the GI Bill to train returning veterans to be silversmiths, using the overlay technique. Today a few Hopi silversmiths use a wide range of techniques, but most rely on the overlay technique, with infrequent use of stones.

The Indian arts and crafts shops of today are a distinct contrast to the turn-of-the-century shops and reservation trading posts of yesterday. The work found today is truly fine art created by craftspeople working with the latest techniques, tools, and materials. The great variety of work coming from tribes of the Southwest and other areas of the country provides the buyer both items to wear and unique artwork that can be proudly displayed in the home. Where once it was sufficient to know the tribal origins of a piece, now as individual styles flourish, the artist's name and history are important.

Indian jewelry is not made solely for the non-Indian collector or tourist. In fact, its earliest and steadiest customers were other Indians. Jewelry was the way many Indians carried their wealth. Among the Navajo, jewelry was pawned for loans between lambing and wool-shearing seasons when money was short. With the proceeds from selling lambs or wool, the pieces were then redeemed. The term "pawn" or "dead pawn" refers to some of this older jewelry that was occasionally not redeemed. Pawning ended on the Navajo Reservation in 1976. Today the term has lost most of its significance and does not mean the piece has any especial value or age. A talented Indian silversmith could become a wealthy man. Atsidi Chon, who often traveled to Zuni to make and sell jewelry, is recorded as being able to trade a good, heavy concha belt for a team of matched horses. After a winter of work he would leave Zuni driving sheep, goats, and horses he had acquired in trade.

Navajo sandcasting is one of the oldest silverworking techniques among the Navajo. A stone that is heat resistant yet can be carved with a knife will be cut in half and the surfaces ground smooth before the pattern is carved. A funnel to pour in the silver and tiny channels to let the air out are carved into one surface. Both faces are covered with soot and wired together, then the molten silver is poured. The result is a rough casting that will need trimming, filing, and polishing.

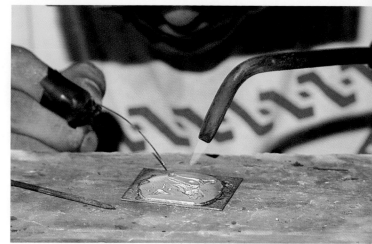

The overlay technique involves sawing the design out of one sheet of silver and then overlaying it on a second sheet to which it is then sweated or soldered. After trimming the edges, the background is darkened with an oxidizing solution before polishing the raised surface. Most Hopi artists use an iron stamp or matting tool to texture the background before oxidizing it.

One of these early silversmiths, Atsidi Chon, "Ugly Smith," traded his work for livestock among the Zuni. He was responsible for teaching his Zuni host, Lanyade, the art of silversmithing about 1872. Interestingly, it was Lanyade who then traded his work among the Hopi and later taught the first Hopi, Sikyatala ("Yellow Light"), silversmithing around 1890.

Two early traders, C. N. Cotton and Lorenzo Hubbell, hired Mexican plateros to teach silversmithing to the Navajos who lived near their trading post at Ganado, beginning in 1884. The arrival of the railroad in the 1890s, and the tourists it brought, increased the demand for Indian jewelry, which motivated more Indians to learn silversmithing. By the early 1920s, the craft had spread eastward to most of the Rio Grande pueblos.

EARLY WORK

The first pieces, fashioned with homemade tools, were often copies of ornaments used by the early Spaniards—among them domed buttons, hollow spherical beads, powder chargers, silver-mounted bridles, loop earrings, and stamped or twisted wire bracelets. Brass and copper, obtained from worn-out utensils, were also used on occasion.

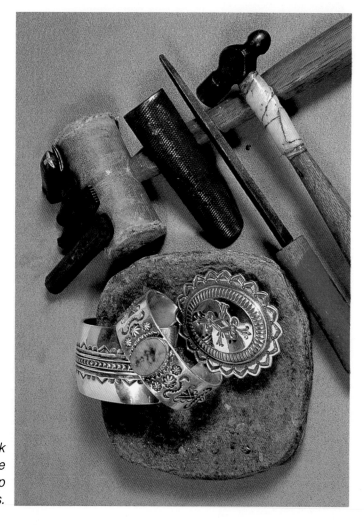

Before Navajo smiths learned to set turquoise, stampwork and file and chisel work were the only ways to decorate their silver jewelry. Stamps were made from any bit of scrap iron, including railroad spikes, old chisels, and broken files.

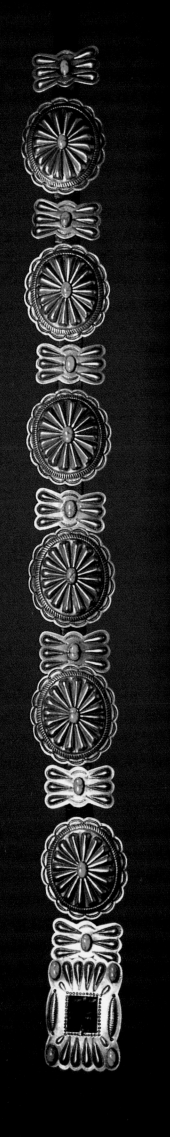

Silverworking is a relatively new craft among the Tohono O'odham of southern Arizona. This distinctive style with desert motifs began in the mid-1970s. Currently there are only a few smiths in the tribe.

The concha belt is one of the earliest styles of jewelry developed by Navajo silversmiths. The oldest had slotted centers through which the leather was strung. This particular style developed after the turn of the century and continues today.

Many of the styles that evolved were adaptations of jewelry made by the Spanish or the Plains Indians. The decorative nickel-silver disks that hung from the cloth belts of the Plains Indian women became the concha belt. The pomegranate blossoms some Spanish gentlemen wore as trouser or cape ornaments, and the crescent-shaped pendants hung from their horse bridles to ward off the "evil eye," caught the attention of Navajo silversmiths. The crescent-shaped pendant, or *nazha*, was hung on a strand of silver beads. On either side of the pendant were strung several pomegranate blossoms, elongated to suit Navajo aesthetics, to create what became known as a squash blossom necklace, which today is regarded as a very traditional example of Indian jewelry.

Indian silversmiths have long made bracelets for Indian men—who continue to outnumber non-Indian men in wearing bracelets.

SILVERWORK

Among the early pieces of jewelry, items such as powder chargers and manta pins have disappeared. Others such as the *ketoh*, or bow guard, have survived to be used for different purposes. The ketoh outlived usage of the bow and arrow to become a piece of men's jewelry worn on special occasions. Still others, such as the tobacco canteen, disappeared but were revived. Beginning with a request from a researcher in the 1930s, the canteen is again being made by a few silversmiths for both other Navajo and collectors.

Coins provided the sole source for silver in the early days of silversmithing. American coins were barred from such use in 1890, but Mexican silver pesos—preferred for their higher silver content which made them more malleable—were used as late as 1930, when Mexico forbade their export. Sterling silver (92.5 percent silver and 7.5 copper) in slug and ingot form replaced coins, and they in turn were replaced by the mid-1930s with silver in ready-made sheets and wire, which had been first introduced two decades earlier as part of an effort to increase productivity. At no time did the Indians mine their own silver.

Hopi jewelry draws much of its design inspiration from other crafts, including painted pottery, woven and embroidered textiles, and katsina spirits, as well as the natural world around them.

One of the biggest bursts of innovation in materials and techniques of jewelry making and design began in the early 1960s with the work of the late Hopi artist Charles Loloma, who created the bracelet at top right. Others have followed his lead, experimenting with techniques like reticulation, and materials ranging from niobium and titanium to charoite from Siberia and sugilite from the Kalahari.

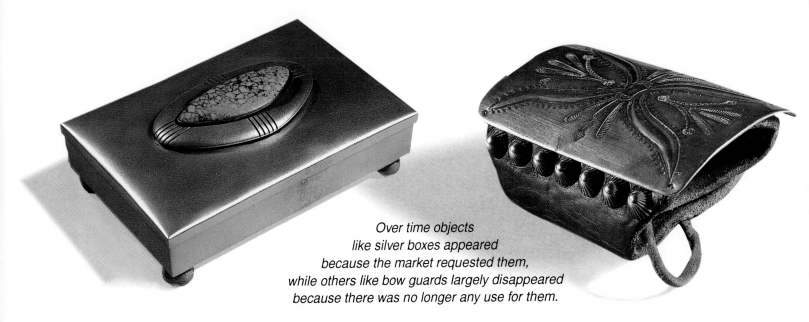

*Over time objects
like silver boxes appeared
because the market requested them,
while others like bow guards largely disappeared
because there was no longer any use for them.*

The first attempt to set turquoise was about 1880. Glass, jet, shell, trade beads, and garnets were also tried, but were not popular. Turquoise was used sparingly for the next several decades, though the trader Lorenzo Hubbell imported Persian turquoise for several years in a successful attempt to produce more turquoise and silver jewelry. American turquoise became readily available by the 1920s, with the opening of mines and lapidary shops—all owned and run by non-Indians.

With the exception of mosaic, cluster, and inlay work, most of the turquoise used by Indian silversmiths is purchased already cut and polished. Coral, from the Mediterranean Sea and now the Sea of Japan, was first imported in the 1930s, and has been used increasingly since the 1950s. Before coral was available artisans relied upon spiny oyster shells, traded from the Pacific Coast of Baja California, for a red-orange material. Artisans now may use stones from virtually anywhere in the world: lapis lazuli from Afghanistan, sugilite from South Africa, charoite from Siberia, and opals from Australia.

New Markets

Until the 1890s most of the silverwork produced was acquired by other Indians. With the appearance of tourists, a new market opened up. Orders from curio companies that catered to the tourists added to their orders items such as napkin rings, salad sets, tie bars, and cuff links. At this time the silversmiths were paid by the ounce, plus so much for each stone set. In order to make the jewelry more affordable for the Eastern buyers, companies requested lighter silverwork from the silversmiths. It should be noted however, that the notion of "heavy, old Navajo silver" does not always square with how the precious and relatively rare metal was used by the early Navajo silversmiths. Some of the heaviest Indian jewelry has been made in the past 20 years. In any event, the weight does not equate with quality.

To fit the Eastern notion of what Indian jewelry should look like, the pieces were decorated with stampwork designs such as crossed arrows, steer heads, and thunderbirds. About this same time a list was created that purported to "interpret" the designs. According to it, a running horse became a symbol of a long journey, and rain clouds of good luck. These "meanings" were concocted for the symbol-minded buyer by

Though best known for their stone and shell jewelry, several artisans from Santo Domingo Pueblo work in silver. These sandcast pendants are based on Pueblo tablita dancers and Pueblo women balancing water jars. They are set with turquoise, orange spiny oyster shell, and purple charoite.

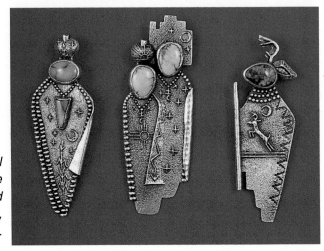

Before a Zuni artisan can begin inlaying stone and shell, a silver frame must be completed. The stone and shell mosaic and inlay work has its roots in a prehistoric tradition of mosaics set on stone and shell. Setting them in silver began about 1930.

This inlay pendant is called a spinner since it rotates and has another, equally intricate design on the reverse side. This type of work is judged not only by its aesthetic qualities but also by the quality of the workmanship. In this case the fit is so precise that the stone and shell pieces are separated by less than the thickness of a sheet of paper.

canny merchants responding to questions of "what does it mean?"

Both markets, Indian and non-Indian, continue today, changing as fashion and usage change. A Navajo silversmith may produce a heavy sandcast bracelet for an Anglo customer, but prefer to wear a Zuni bracelet himself. Both may covet an old bracelet, but the Anglo may prize the patina of age while the Navajo wearer is more likely to have it cleaned and brightly polished.

Silversmithing is one of the native crafts at which an artisan, employed full time, can earn a living. However, much of the work produced is still the result of part-time labor, even in cases where the entire family participates in jewelry making. An increasing number of Indian

silversmiths and lapidarists are employed (largely in the Gallup, New Mexico area) doing benchwork for an hourly wage or on a piecework basis.

Many people lament the passing of "fine old silverwork." The truth is that more fine silverwork is being produced today than in any period in the past. A wider range of materials are being used, new techniques are being incorporated, and new styles are constantly being introduced. Part of the increase in the quality of the work is the result of new and better tools, but it is primarily the result of continuing efforts by the artisans themselves to improve both design and craftsmanship.

Zuni jewelry techniques include mosaic, channel, inlay, cluster (the larger stones), needlepoint (the long thin stones), and petitpoint (very tiny, usually round stones). The latter three categories are judged for quality based upon symmetry and consistency.

Turquoise

Turquoise is a semiprecious stone found in many arid regions of the world including the Middle East, China, Australia, and Chile as well as the American Southwest where it has been mined and used for over 1,500 years. In pre-Hispanic times Southwestern Indians mined turquoise with stone hammers and picks made of antler. Fire was used to crack bedrock containing the blue gem. The largest of these early mines was near Cerillos, New Mexico, near present-day Santa Fe. It extended 200 feet underground and was 300 feet wide in places. Turquoise from pre-Columbian mines in the Southwest was widely traded, some traveling as far as the Aztec Empire in Mexico.

Cut turquoise was not readily available in the late 1800s when Indian silversmiths began setting it in their jewelry. The stones used often were broken earrings or pendants from necklaces. For a few years during this period a trader at Ganado, Lorenzo Hubbell, imported turquoise from Iran in order to supply silversmiths in his area. By the 1920s several American turquoise mines were in operation and producing cut stone.

Today turquoise is mined in a number of locations in Colorado, New Mexico, Arizona, and Nevada as well as northern Mexico. None of the mines are owned by Indians, and most of the mining is done on a small scale by private individuals or small companies although some turquoise is recovered as a by-product of copper mining. With the exception of inlay, cluster, and mosaic work, most of the stone set in Indian jewelry over the past 75 years has been cut and polished by non-Indians.

Indian jewelry artists have always used the full range of colors in turquoise, sometimes seeking the unusual stone for inspiration and other times looking for a specific type of turquoise to complement their silver design. When multiple stones are used, matching them can become a problem. Additionally, as such a piece is worn, soaps and oils can cause the colors to change at different rates even though the stones may have come from the same mine.

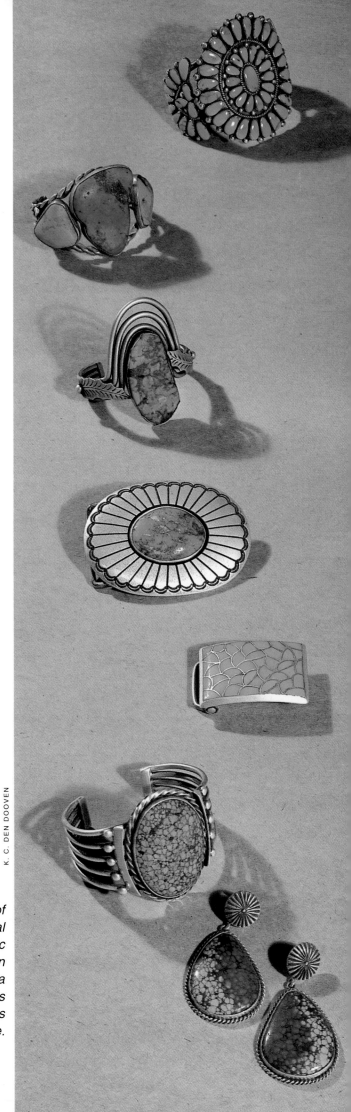

K. C. DEN DOOVEN

The double strand of beads hanging from this multi-strand nugget necklace is called a jocla, *which is a Navajo word meaning simply "earrings." The earrings were once often hung from the bottom of necklaces while riding, lest they be torn from the ear by a tree branch. Eventually they became a design element of the necklace itself, although ones small enough to wear as earrings are still made. The shell beads at the bottom of the jocla are referred to as "corn" because of their resemblance to corn kernels. The style of wrapping at the top of the necklace, usually done with cotton string, predates the use of catches and hooks. It is still popular, however, because it makes wearing a heavier necklace more comfortable.*

Determining the origin of a stone based upon its appearance is usually a matter of educated guesswork. This turquoise is from mines around the world. While known for producing stones of a particular color and markings, each mine produces turquoise of widely varying appearance. It is entirely possible to have a piece of Persian turquoise that matches a piece from Bisbee, Arizona, or one from China that is a perfect match for spider-web turquoise from a Nevada source.

K. C. DEN DOOVEN

Since it was first used, turquoise has been treated to alter its color. Earliest methods involved immersing it in wax or oil. More recently, fiberglass resin has been used to stabilize or harden lower, softer grades. The stone on the right has been treated this way but the resin did not fully penetrate the stone. The piece at left is an example of the synthetic turquoise blocks that have become available and are sometimes used for inlay work and even beads.

Turquoise can vary in color in a single nugget, as demonstrated here. The bracelet atop the nugget is set with spider-web turquoise—a more costly grade that is rarely used this way because of the amount lost to waste in cutting tiny stones.

Turquoise is a hydrous aluminum phosphate colored by copper salts. It is deposited by water action, and found as either nuggets or veins in mother rock. This mother rock or matrix is responsible for the markings in turquoise. The matrix may be composed of thin black lines (sometimes forming a "spider-web matrix"), brown or black mineral inclusions, iron pyrites, or quartz.

THE COLORS OF TURQUOISE

The color of turquoise ranges from a very pale chalky blue—almost white—to a very deep green, with literally dozens of shades in between. The price of an individual stone will depend upon its hardness, color, and markings. Its value as a cut and polished stone can range from as little as 10 cents a carat for the poorest grades to as much as 20 dollars per carat for the finest and rarest.

In the Southwest the most highly prized turquoise is deep blue with a black spider-web matrix. Both color and markings, however, are a matter of personal preference. Hard stones are more desirable as they are less porous than the softer grades and therefore less likely to change color. Repeated or prolonged contact with soaps or oils will change the color of more porous softer stones, usually to a dark green.

While turquoise was sometimes treated with oils, wax, animal fats, and even dyes to enhance the color, the practice did not become commonplace until the 1970s. It was then that growing demand for Indian jewelry outstripped the limited supply of good turquoise, and poorer grades were treated for color and hardness (by immersion in a plastic resin) in great quantities. This process goes by many names—treating, stabilizing, and enhancing, among others. It makes usable otherwise unusable grades of turquoise that are either too soft or badly fractured. It is most commonly seen in *heishe* necklaces. Bead makers use stabilized turquoise extensively because of its lower cost and lower incidence of chipping and breaking while being worked. Also, it will not change color, even through repeated exposure to soaps and oils. As one might expect, there is a considerable difference in price between a strand of treated turquoise beads and one of untreated good quality natural turquoise.

Although its primary use in the Southwest is for adornment, turquoise can also serve as a prayer offering, and is sometimes crushed for use in sandpaintings.

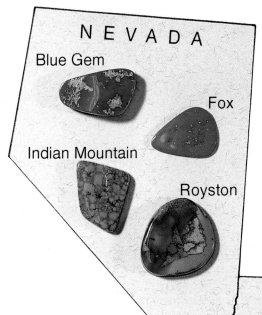

There are many mines in the Southwest that produce turquoise. However, their output is often sporadic and limited. Many small mining operations close or change ownership frequently, with their names also changing. In prehistoric times turquoise mined in what is now Arizona and New Mexico was widely traded, with some of the hardest, bluest stone finding its way to the Aztec Empire.

Bead Making

Bead making is an ancient craft that remained virtually unchanged until very recently. Even today a few stone and shell workers among the Indians of Santo Domingo Pueblo use the old style pump drills on occasion, though with the finest diamond and tungsten-carbide drill points that modern technology can provide. Some even make their own drill points, especially for the exceptionally fine work produced by a few highly skilled bead makers.

Bead necklaces are often called *heishe*, from the Keresan-speaking Santo Domingo Pueblo word for shell. Seashells are the most common material used for beads, and have been an important trade item in the Southwest for over 1,000 years. Seashells were prized over more available freshwater shells because of their association with the ocean, which was the source of the life-

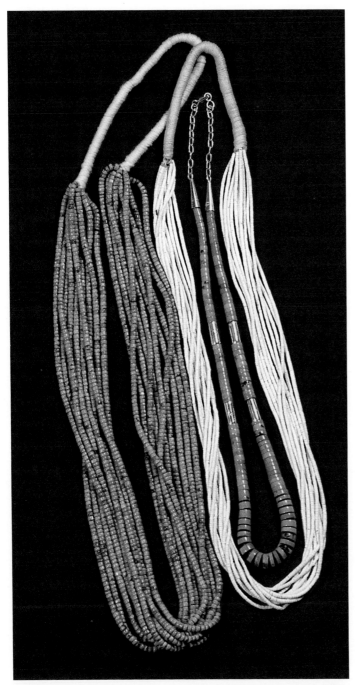

The fineness of strands on a bead necklace (as measured by their diameter) and the number of beads per inch are a measure of the skill of the bead maker. However, the style and the design of a necklace can also dictate the size and shape of the beads.

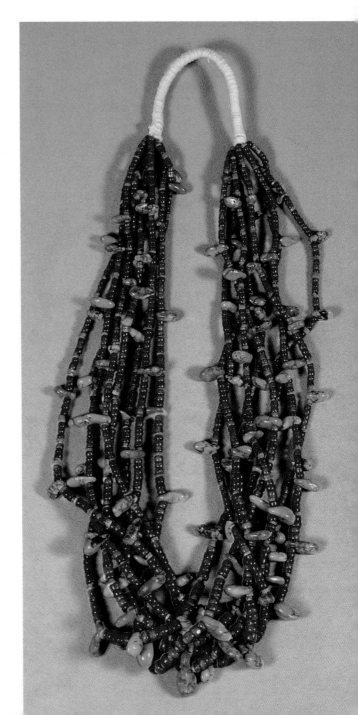

BEAD MAKING

giving summer rains. Among the many species of shells used are clam, conus, olivella, abalone, mother-of-pearl, conch, and spiny oyster. Most of these are obtained from the coasts of the Pacific Ocean and the Sea of Cortez. They were carried inland over well-established trade routes by pre-historic Indian traders. Even in historic times, many tribes trekked across the desert in search of both shells and salt. Today the shells used may come from any ocean in the world.

Beads are made by first breaking or sawing the shell into small irregular pieces and individually drilling each one. Short lengths of the drilled fragments are then strung on wire and carefully ground until they become disc-shaped and are the desired diameter. There are a number of steps from grinding to polishing as progressively finer abrasives and polishing agents are used.

The fineness of the beads, determined by the number per inch and their diameter, as well as smooth finish and uniform size, is a result of the maker's skill, time, and tools. The finer strands require far more time and skill and are thus more expensive. A few bead makers today are able to produce a strand of beads so fine that they exceed the finest of the prehistoric bead necklaces.

At one time most of the tribes in the Southwest produced stone and shell bead necklaces. Today bead making is largely limited to the pueblo of Santo Domingo, which trades widely with other tribes.

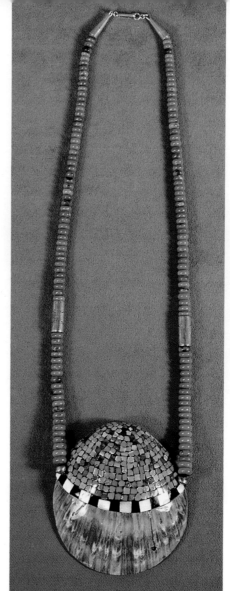

The ancient tradition of shell and stone mosaics on shells remains strong. The shells, once traded over hundreds of miles from the coastal regions, now may come from oceans anywhere in the world.

Prehistoric artisans used drills that were spun between the palms of the hand, with the pump drill appearing much later. The pump drill is in turn being replaced by the electric drill. Stone drill points were replaced by iron ones, and then by diamond drill bits. The work still requires much time and a skill level that goes up as the fineness of the beads increases.

K. CAMILLE DEN DOOVEN

Coral is still highly valued for its rich red to red-orange color. When first introduced into the Southwest by the Spanish, a single strand of scarce fine red coral beads was regarded as being equal in value to several strands of the finest, but more readily available, turquoise.

Fetishes

The use of fetishes by Indians of the Southwest is of prehistoric origin. A fetish is an object in which a spirit dwells. If treated with proper respect and reverence, the spirit will provide the owner of the fetish with assistance in the form of supernatural power. Any object may be used as a fetish, including arrowpoints, unusual stone concretions, shells, carvings, or a perfect ear of corn.

Among the Zuni there is a legend that tells of a time when all the animals were shrunken and turned to stone by certain supernatural beings. When they were finally restored to life, some were overlooked. Stones that naturally resemble an animal or internal organ are believed to date from this time and are especially prized.

Fetishes may be the property of individuals, households, kivas, clans, or religious societies. They are treated with reverence, and when not

This Mountain Lion has turquoise and shell offerings attached to increase its strength or willingness to help, and an arrowhead that may be to protect or increase its strength or mean it is a hunting fetish. Some pueblos once used mountain lion fetishes for protection while traveling.

in actual use may be stored in a jar, basket, or leather pouch, or wrapped in corn husks. They are usually fed periodically—generally with corn pollen or cornmeal, although hunting fetishes, like the mountain lion, may be ritually fed the blood of a kill.

Most tribes use and many still make fetishes, but the Zuni are the best known, using and making the greatest variety and number. In recent years both Navajo and Zuni carvers have begun

A number of tribes make and use fetishes for widely varying purposes. Some, like the Zuni, also make carvings that are not fetishes in their tradition—such as frogs and turtles—but may be in the tradition of other tribes to which they are sold. Additionally, they make a wide range of carvings that are not intended for use as fetishes but which shops may lump into that category. They have become very popular with non-Indians who either collect them for their aesthetic qualities or assign their own meanings and significance to them. Traditionally, stones are used according to the color of the animal, which depends upon the direction it is believed to represent. Among the Zuni, who assign an animal for each of the six directions, the stones used vary according to the direction the animal represents.

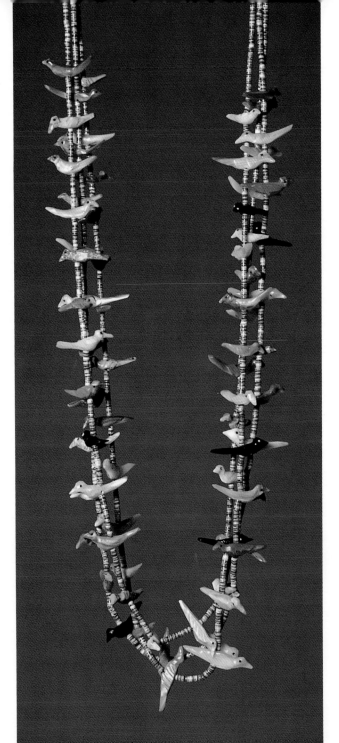

to carve animals that they do not traditionally recognize as fetishes themselves such as owls, frogs, turtles, rabbits, and fish.

The distinction between a carving and a fetish is a fine one, resting less on the intent of the maker than the use of the owner. Even store-bought plastic horses have been adorned with prayer feathers and used as fetishes. The traditional viewpoint is simple: if you believe it is a fetish, it is—if you don't, it isn't, for the spirit within the fetish won't assist an owner who doesn't believe in it.

The most commonly seen fetishes are hunting fetishes, which generally have a small replica of an arrowhead attached. According to some, an arrowpoint can be added simply as an offering, or as protection for the fetish itself as in the case of a livestock fetish. Bits of shell, coral, or turquoise and feathers may be tied to these stone animals to increase their power, or as offerings to the fetish spirits to increase their inclination to honor requests.

This Navajo bison carving was made from septarian—limestone and quartz crystals—with turquoise horns.

Though called fetish necklaces, in the traditional Zuni sense fetishes cannot be used for jewelry. These are simply animal carvings on a necklace. Prehistoric drilled stone and shell animals found during an excavation in the early 20th century inspired several Zuni to begin making them for sale and trade.

The stone used can contribute as much to the "personality" of a carving as the personal style of the carver. (The two bears with fish would be considered carvings, not fetishes.)

FETISHES

Early fetishes were often carved from stones that already resembled an animal and needed only a little work with a piece of rough sandstone to highlight certain features.

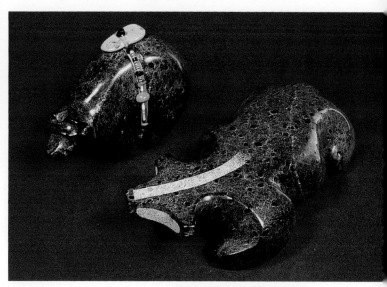

Modern equipment now allows for much greater detail but a steady hand and a good eye are still required. The new equipment means that stones once too hard to work can be carved with relative ease.

Some carvers prefer to work with stones from the traditional boundaries of their land while others actively seek out interesting and unusual stones from around the world. Regardless of materials and tools used, each carver has his or her own distinct style. Mike Romero, from the Tewa Indian pueblo of Santa Clara, not only makes fetishes but also much larger pieces which are intended for use as sculpture.

Overleaf: The Indian art and symbols of the center spread were collected by Tom Bahti over many years of working directly with people of individual tribes in the Southwest. Some elements came from kiva mural paintings excavated by the University of New Mexico, where Tom was a student. Artwork by Tom Bahti, 1962.

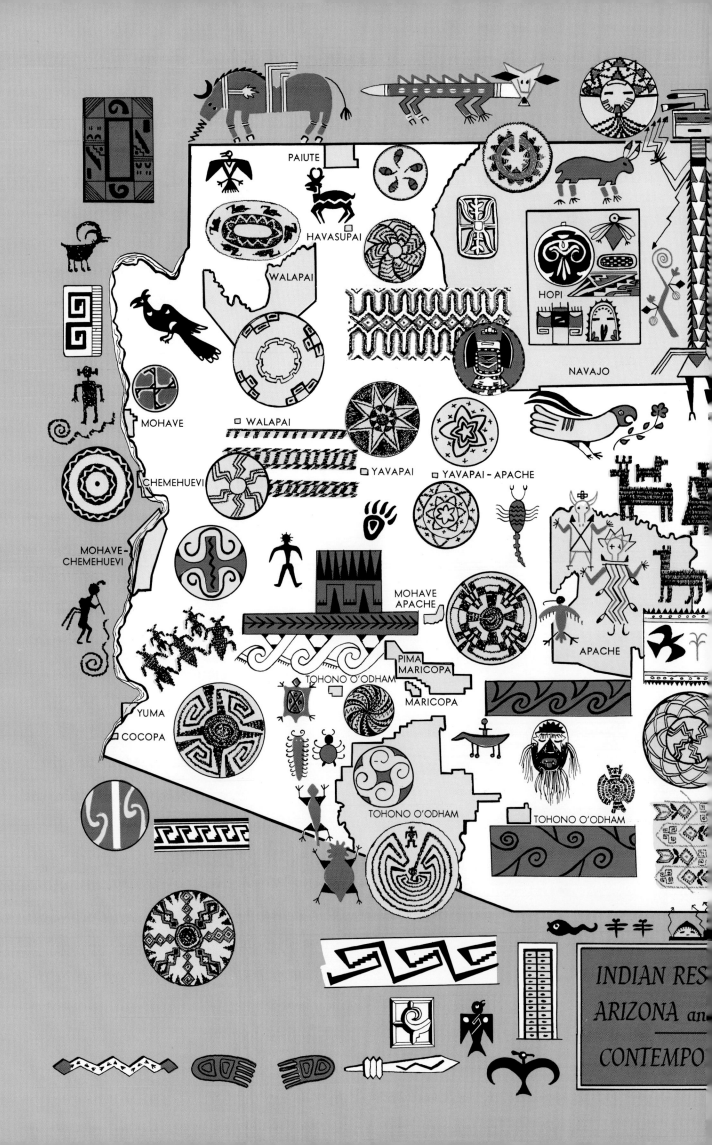

PAIUTE

HAVASUPAI

WALAPAI

MOHAVE

□ WALAPAI

CHEMEHUEVI

□ YAVAPAI

□ YAVAPAI – APACHE

MOHAVE-
CHEMEHUEVI

MOHAVE
APACHE

HOPI

NAVAJO

APACHE

PIMA
MARICOPA

TOHONO O'ODHAM

MARICOPA

YUMA

□ COCOPA

TOHONO O'ODHAM

TOHONO O'ODHAM

INDIAN RES

ARIZONA an

CONTEMPO

JICARILLA

TAOS

PICURIS

SAN JUAN
SANTA CLARA
SAN ILDEFONSO
NAMBE
TESUQUE

JEMEZ   COCHITI
ZIA   SANTO
       DOMINGO
SANTA ANA   SAN FELIPE

SANDIA

ZUNI

ACOMA   LAGUNA

ISLETA

MESCALERO

TIONS of

MEXICO

DESIGNS

Reservation Area

Navajo Rugs

According to anthropologists, the Navajo learned weaving from the Pueblo Indians—where weaving is done exclusively by the men. By Navajo traditions it was Spiderwoman who first taught Navajo women how to weave. (Only a very few Navajo men practice the craft.) Regardless of origin, it has become a vital part of Navajo economic life and culture. Though yarn preparation has changed over the years, the basic weaving technique has been unchanged for centuries. As early as three centuries ago the quality of Navajo weaving was acknowledged; a Spanish territorial governor wrote that Navajo weaving surpassed that of the finest Spanish weavers.

Relative newcomers among the Indians of the Southwest, the Navajo entered this region as hunter-gatherers 600 to 800 years ago. Under the influence of the Pueblo Indians many Navajo groups had begun to farm when the Spanish entered the Southwest and introduced both horses and livestock. From them the Navajo obtained sheep, substituting its wool for the cotton with which they had learned from the Pueblo Indians to weave. (According to Navajo tradition it was Spiderwoman who taught them to weave.) Soon

NAVAJO RUGS (continued on page 38)

JOHN RUNNING

Traditionally the shearing, cleaning, carding, dyeing, and spinning of the wool comprised much of the time necessary to complete a weaving. While Navajo still raise and shear sheep, most weavers now rely upon processed wool which is ready for the final spinning and a few even prefer ready-to-use commercially spun wool. Regardless, the hours before the loom remain unchanged. For over a century non-Navajo experts have predicted the end of Navajo weaving, but the tradition continues to be passed on to new generations of young Navajo women. Though many may never weave much, they carry with them a rich and vital part of Navajo culture.

Weaving involves many long hours. For a young woman being taught the art, it becomes an opportunity to learn more than just the technique—it becomes a time to learn more of Navajo traditions and values, becoming a part of the tapestry of Navajo culture.

35

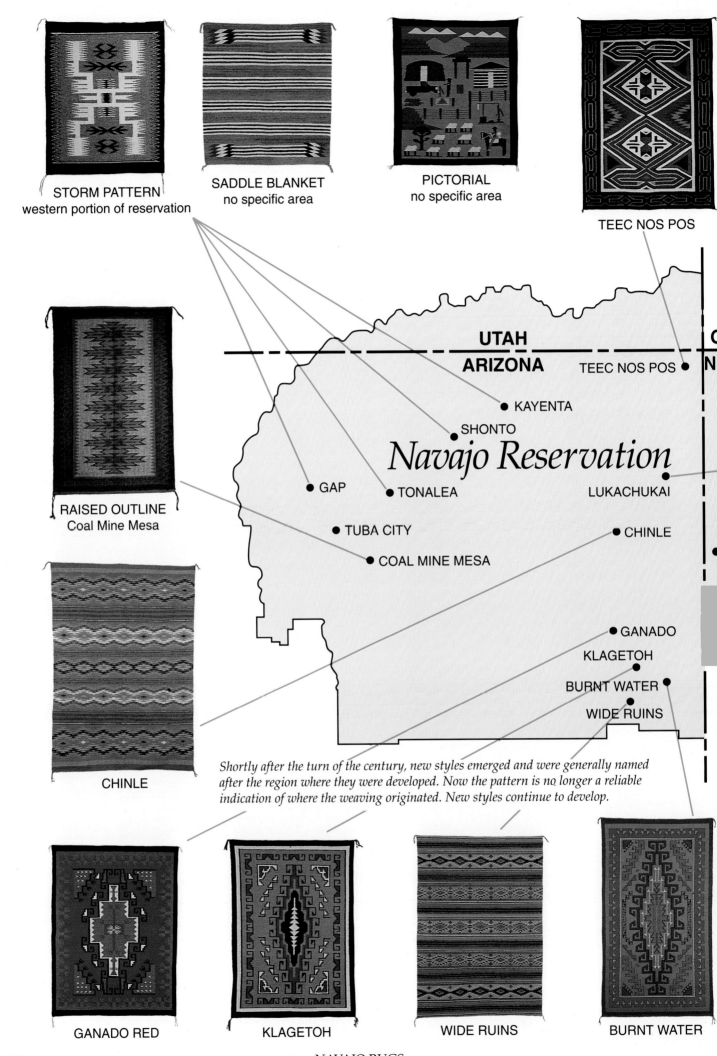

STORM PATTERN
western portion of reservation

SADDLE BLANKET
no specific area

PICTORIAL
no specific area

TEEC NOS POS

RAISED OUTLINE
Coal Mine Mesa

CHINLE

UTAH
ARIZONA
TEEC NOS POS ●
C
NE

● KAYENTA
SHONTO ●

Navajo Reservation

● GAP
● TONALEA
LUKACHUKAI

● TUBA CITY
● CHINLE
C

● COAL MINE MESA

● GANADO
KLAGETOH
BURNT WATER ●
WIDE RUINS

Shortly after the turn of the century, new styles emerged and were generally named after the region where they were developed. Now the pattern is no longer a reliable indication of where the weaving originated. New styles continue to develop.

GANADO RED

KLAGETOH

WIDE RUINS

BURNT WATER

NAVAJO RUGS

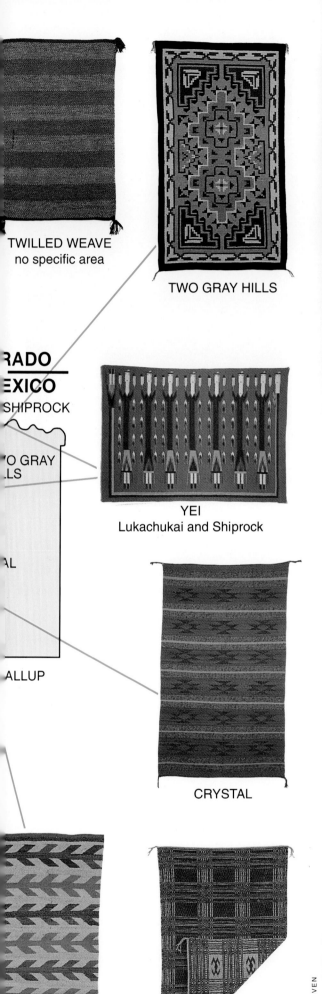

TWILLED WEAVE
no specific area

TWO GRAY HILLS

RADO

EXICO

SHIPROCK

O GRAY
LS

AL

ALLUP

YEI
Lukachukai and Shiprock

CRYSTAL

THROW
Gallup area

TWO-FACE
no specific area

the Navajo were well-known for their weaving skills. Even the Spanish territorial government conceded that Navajo weaving surpassed that being produced by the best Spanish weavers.

From the 1700s through the late 1800s, Navajo women wove blankets that were highly prized and traded throughout the Southwest and beyond. The introduction of machine-woven blankets in the late 1800s began a decline in the quantity of Navajo weaving, with a consequent rise in the bags of wool from Navajo flocks exported to the East. That reversed when traders found a more profitable market in selling wool as rugs to the tourists who were then beginning to come out West on the Santa Fe Railroad. The new market was for floor rugs rather than wearing blankets, and weavers were paid by the pound, depending upon the grade, which was determined by the fineness of the weave.

There were changes as well in patterns, with large geometric designs with borders replacing the earlier banded styles. Most of the regional styles we are familiar with today, such as Ganado and Two Gray Hills, began after the turn of the century. Traders began to encourage weavers to go back to finer weaves and experiment with more vegetal dyes, which have in turn been replaced by commercial dyes that match those colors.

A TIME-CONSUMING PROCESS

The casual visitor seldom realizes the hours of labor involved in making a rug. Traditionally it begins with the shearing of the wool, cleaning, carding, washing, dyeing, and more spinning. The amount of time spent in spinning determines the fineness of the weave. Yarn preparation easily exceeds the time spent in weaving for a tapestry-quality example. For this reason processed wool and commercially spun wool are becoming more prevalent.

When one includes the time spent setting up the loom, the entire procedure can result in a 3 x 5-foot rug of average quality (about 8 warp and 25 weft threads per inch) that required between 300 and 400 hours of work, depending upon the intricacy of the design. The same size textile, executed in a tapestry weave of about 25 warp and 80 weft threads per inch, would require in excess of 2,000 hours work by a master weaver.

The "spirit line" is used only by some weavers. Stories purporting to explain it vary wildly between weavers and traders. Basically, if the design is too symmetrical, the eye can be "trapped" looking for a variation. The spirit line "lets the eye out."

Once used for saddle blankets and personal wear, Navajo weaving was re-directed towards floor rugs and decorative wall hangings around the turn of the century. It has since been recognized as a textile art and used much as one would paintings.

Like those who weave baskets, no rug weaver can truly earn a living at her craft. The very best weavers generally command scarcely more than the equivalent of minimum wage for their work. Navajo weaving skills are still being passed down to the younger women (only a very few men weave), but the craft is surviving as an avocation rather than an occupation. It is the cultural importance more than the financial aspect that keeps the craft alive among the Navajo.

THE FUTURE OF NAVAJO RUGS

Navajo rugs are justly famous not only for their beauty, but also for their durability. It is the hand-spun yarn with its natural lanolin, which traditional processes leave in the yarn, that helps give these rugs their strength. It is not uncommon for a Navajo rug, given proper care, to last 30 to 40 years on the floor. However, today rugs are more commonly used as wall hangings than as floor coverings.

The demise of Navajo rugs has been predicted as imminent for over a century, and the end is not yet in sight—for either the weaving or the predictions. The craft is still being learned by young Navajo women, though many weave only a few rugs—often for their own use and enjoyment rather than for sale.

With each passing year the quantity of weavings declines somewhat, but the quality remains high. A few weavers produce rugs so fine that they far surpass the best of the pre-1900 textiles. Design innovations continue, but the regional styles have begun to blur: a Ganado rug may be woven not only at Ganado, but anywhere on (or off) the reservation. Navajo weavings also remain a popular trade item and prestige symbol among the tribes themselves.

Navajo Sandpainting Art

According to Navajo philosophy, the Universe is a very delicately balanced place full of enormously powerful forces. If the balance is upset it can cause illness or other disasters. It is believed that only humans can upset this balance. Should someone fall ill, a Navajo Chantway must be given to restore the patient to harmony. The particular chantway will depend upon the cause of the illness. For example, painful, swollen joints may be determined to have resulted from offending a bear, and the Mountainway will be prescribed.

These ceremonies, which may last from one to nine days, include prayers, medicinal herbs, songs, and sandpaintings under the guidance of a *hatathli,* or medicine man. The patient ceremonially identifies with the hero of the chantway to gain the hero's strength. Health returns as *huzho,* balance or harmony, is restored.

The sandpaintings, called *ikaah,* used in these ceremonies are created between sunrise and sunset of the same day. Until the mid-1950s only photographs or painted reproductions served as

Sometimes mistakenly referred to as Sun and Eagle, this sandpainting represents Pollen Boy on the Sun.

K. C. DEN DOOVEN

a permanent record of these creations. It was then that the new craft began to evolve.

Sand is acquired by grinding up rock found at a number of locations within the traditional—as opposed to the modern legal—boundaries of Navajoland. After grinding, sifting, and grading the sand, the background sand is sprinkled across a sheet of particle board that has been prepared by the sandpainter with a specially mixed and thinned white glue.

The sandpainter uses the same glue and a fine paintbrush to begin the design. Working freehand, each color is applied separately, allowing plenty of time between colors for drying in order to avoid any blurring or mixing. The flow of sand is regulated by placing a pinch of sand in the palm of one hand and allowing it to trickle out between the index finger and the thumb. A soft, even flow over a glue line that is neither too thick nor too thin is necessary for an even line. After the sandpainting is completed and dry, the entire surface is usually sprayed with a very fine mist of shellac for additional protection.

Hatathlis warn that duplicating religious images can cause an illness to befall the maker. For this reason many who use a significant number of elements from religious sandpaintings will deliberately make certain changes, such as altering a color sequence or deleting a significant detail.

Since the mid-1970s Navajo sandpainting artists have been turning increasingly to non-religious subjects, including landscapes, portraits, still lifes, and abstracts. The artists are presently refining and expanding their techniques, taking on more elements of fine art.

Many Navajo sandpainting artists use elements from the larger, more complex images that are a part of traditional Navajo healing ceremonies. Navajo hatathli or healers do not necessarily approve of this practice. For that reason, and to express personal creativity and vision, many younger artists are moving into other subject areas and developing and perfecting new techniques.
Eugene Baatsoslanii Joe

Baskets

Basketry is the oldest of all the present-day crafts. The importance of baskets in the religious activities of the many tribes is great, and exceeds any monetary consideration. From a purely economic standpoint, Indian basketry should have disappeared completely years ago. The hours involved in weaving a basket are considerable, yet a weaver can expect to earn little more than a dollar or two an hour for her labor. Even the finest baskets by the most skillful weavers sold directly to museums or collectors will net the weaver no more than the equivalent of minimum wage.

Even among tribes in which basket weaving has disappeared, baskets are in demand, creating a lively trade for weavers from tribes that still produce them. Most Navajo curing rites require the use of a basket in some portion of the ceremony. The Hopi present coiled basketry plaques to winners of footraces, and baskets of all sorts are used in the Basket Dance held in the fall. Sifter baskets are still in use in many Hopi households.

The Apache puberty rites, held for a young woman who has come of age, generally include one or more burden baskets. Baskets may be used in some pueblos as partial payment for ceremonial work performed. Among many tribes cornmeal is placed in the baskets for use as a prayer offering or blessing during religious ceremonies.

Few people appreciate baskets as do the Indians, who fully realize the time and skill that go into creating them. A basket weaver must know the seasons for gathering her materials (like rug weaving, it is primarily a woman's activity)

Basic coiled basketry involves a coil that is stitched together. This Tohono O'odham basket uses bear grass for the coil and bleached yucca for the stitching.

Much of the time in basket weaving is the gathering and preparation of materials. For Tohono O'odham baskets that means gathering bear grass from certain areas, yucca from other regions of their land, and devil's-claw seed pods, available only one time during the year. Preparation includes trimming, splitting, and soaking.

Hopi weavers use the greatest variety of basketry techniques, including coiling, plaiting, and twining. Villagers on Third Mesa weave willow wicker baskets, while those on Second Mesa make coiled baskets; all the villagers make yucca plaited baskets. Baskets are traded between villages, used in religious ceremonies and for special occasions, and sold or traded to non-Hopi.

and the places where they grow. It is not unusual for a Tohono O'odham weaver to travel 50 to 100 miles to gather a specific plant for her basketry. Additionally she must harvest, dry, preserve, and prepare the plants for use. Preparing the materials can include bleaching, dyeing, soaking, stripping, and trimming. Only then can the equally time-consuming task of actually weaving the basket begin.

STYLES OF BASKETS

The Rio Grande pueblos of New Mexico produce relatively few baskets, primarily plaited yucca baskets from Jemez and openwork willow baskets at a few other pueblos, notably Santo Domingo.

The Indians of Arizona produce a great quantity and diversity of basketry. The Hopi of Third Mesa make wicker trays, bowls, and plaques of rabbitbrush dyed with either vegetal or aniline

HELGA TEIWES

The number of O'odham basket weavers has been increasing over the last few decades, as has the number of baskets produced and the creativity in the designs used. Severely depressed economic conditions on their main reservation provide very limited job opportunities. As little as a basket weaver makes at this time-consuming craft (significantly less than minimum wage), it often represents the only alternative. Basketmaking is also part of efforts by the O'odham people to preserve their culture—material and spiritual—by passing down traditional skills and knowledge to each new generation.

dyes. Second Mesa villagers produce tightly woven coiled plaques of grass coils sewn with narrow strips of dyed yucca. The villagers of all three mesas make plaited yucca sifter baskets woven over a willow ring, a style that dates back over 1,500 years. Many weavers now use a metal ring for greater strength and durability. Occasionally the Hopi also weave plain plaited willow baskets for use as piki bread trays, peach baskets, and cradleboards. The Hopis themselves are the greatest consumers of their own basketry, but they do produce a surplus for sale or trade.

The Tohono O'odham of southern Arizona weave more baskets than all the other tribes in the United States combined. The craft was slowly declining in quantity in the 1950s when the American Friends Service Committee, involved in a struggle to help the O'odham acquire the mineral rights to their own land, helped stimulate basketmaking by encouraging weavers to

Traditionally made of baling wire, this type of basketry dates to the late 1800s. Handled baskets were often used to keep perishable food cool by lowering it into a well. Only a few weavers—mostly men—make them.

BASKETS

MARK BAHTI

The tinklers on Apache burden baskets made noise to avoid startling bears while carrying heavy loads in their mountainous homelands.

pass on their skills, and by broadening the market for their craft. In 1963, an estimated 8,000 baskets were produced by weavers ranging in age from under 10 to over 80. In 1985, it was estimated that over 30,000 baskets had been woven. It is expected that a better economic situation will cause the number of baskets produced to eventually level off and ultimately decline.

Old-style baskets woven of cattails sewn with devil's claw, yucca, or even willow are occasionally seen, as are the more common baskets of bear grass coils sewn in an open stitch with yucca. Miniature baskets of horsehair, which have their origins around 1930, are also woven in considerable quantity.

The Tohono O'odham's neighbors to the north, the Pima, also produce baskets similar in both design and technique, though they use willow rather than yucca to stitch the coils, which are also made of willow. Very few weavers are still active among the Pima, and designs used by the Pima are now increasingly being woven by Tohono O'odham basket makers.

The Western Apache, famous for their tightly

K. C. DEN DOOVEN

Horsehair used to make ropes also became a source of material for miniature baskets beginning around the 1930s. Though good eyesight is required, little time is needed to prepare the material for weaving.

Beaded baskets date back to the late 1800s. The beading is done after the basket is complete rather than during weaving. Some Ute beading is done on baskets woven by artists of other tribes, notably the Tohono O'odham.

Years ago Jicarilla Apache willow baskets, with their bright aniline-dyed colors, were expected to eventually disappear. Instead, a modest revival has taken place.

Paiute willow baskets have also undergone a revival. In addition to traditional Paiute designs, weavers have created new ones and also responded to market demands by creating baskets using patterns from tribes whose baskets are disappearing or are no longer made.

BASKETS

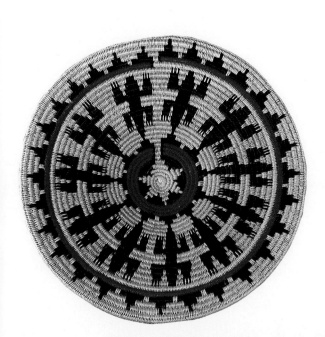

Navajo weavers, working in sturdy, durable willow,
are also experimenting with and creating new designs.
They sometimes incorporate elements of older motifs. The basket
to the right, commonly called a "wedding" basket, is a type used in many ceremonies.

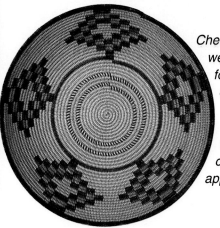

Chemehuevi basket weaving, once readily found, may be disappearing. At present there are but two weavers—an elderly woman master of the craft and her young apprentice.

woven, intricately designed willow coiled baskets, produce primarily twined willow burden baskets today. These are decorated with long buckskin fringe, usually with metal tinklers attached at the bottom. A few pitch-covered *tus,* or water baskets, are also made. The Jicarilla Apaches of northern New Mexico still make a few bright aniline-dyed coiled willow baskets.

The Havasupai, Hualapai, and Chemehuevi still produce baskets, but in very limited quantity. In northwest Mexico, along the desert coast of the Sea of Cortez, the Seri Indians weave coiled baskets of *torote* dyed with vegetal and aniline dyes. Metal pots and pans have replaced baskets in daily life since the 1960s. The Seri continue to weave baskets, however, because of the demand from American collectors for their beautiful, exceptionally sturdy baskets.

Basket prices are determined by the fineness of weave (number of stitches and coils per inch), symmetry, complexity of design, size, and shape, as well as materials, with willow being more durable but more difficult to work with than yucca. Understandably, the more time and skill that go into them, the more they will cost.

Willow wicker baskets are still woven in several
Rio Grande pueblos and by a few Mexican-American weavers.

Hopi Katsina Carvings

The Hopi word *katsina* is used in three ways. It may refer to the actual spirit being, the impersonation by Hopi men in religious dances, or the painted, carved, wooden figurines.

The importance of the katsina in the religious life of the Pueblo people is indicated by the numerous depictions of their masks on pottery vessels and baskets, in kiva murals, and as petroglyphs on canyon walls throughout the Southwest. Today katsinas appear in ceremonies of most pueblos, but are more prevalent among the Hopi and Zuni villages. Among the Zuni, katsinas are known as *koko*.

The katsina is a very old concept and though made far more frequently today, the *katsin tihu* or katsina doll probably extends back to the pre-Columbian era. Early Spanish missionaries believed them to be a form of idolatry, and reported confiscating and burning a large number in the Rio Grande pueblos. These dolls are not idols, nor are they worshipped or prayed to. Similarly they are not toys. They are used in the religious training of young Hopi children, and traditionally were given to women of childbearing years to help ensure fertility. The children and women receive the dolls as gifts or blessings from the masked katsina dancers who appear in the village during katsina ceremonies.

Non-Indians are often astonished to learn that the Hopi have well over 200 katsinas and cannot imagine why there is a need for so many. Similarly, some Hopi are astounded that there are over 1,000 saints in the Catholic faith. This comparison is somewhat appropriate in that some of the functions of the saint and the katsina are roughly parallel. Each serves to intercede on

In the past 20 years carvers have begun to work in more detail and with better tools. Unlike the earlier style, many pieces are now largely crafted from a single piece of wood. In this Pahi-Ala katsina hand-carved of cottonwood root, only the rattle and bow are carved separately and attached.

K. C. DEN DOOVEN

Though there are fixed elements that must be included to correctly portray any given katsina, the work of carvers also reflects their individual artistic styles.

Some carvers utilize a sculptural style, meant more to represent the katsina spirit, while others prefer a more detailed approach that represents the katsina dancer.

To evoke the feeling of a particular katsina, great detail in carving and painting is not necessary as this old-style So-wing or Deer katsina illustrates. Once disdained by collectors, their consequent disappearance from the market has fueled interest in a revival of the old style.

The Kwahu *or Eagle katsina is one of the most popular katsina dolls among collectors; yet it is rarely seen in ceremonies, and even then usually appears in a very different form. It is a popular doll among carvers wishing to showcase their talent.*

This Palhik Mana *or Butterfly Maiden is done in the style that one would have seen in the latter part of the 1800s. The butterfly was important not only because it is so beautiful but because it is one of the few pollinators of crops in Hopiland. Her tablita incorporates cloud, rain, rainbow, and corn motifs.*

Koshares are one of several types of clowns that can appear during Hopi ceremonies to amuse and instruct by using their extreme behavior to reinforce Hopi values. This one is just plain lost.

behalf of mortals with the more important deities. Persons unfamiliar with Pueblo Indian culture sometimes find the katsina dolls grotesque in appearance, but many tribes had a similar reaction to their first view of a crucifix.

Katsinas can be the spirits of birds, animals, places, objects, forces of nature, insects, plants, and even other tribes. Some are named for what they represent such as the *Nuvak* or Snow katsina, and the *Hon* or Bear katsina. Often the name cannot be translated, such as the *Qöqöle*. A katsina may also be named for its distinctive call, as is the case with the *Hololo* katsina.

Many of the katsinas have well-defined functions such as disciplining children, or opening the kivas at the Winter Solstice. A few, like the Bear, are credited with the power to cure specific ailments. One group, the *tsuku* or clowns, perform antics for the spectators. These

performances do more than simply relieve the solemnity of the occasion—they also reinforce certain rules of Hopi behavior through their humorously excessive acts.

The *Wawas Katsinam* or runner katsinas may challenge the men of the village to footraces and reward them with a basket if they win. If the katsina wins the loser may be switched, his hair cut, or his face rubbed with soot, depending upon which runner he lost to. These katsinas, along with some of the soyoko or "ogre" katsinas, also perform the task of keeping spectators at a proper distance and singling out those behaving inappropriately.

Katsinas are believed to live on the San Francisco Peaks north of Flagstaff, Arizona. At the time of the Winter Solstice, they leave their home to visit the Hopi villages where they dance for the residents. Their main objectives

There are several hundred katsinas, depending upon who is counting and how they are counting. The exact number seems to be more important to non-Hopi than Hopi. Their appearances can vary somewhat from mesa to mesa and a few appear only at certain villages. Their functions can also vary depending upon the religious ceremony in which they appear. From left to right these are: Hozro Wuuhti (Cold-Bringing Woman), Koyemsi (Mudhead), Qöqöle, Hilili, Pookonghoya, Kocha Hon (White Bear), Wakas (Cow), Tawa (Sun), Avats'hoya (Spotted Corn), and Anuthlona. Not all have names that can be translated, and some commonly accepted English names are not accurate.

are to ensure the continuation of the life cycle of all living things and to promote the general well-being of the people. Benefits are not limited to the Hopi, for they believe that a katsina dance, performed in the proper spirit, extends its blessings beyond the borders of their land. The katsina religious cycle ends in late July with the *Niman* or Home Dance, which marks the return of the katsinas to their mountain home until the next Winter Solstice.

Hopi men (a few women have begun to carve in the past 20 years) carve katsina figures from the root of the cottonwood tree. Using a variety of carving tools (including hand-held electric tools in some cases) and files they form the figure and then sand it smooth. Sandpaper and emery paper have replaced the traditional piece of sandstone for smoothing. The figure is then coated with either gesso or kaolin, a white clay, to seal the wood. Mineral and vegetal paints were traditionally used; however, much to the dismay of non-Hopi buyers, they rubbed off too easily when the figures were handled. The artists then began to use tempera and poster paints, which in turn were replaced by acrylic paints in the 1960s. Both the poster paints and the acrylics also offered a wider range of colors

than the traditional mineral and vegetal paints. Since 1990 several carvers have gone back to the more muted traditional pigments, with some using an acrylic base as a fixative.

THE SIGNIFICANCE OF COLORS

The colors with which a katsina is painted can be significant. The Hopi assign a different color for each of the six directions: yellow for the north, white for the east, red for the south, blue-green for the west, black for the zenith, and spotted or all colors for the nadir. Certain katsinas can appear with different directional-colored masks, or the color can simply be part of the name as with the *Sakwa Hu* or Blue Whipper.

Similarly, the feathers used are significant. Certain katsinas and their dolls are decorated with the feathers from specific birds. Feather use on katsinas that are sold is restricted by the Fish and Wildlife Service to most (but not all) species of domestic fowl, sparrow, quail, parrot, pigeon, and pheasant. Even feathers from most game birds cannot legally be used, causing most carvers to make feathers from wood instead.

Katsina figures range from the simple *putska tihu* or flat dolls, sometimes called cradle dolls, that are given to infants, to elaborately

Hopis receive their first doll or tihu *when in infancy. ("Doll" is a misleading word as they are not played with like toys.) The style of doll they are given is a* putska tihu *or flat doll. Traditionally this was also the type given to women of childbearing age during the katsina rites. Hopi boys traditionally no longer received dolls after they had been initiated into the Katsina Society. From left are:* Hahai Wuuhti, Susopa *(Cricket), and* Qöqöle. *Hahai Wuuhti is one of two regarded as being the grandmother of the katsinas. She is also usually the first putska tihu a Hopi infant is given.*

carved and painstakingly painted figures in action poses created basically from a single piece of wood—with virtually nothing added or glued on. Most katsina dolls have arms and accessories, such as bows or rattles, that are carved separately and then attached to the body with pegs and glue. Beginning in the 1980s a sculptural style has evolved, meant to evoke more the katsina spirit than the katsina dancer.

A particular katsina can differ in appearance from one village or mesa to the next. In fact, some known at one may not appear at all in another. This variance has led to the mistaken belief that Hopi carvers deliberately leave out certain details on katsinas that are carved "for sale." This is generally untrue. Detail and proportions of a katsina will vary depending upon the carver's skill and style of work, and be reflected in the price, but in Hopi eyes skill does not make for a "better" doll—only accuracy in its depiction is important.

Pottery

A new pottery tradition—the making of storyteller figurines—has arisen to commemorate an old tradition—that of the storyteller who passed on the traditions and beliefs of the tribe to succeeding generations.

The art of pottery making in the Southwest is nearly 2,000 years old. Early pieces were used as cooking pots, water jars, storage jars, and ceremonial vessels. Both form and design varied from one tribe to the next, just as they do today. Change was the rule rather than the exception. Archaeologists employ a chronology based upon progressive changes in Pueblo pottery types as a method of dating prehistoric sites.

Introduction of metal containers had a profound effect on the ceramic arts. By the early 1900s large storage jars were infrequently produced, and the use of cooking vessels had sharply declined. At the same time, demand by non-Indians for smaller, more decorative pieces increased and pottery production was tailored to fit the new market.

Most modern Southwest Indian pottery is made in the same manner as prehistoric ware. Clay is dug from local deposits and ground, soaked, refined, and mixed with a grit or temper.

Most pottery construction is by the coil and scrape method—building the vessel by coiling long ropes of clay into the desired shape and then pinching them together. Next the vessel is scraped smooth with a piece of gourd or metal to obliterate any sign of the coils. A few tribes, such as the Tohono O'odham, use a paddle and anvil technique, by which the pieces of clay are flattened and molded piece by piece to build the vessel. The potter's wheel was never used by traditional Indian potters.

Often a coat of clay, called a clay slip, is applied. The slip is a mixture of water and very fine clay which is painted or wiped over the surface of the pot. Then, depending upon the pueblo, the surface may be polished with a small, smooth stone. If there are to be painted designs they are

Since its beginning at Cochiti in 1964, the making of storyteller figurines has spread to other pueblos in the Rio Grande Valley and west to Acoma, where this one was made. Each pueblo has a unique general style range within which artists express their individuality.

The Tewa potters have long made a carved ware but only since the 1960s have they employed a technique called sgraffito. This technique differs from earlier methods in two distinct ways: it is shallower and it is done after the piece has been polished and fired.

applied at this point. Specific designs and colors used depend largely on the potter's tribal affiliation, though stylistic boundaries are beginning to break down. Experimentation and innovation continue, with the creation of new designs and the borrowing or resurrection of older, often prehistoric designs, as well as the reinterpretation of those early designs. The painting, in either mineral or vegetal paints, is usually applied with a brush made of yucca, though a few potters now use conventional paintbrushes.

FIRING OF THE POTTERY

After it dries, the pottery is fired by placing it on a grate or bed of potsherds around which a wood fire is lit. In some cases the pottery is covered with sheet metal (usually tin) and large shards, and a fire is built under and around the pottery. Dried dung, usually sheep manure, is often used for firing, although coal or wood are also used by some Pueblo potters. The firing itself generally lasts no more than a few hours from start to finish, with temperatures ranging from 850 to 1,300 degrees Fahrenheit—higher for coal-fired kilns.

Pottery fired in this manner is fairly porous. Glazes were known in prehistoric times but were used exclusively for decoration, not

(continued on page 60)

SAN JUAN—The most common types are a plain polished redware, a light brown incised ware made of a clay that contains mica, and a polychrome. Some pieces are carved in low-relief.

TAOS-PICURIS—The micaceous clay used by potters from these villages gives their pottery a golden glitter. This ware is well-fired, and their wide-mouthed bean pots are much sought after for use as cooking vessels.

SANTA CLARA—Styles include polished red and blackware, carved, sgraffito, or with matte paint designs, and a polychrome redware with blue-gray and white designs, as well as some white-slipped polychrome ware. Animal, bird, and human figurines are also made.

SAN ILDEFONSO—Highly polished red and blackware with matte paint designs were revived by the renowned potter Maria Martinez beginning in the1920s. Carved ware was begun in the early 1930s and sgraffito work in the 1960s. A little polychrome redware is occasionally produced. Pottery from Santa Clara and San Ildefonso are identical in appearance.

POJOAQUE—Pottery here has been revived in recent years much as the pueblo itself was resettled and revived over 60 years ago. Micaceous ware, blackware, polychrome redware, and some carved ware and sgraffito are now produced here.

POTTERY

NAMBE—Micaceous clay pottery from this pueblo's pottery revival includes sculptural pieces as well as carved ware, polychrome ware, polished redware, and sgraffito work—similar to types produced at Santa Clara.

TESUQUE—The poster-painted, sun-dried pottery once associated with this pueblo has nearly disappeared. In its place is a rebirth of traditional pottery— some of it black on gray-white, a little polychrome, and some micaceous ware.

COCHITI—Storyteller figurines are the primary pottery form at this pueblo. Though they once produced bowls and jars, those have now nearly disappeared.

SANTO DOMINGO—Though best known for black on white with a red bottom, a little polychrome work is done, along with a matte on polished black and some black or polychrome on redware.

SAN FELIPE—The older style polychrome work has disappeared, but there are a few remaining potters who produce a black on red and a polished ware made from mica-flecked clay.

JEMEZ—Known for years for its poster-paint and later its acrylic-paint pottery, this pueblo has undergone a major revival with sgraffito work, polished redware that includes black on red, cream on red and polychrome, a polychrome on cream, and figurative work including storytellers.

ZIA—Classic pottery from this pueblo is a black and red on a cream- or sand-colored slip with a red base, but a few potters use acrylic paints in executing intricate designs after firing.

ISLETA—Most of the pottery here is produced by two families and is primarily polychrome though a few potters have experimented with polished redware and sgraffito. Storytellers are also made.

LAGUNA—A Keresan-speaking Pueblo people like Acoma, their pottery, while limited in quantity, is very similar in appearance to classic Acoma pottery.

ACOMA—This pueblo produces very fine black on white, polychrome, and plain white—sometimes corrugated—ware. A few potters also make storytellers and figurines.

POTTERY

ZUNI—In the last two decades Zuni pottery has undergone
a revival of its polychrome wares and figurative work. A few potters use a sand-colored
slip rather than white and a number model small lizards and frogs atop their bowls.

NAVAJO—For more than
30 years Navajo pottery has edged
away from near-disappearance of
utility ware to a thriving craft, with several
potters creating new styles—
including a subtle polychrome, a "folk-art"
style, and an exceptional polished
ware—all coated with a pinyon pitch
that is sometimes mistaken for a glaze.

HOPI—A range of types can be found
here beginning with a redware, a
whiteware, and a yellowware with
either black or polychrome designs.
Some plainware, corrugated
pottery, painted tiles, and carved
or sgraffito work are also made.

TOHONO O'ODHAM—Once limited
primarily to an undecorated brownware, potters
have created new forms like the friendship
bowl, and are reviving and improvising on
both historic patterns and ancient Hohokam pottery.
Mesquite sap is used for the black paint.

waterproofing. A porous pot used for water storage allows for the evaporation of moisture seeping through the sides, which cools the water inside the jar. In southern Arizona, water jars made by the Tohono O'odham were popular for this reason and used by residents of towns in southern Arizona until after the turn of the century.

Black and red polished ware from the Tewa pueblos of Santa Clara and San Ildefonso owe their colors primarily to two different methods of firing. To achieve a polished red finish the smoothed pot is coated with a red clay slip, polished, and then fired in an oxidizing atmosphere where the air is allowed to freely circulate and the fire burns cleanly. For the black finish, the same slip is applied and polished, but the pot is then fired in a reducing atmosphere in which the fire is smothered and a dense smoke created. The carbon in this smoke is absorbed by the iron oxide in the clay and "locked in." It will not rub off.

The traditional method of firing is filled with potential pitfalls. If the ground is too damp, or the wind comes up, or the pottery is exposed too soon to a cold atmosphere, or if there is a sudden change in the weather while firing, or there is an air pocket in the clay wall of a pot, the entire kiln-load of pottery, representing weeks or even months of work, can be ruined.

Some pottery produced for the non-Indian tourist trade is sun-dried or simply oven-baked rather than fired, and then painted with poster paint or acrylic paint, but it is less often seen these days. Its more modern counterpart is greenware—a commercially produced, mold-made pot—paint-

Whether creating bowls for serving stew or one-of-a-kind masterpieces bound for private art collections, the basic techniques remain the same.

ed with commercial paints, which may be applied either before or after firing.

Other recent changes in pottery making include *sgraffito* (a carving technique employed after firing), secondary firings to create two-toned pots, new mineral paints and glazes, gas or electric kilns and, occasionally, the potter's wheel. A few potters even add turquoise, coral, or shell beads to highlight their design work, or draw upon old design traditions to create highly individualistic work that exhibits great skill and artistry.

POTTERY

Buying Indian Crafts

With few exceptions, the first Indian-owned and operated Indian arts businesses were primarily tribal guilds and coops opened shortly after World War II. A growing number of Indian entrepreneurs—some of them artists—are now opening their own shops.

Every art has its imitators, and Indian art is no exception. Its broad appeal makes Indian jewelry the craft most often imitated. Misleading advertising is responsible for much of the fraud perpetrated on the public. The words "Indian design" or "Indian style" are no guarantee that the items are Indian handmade. In fact, they often indicate the opposite. Similarly, "silver metal" and "turquoise-blue stones" are simply descriptive terms that a careless buyer may misinterpret. "Reservation-made" is another meaningless phrase, for an Indian handmade item is no more or less authentic for having been created on or off a reservation.

Beware of major "discounts" as they are usually meaningless. The Indian artisans normally have a set price—the only variable is the store's markup. A store that quadruples its jewelry prices can offer a 50 percent discount that winds up being the same as the regular price of a store that doubles but does not "discount."

A purchase made directly from an Indian is not always a guarantee of authenticity either. Many an imitation has been bought from a genuine Indian by unwary buyers. A person who would never consider buying a diamond from a street-corner vendor will not hesitate to buy an imported Indian-style rug or a pair of earrings if the seller is picturesque enough.

As with any craft there are shortcuts that artisans can take that influence the value. There is also an extensive range of imitations and imitation materials. Obviously no one can become an expert on Indian crafts in a short period of time. Therefore it is necessary to rely upon dealers who have a reputation for handling authentic crafts. The Indian Arts and Crafts Association in Albuquerque, New Mexico, museums, and even the craftspeople themselves can be good sources to inquire about the names of reputable shops. A few Indian tribes operate guilds or cooperatives that are also good places to buy the crafts of that tribe.

Another way to become a careful, informed shopper, is to familiarize oneself with Indian crafts by attending some of the many exhibitions of Indian art held in the Southwest, and asking questions of the traders and craftspeople. State offices of tourism can be contacted for specific places and dates.

Even the most knowledgeable buyer is well-advised to obtain all claims in writing on the receipt. Certificates of authenticity are no guarantee but, like a well-written receipt, they can provide the basis for a refund if the item turns out not to be as claimed.

In recent years many Indian artists have become the focus of brochures, articles, and other promotional material. Many will list awards, ribbons, and recognition they have received for their work. While this can be an indication that you are looking at the work of a talented artist, some exceptionally fine artists choose not to enter competitions and shun the limelight or have been ignored by it. Additionally, a famous artist can have a bad day and an unknown artist can have a moment of glorious inspiration. Buy a piece because *you* like it, not because the salesperson, a crafts judge, or a magazine writer likes it.

The suggested reading list at the end of this book can provide additional information to assist the reader in becoming a more knowledgeable, discriminating buyer, and to develop an appreciation and understanding of not only Southwestern Indian arts and crafts, but Southwestern Indian culture as well.

Care of Indian Crafts

Silver jewelry usually has areas that have been deliberately oxidized, or darkened, to heighten the contrast that creates the design. If this patina is accidentally removed, it can be restored by using a little "liver of sulfur" mixed in a bit of water and applied with a toothpick or small paintbrush. Craft shops sell this and other solutions for oxidizing jewelry. Allow it to dry before polishing the raised areas.

Some people like a high polish on their jewelry while others like the softer patina that comes with age and use. To restore the polish, use a jeweler's rough cloth. Paste can get caught in the recessed areas, and dips can harm the stones and remove all the oxidation. Household ammonia, applied carefully with a Q-tip, can remove heavy tarnish.

To avoid continually bending a bracelet, which will cause it to eventually crack and break, put it on just above the wrist bone from the inside of the arm. Then rotate it over the wrist. To take it off, reverse the procedure. The bracelet should fit loosely enough to be comfortable without falling off.

When putting on a bracelet, especially one set with stones, one must exercise care to avoid bending the bracelet. It should be put on from the inside of the arm, just above the wrist bone, with a rolling motion. To take it off, simply reverse the action. If a bracelet is bent, even slightly, each time it is taken on and off, it will crack and eventually break. Bending will also crack or loosen the stones in their settings.

Stones set in bezels usually have a cushion of either sawdust or a bit of cardboard to help absorb minor impacts without cracking. If it is immersed in water the backing can swell, causing the stone to loosen and fall out. Inlaid stones can be susceptible to soaps and oils loosening their bond with the epoxy that holds them in place. Coral, as well as medium to soft grades of turquoise, can also be harmed by repeated exposure to soaps and oils.

Silver bead necklaces, including squash blossom necklaces, are best strung on foxtail—a braided steel wire.

Heishe should be strung on braided nylon. Monofilaments (single strands of nylon or wire) and fine silver chains do not wear well or last long. Very fine necklaces may be strung on silk thread. Care should be taken to avoid contact with water and oils, which might shrink or weaken the stringing material.

Navajo rugs should never be shaken clean as the snapping motion tends to fray the ends and break the warp threads. Vacuuming is preferable. Floor rugs should be turned end for end and reversed from time to time to ensure even wear and mellowing of the colors. They should also have a rubber pad—preferably a waffle pad—to prevent slipping and reduce wear and tear.

Navajo rugs that are hung should also be turned end for end and reversed periodically as this not only ensures that any mellowing of the color over the years occurs uniformly, but also provides an opportunity to check for the presence of bugs that might harm the weaving. Hangings should be mothproofed annually and vacuumed regularly.

The best way to hang a Navajo rug is with Velcro™. A strip of the wide, self-adhesive hook side of Velcro™ can be applied either directly to the wall or to a strip of wood, which is then hung from the wall. When the rug is pressed against it, the thousands of tiny nylon hooks catch and hold the rug. If the rug is older there may not be enough nap left for the Velcro™ to hold. Specially designed, often decorative, wooden clamps are made that permit hanging the rug without sewing or otherwise piercing it.

If a rug is to be stored for any length of time it should be mothproofed and then rolled to avoid creases from folding. Also, it is best wrapped in a clean white sheet rather than plastic. If the rug needs a spot removed, take it to a cleaner who handles fine oriental textiles, as Navajo rugs require the same type of care and attention in the cleaning process. Navajo rugs can be dry-cleaned, but the harsh chemicals can leave the wool fibers brittle over time, which can shorten the life of a rug intended for floor use.

Indian baskets can be hung by using thread or a bit of fine wire. Hold the basket up to the light and with an awl or needle enlarge two holes to run the wire or thread through. If the basket is so tightly woven that no light shines through, then carefully select two points in between the coils and in between the stitches. This is advisable only for new baskets, not older baskets that have become somewhat brittle. To use a basket for serving bread or fruit, line it with a napkin. Avoid hanging the basket where it might receive direct sunlight that can fade or discolor it, or near

The best way to hang a Navajo rug is using the hook side of Velcro™. This will allow you to easily attach and remove the rug. If it has been used on a floor, however, there may not be enough nap to hold it.

a kitchen where it can absorb cooking oils from the air and discolor.

Traditional *Indian pottery* should not be used as a planter unless a glass jar is used as a liner; otherwise the moisture will seep through the pot and begin to blister and disintegrate the design and the surface itself. In order to prevent the bottom of the pot from marring a table, or erasing the potter's signature through wear, place it on a felt or buckskin pad. Dust with a very light touch and only with a clean, dry cloth.

Though some Indian pottery was meant to hold water, it isn't fired at a high enough temperature to hold it without eventually sustaining damage. Those collecting it as art should keep it away from any moisture. Frequent or rough, careless handling can rub away the painted surface. Similarly, repeated handling of a fine pot can deposit oils from the skin on the surface, causing discoloration. Some damage can be restored by professionals, but the finish of polished Santa Clara pottery, for example, cannot be fully restored.

*The lands of the Southwestern Indian tribes
have shaped them in many ways. In turn, the hand of
the Indian has left its mark on the Southwest.*

Chapter II

SOUTHWESTERN INDIAN TRIBES

E*ach tribe in the Southwest has its own unique history. Though some may share a common language with other groups, each has an identity that has evolved over time, an identity that has helped shape their history.*

Not only does each tribe have a story to tell, but often smaller groups within a tribe have their own histories. This section attempts to provide the reader with a sense of the relationships among tribes as well as the history of Indian-European contact.

Corn, highlighted by Jemez potter Marie Romero.

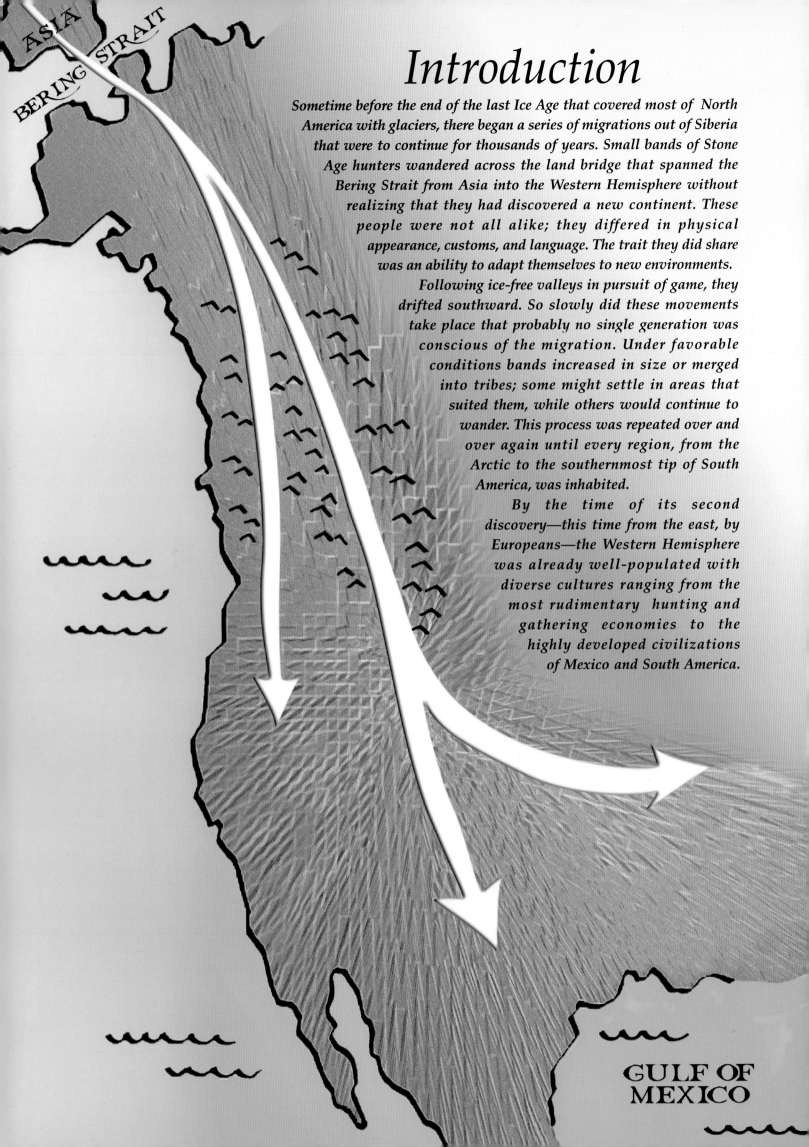

Introduction

Sometime before the end of the last Ice Age that covered most of North America with glaciers, there began a series of migrations out of Siberia that were to continue for thousands of years. Small bands of Stone Age hunters wandered across the land bridge that spanned the Bering Strait from Asia into the Western Hemisphere without realizing that they had discovered a new continent. These people were not all alike; they differed in physical appearance, customs, and language. The trait they did share was an ability to adapt themselves to new environments. Following ice-free valleys in pursuit of game, they drifted southward. So slowly did these movements take place that probably no single generation was conscious of the migration. Under favorable conditions bands increased in size or merged into tribes; some might settle in areas that suited them, while others would continue to wander. This process was repeated over and over again until every region, from the Arctic to the southernmost tip of South America, was inhabited.

By the time of its second discovery—this time from the east, by Europeans—the Western Hemisphere was already well-populated with diverse cultures ranging from the most rudimentary hunting and gathering economies to the highly developed civilizations of Mexico and South America.

ASIA

BERING STRAIT

GULF OF MEXICO

Early People in the Southwest

The story of people in the Southwest begins between 25,000 to 40,000 years ago with the appearance of small bands of nomads who used spears to hunt the mammoth, camel, bison, and ground sloth. Evidence of their passing is found only in stone implements they made and left in their caves and campsites, or embedded in the skeletal remains of the animals they killed.

With the retreat of the glaciers the climate slowly changed. The once-lush land, which supported the herds of animals these people hunted, became progressively drier. Lakes and swamps disappeared and streams ran intermittently. Once-plentiful game diminished, and these early hunters were forced to alter their way of life to meet these changes in their environment. They began to supplement their diet of meat with more seeds and edible plants they gathered. As plant foods became increasingly important in their diet, the rudiments of agriculture developed.

Agriculture does not allow for a nomadic existence, so these early people built semipermanent dwellings near their fields. Villages soon followed, and with them came all of the complexities of social and religious life that occur when people live together in communities.

Not all groups developed at the same pace, but contact between them increased and new ideas were exchanged. Basketry and weaving were highly developed and widespread. Pottery, a craft usually associated with sedentary, agricultural people, was either invented independently or introduced from Mexico around A.D. 100. By A.D. 600, it was known throughout the Southwest.

Movements of people still occurred, however, as local populations were subjected to droughts, erosion of farmlands, internal conflicts, or merely the human urge to move to a new area.

Cultivation of the "Sacred Triad"—corn, squash, and beans—now provided a relatively plentiful, stable food supply, and populations and villages increased in size and number. Social organization, ceremonialism, architecture, and crafts became more complex. Trade with the civilizations of Mexico grew and further enriched the life of the people. By A.D. 1000, these village dwellers, or Pueblo Indians, had reached a "golden age."

Evidence of the ancestors of present-day Indians can be seen in the ruins of their pueblos and heard in the ancient oral traditions of today's tribes.

Not long after this, the ancestors of the Athabascan-speaking Navajo and Apache entered the Pueblo domain. Their constant raiding forced the Pueblo farmers to fortify their towns or abandon them entirely. Depletion of natural resources, probably internal dissension, and a prolonged drought that began in the mid-1200s, resulted in more forced migrations. By A.D. 1250, many of the great pueblos were deserted and the people had sought refuge elsewhere. When the Spaniards arrived on the scene in the mid-1500s, most of the Pueblo population was concentrated at Hopi, Zuni, Acoma, and in the Rio Grande Valley.

Between A.D. 1200 and A.D. 1400 the Piman-speaking tribes, who may be the descendants of the earlier Hohokam people, settled southern Arizona, and Yuman-speaking groups moved eastward from California into Arizona and settled along the Colorado River.

By the late 1600s most of these tribes were occupying the same areas they do today, with the Navajo and Apache people moving into the intervening areas.

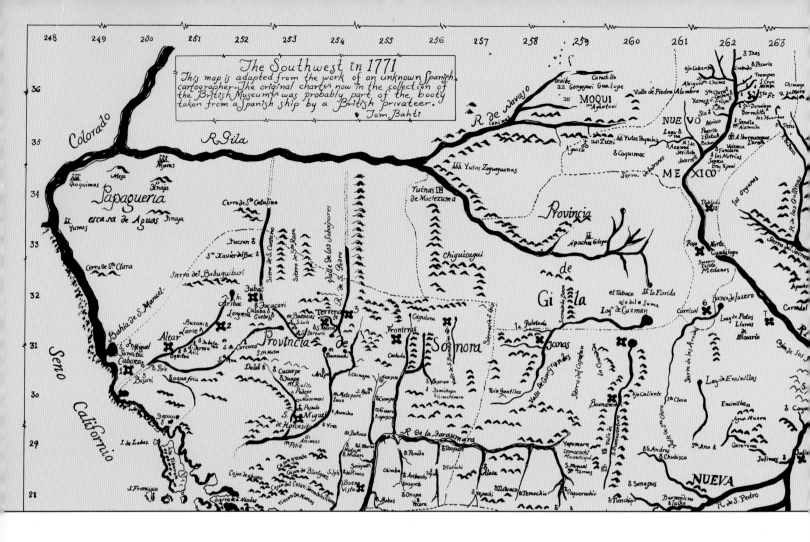

European Contact

The search for Cibola, a mythical province containing seven cities of silver and gold, brought the Spanish *conquistadores* to the Southwest. A series of explorations, beginning in 1539 with one led by Fray Marcos de Niza, failed to locate anything more spectacular than villages of mud and stone inhabited by people rich in ceremonialism but poor in material possessions.

In 1595, Juan de Oñate was awarded a contract to colonize New Mexico. Leaving from California in 1598, he arrived in New Mexico the same year to declare formal possession of Indian lands and begin colonization. The Pueblo Indians were required to swear obedience to the King of Spain and the Catholic Church. The Indians were not ousted from their lands as the Spaniards preferred to have them remain to be exploited by civil and church authorities. Tribute was demanded in the form of forced labor, food, crops, buckskins, and textiles. In return each pueblo received a Spanish name, Catholic religious instruction, and the promise of protection from Apache and Comanche raids—though much of the trouble with the marauders occurred because the Spaniards forced the Pueblo people to aid in attacks against those

tribes. Of far greater importance to the Indians was the acquisition of iron tools, fruit trees, new domestic plants, cattle, horses, and sheep.

The Spaniards also imposed the Law of the Indies which decreed that each village elect a governor, lieutenant governor, and other officials to handle secular affairs. The Indians obligingly added this new political system to their theocratic form of government, and the *cacique* or priest-chief continued to function as the real head of the village.

Life under Spanish authority became increasingly oppressive—taxation, forced labor, and harsh suppression of native religion resulted in the Great Pueblo Revolt of 1680. The tribes united in an unprecedented effort to drive out the invaders. The uprising was a success. The Spaniards retreated to El Paso and for the next 12 years the Indians once again ruled their own villages. In 1693, Diego de Vargas reconquered the Indians and reestablished Spanish authority in New Mexico.

Under Spanish rule the Indian population was centralized for ease of administration and control. In doing so, the number of pueblos in Rio Grande Valley decreased from 66 in 1540 to 19 in

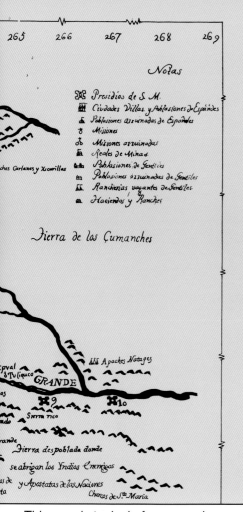

Notas

🏰 *Presidios de S. M.*
🏛 *Ciudades Villas y Poblasiones de Españoles*
⚑ *Poblasiones arruinadas de Españoles*
✝ *Misiones*
✝ *Misiones arruinadas*
🏭 *Reales de Minas*
🏘 *Poblasiones de Gentiles*
🏚 *Poblasiones arruinadas de Gentiles*
⚒ *Ranchenias vagantes de Gentiles*
🏠 *Haciendas y Ranchos*

Tierra de las Çumanches

Apaches Natages

GRANDE

Sierra Tica

Tierra despoblada donde se abrigan los Yndios Enemigos y Apostatas de las Naciones

Charcos de Sta. Maria

This map is typical of ones made by Europeans as a first step in claiming Indian land and dividing it up among themselves.

In 1934, the Indian Reorganization Act was passed with the idea of enabling tribes to reestablish self-government. Unfortunately, the form of self-government required by the U.S. was a non-traditional model designed for the convenience of the federal government.

Almost 20 years later, as an effort to reduce federal expenditures, a termination policy was established, which included relocations of Indians from the reservations to major urban areas across the country.

Finally, in 1975 Congress passed the Indian Self-Determination Act. Since then the tribes have sought, and often obtained, greater control over their own affairs including financial, medical, housing, educational, planning, and governance issues. The Indian Gaming Regulatory Act of 1988 has also had an immense impact on tribes in the Southwest, allowing many to boost sagging or virtually non-existent revenues and offset diminished federal funding. The new revenue source has also given tribes greater freedom to plan their futures.

1700. In this same time-frame disease, famine, and warfare reduced the native population by one-half.

The War of Independence transferred jurisdiction of New Mexico from Spain to Mexico in 1821. Mexico, unlike Spain, bestowed full rights of citizenship upon the Indians. (By contrast, the United States did not grant Indians full citizenship—the right to vote—until 1924, and Arizona and New Mexico did so only after a federal lawsuit in 1948.)

The Treaty of Guadalupe Hidalgo in 1848 marked the end of the war between the United States and Mexico, and New Mexico became a territory of the U.S. Much Indian land was lost to the new flood of settlers.

In 1849, jurisdiction over Indians was transferred from the War Department to the Bureau of Indian Affairs under the Department of the Interior, where it remains today. This transfer also marked the beginning of the reservation era, which was a policy designed to free up more land for settlement by non-Indians and to act as a "civilizing" agent.

Many Rio Grande pueblos retain as symbols of authority the silver-headed canes given them by President Lincoln in 1863. Former Taos Pueblo governor Tony Reyna holds the Lincoln cane, along with that given by King Phillip II of Spain in 1620 and ones from President Nixon (1970) and the state of New Mexico (1981).

Here at San Juan—during a Deer Dance—is evidence that while churches have a visible presence in many pueblos, the ancient traditions that preceded the European arrival remain strong.

Rio Grande Pueblos Today

Pueblo Indian life is based on the fundamental religious conviction that people must live in harmony with the natural world around them. So strong is this belief that it is not possible to separate religion from everyday life. The religious ceremonies that are held throughout the year are enactments of this philosophy.

Societies, headed by priests, within each pueblo are responsible for maintaining harmony with the supernatural world. Properly conducted ceremonies control the weather, effect cures, bring rain, mature crops, lead to success in hunting, and generally ensure that the cycle of life continues.

Harmony must also be maintained within the pueblo—family, clan, and society relationships require specific behavior of the individual, and children are reared to accept these duties. In such a tightly knit society it is not surprising to find that the welfare of the group traditionally ranks before that of the individual.

Each Tewa-speaking pueblo is divided into two groups, or moieties, known as the Winter People and the Summer People, or the Squash and

At the Tewa village of Santa Clara, the Corn Dance is observed much as it has been for centuries. At other pueblos where such ceremonies lapsed, there has been a revival of the old traditions.

TRIBES

Laguna is the newest pueblo in New Mexico, founded roughly 300 years ago by survivors of the Spanish re-conquest of northern New Mexico. A Keresan-speaking pueblo, it was founded by refugees from Cochiti and Santo Domingo who were later joined by settlers from Acoma, Jemez, Oraibi, Sandia, San Felipe, Zia, and Zuni.

the Turquoise. Each moiety, under leadership of a cacique, has its own kiva and ceremonial chambers and directs the ceremonial life of the village for half of the year. Keresan-speaking pueblos have only one cacique who is responsible for the spiritual well-being of the entire pueblo. Ordinarily, it is he who selects the officers to handle secular affairs. Each pueblo is politically autonomous.

Although the Catholic Church has claimed converts among the Rio Grande pueblos for over 300 years, and most of the Indians make use of some services provided by the church (baptism, confirmation, marriage, burial), the importance of native religion has not diminished. The two religious systems are separate and the Indians find nothing inconsistent in making use of both.

In recent years there has been a revival in the native religions—old ceremonies have been renewed and more people, especially younger members, participate in the ceremonial life of the pueblos.

Problems that face the pueblos are serious and numerous. Increased intermarriage with non-Indians tends to weaken pueblo authority. Population increases render present land resources inadequate. Outmoded and inequitable systems of land inheritance have fractionalized holdings until they have become impractical to farm. Agriculture, once the economic foundation of pueblo life, has become less and less important, being supplanted by other forms of economic development ranging from resorts, golf courses, and casinos, to shopping centers and even housing developments aimed at non-Indian markets.

Encroachments from non-Indian cultures combined with internal frictions, factionalism, and substance abuse, all symptoms of a culture under pressure and in the process of social change, weaken tribal solidarity.

A strong love for the tribal lands, a common language, and a deep attachment to and respect for the religious life of the village seem to hold each pueblo group together in the face of these difficulties.

Life in the pueblos is neither ideal nor idyllic, but it obviously holds a greater attraction and greater satisfaction for most of these people than an existence in the mainstream of American life.

These Indian tribes have not only survived 400 years of occupation by alien cultures, but have managed to retain more of their native life than they have lost. It is probably not overly optimistic to believe that they can continue in the same manner.

ACOMA

(ah'-ko-mah) — from the native word *Ah'-ku-me*, meaning "people of the white rock." Language: Keresan. Reservation: 378,345 acres. Population: 5,029. Government: Cacique chooses secular officers and council members. Dances: Sept. 2 - Harvest Dance and annual Feast Day of San Estevan. Dec. 24 - Christmas Eve festival.

Acoma, the Southwest's "Sky City," is located atop a mesa that stands nearly 400 feet above the surrounding valley. Acoma vies with the Hopi pueblo of Oraibi for the claim to being "the oldest continuously inhabited community in the U.S." Archaeological evidence indicates that the site has been occupied since at least A.D. 1150.

The first Europeans to visit the pueblo were part of Coronado's expedition, who arrived in 1540. At the time there were 5,000 Acoma occupying several villages in the area.

The Spaniards feared Acoma's military potential and its control over neighboring pueblos. In 1599, the Spanish territorial governor Juan de Oñate sent a military force to demand tribute and supplies. The Acoma responded by attacking the soldiers. The following month a larger force was sent to lay siege to Acoma. Over a three-day battle, 800 Indians were slaughtered and the mesa-top town largely destroyed. The survivors were taken captive and marched to Santo Domingo Pueblo to stand trial. Women over 12 years of age were sentenced to 20 years slave labor; men between 12 and 25 received the same fate in addition to having one foot chopped off. (Those over 25 were deemed too old for 20 years of servitude, and so had one foot amputated before being sent home.) Young girls were given to the Church, and the boys to the officer who led the soldiers as a reward for his victory.

In 1629, the Franciscans established the mission of San Estevan del Rey at the pueblo under the direction of Fray Ramirez. This impressive structure, which has been rebuilt and remodeled many times, loses some of its charm when it is remembered that it was originally built (like most church buildings at Indian pueblos) with forced labor. The enormous logs that form the beamed ceiling, for example, were carried from Mount Taylor, which lies a hard two days walk from the village.

Acoma participated in the Great Pueblo Revolt of 1680, and later served as a refuge from the Spaniards for other Indians. During the reconquest, the Spanish attacked Acoma in 1696 and laid waste their fields to try and starve them into submission. It was three years before Acoma was finally forced to submit to Spanish authority.

Only a few families live in the mesa-top village year-round. Most occupy the permanent farming communities of Acomita, Anzac, and McCartys. All of them, however, return to the main pueblo for ceremonies.

Farming, ranching, wage work, and some mining are the primary occupations. Uranium mining, once the major source of tribal income, has collapsed. A casino is now providing a source of considerable income as well as employment for the Acoma people. Lakes built for recreation were polluted by communities and mining activities upstream, forcing the Acoma to shut down the lakes, drain, and dredge them. They are now in the process of refilling the lakes, which they hope will become a significant source of income.

Acoma has long been noted for producing very fine polychrome pottery with the thinnest walls of any pueblo pottery, but corrugated pots are also made. This corrugated vessel is meant to represent the rock cisterns atop the mesa which catch run-off rainwater. While no longer vital to the existence of the pueblo, they are still an attraction for children—and visitors.

ACOMA

The high mesa upon which Acoma rests provided security and protection from its enemies for over 400 years. In 1599 Spanish soldiers lay siege to the pueblo killing hundreds and brutally mistreating the survivors.

The best-known craft of Acoma Pueblo is pottery. Many potters still produce large quantities of carefully painted, thin-walled ware. In addition to the traditional jars and bowl forms, copies of prehistoric vessels, figurines of animals, birds, and humans are produced. Several potters are producing new, innovative forms. Most potters use conventional kilns to fire their work, and a number have begun to paint and fire ready-made "greenware."

Visitors to Acoma are charged an admission fee (a practice begun in 1928), which includes a guide and transportation up and down the mesa in a bus. Picture-taking anywhere on Acoma land also requires payment of a fee.

Famous for their pottery, Acoma artists still produce vessels shaped like the ones once used to hold water, store seeds, and serve food. Acoma used to be known for its beautifully woven and embroidered mantas or dresses, but textile arts have disappeared here as at most other pueblos.

K. C. DEN DOOVEN

ISLETA

ISLETA (iss-leh'-tah) — from the Spanish word for "little island." Native name is *Cheh-wib-ahg*, meaning "flint kick-stick place." Both names are descriptive of the physical location of the pueblo. Language: Tiwa. Reservation: 211,103 acres. Population: 4,105. Government: Constitution adopted in 1947. Adult members (women received the vote in 1971) annually elect governor, president, and vice-president of the council. These officers then select council members and minor officials. Dances: Jan. 3 - Corn and Turtle Dance. Aug. 28 - Corn Dance and fiesta. Sept. 4 - San Agustin Feast Day. Dec. 24 - Christmas Eve dance.

Unlike other Rio Grande pueblos, Isleta legend states that their ancestors came from the south as well as the north. The present site has been occupied since the early 1700s, and may have been used at least seasonally since the early 1500s.

The population of Isleta was greatly increased in the 1600s by an influx of refugees from other Tiwa villages who sought protection from Apache raids. In 1680, the population was estimated to be 2,000. Of the 20 villages that comprised the Southern Tiwa province at the time of Spanish contact, only Isleta remained by the late 1700s.

The large numbers of Spanish settlers who moved to Isleta prior to the 1680 revolt unwittingly prevented that village from taking part in the initial uprising. However, before the fleeing Spanish reached Isleta on their retreat south to El Paso, most of the villagers had abandoned their pueblo and joined the insurgents.

In 1681, Governor Otermin, during an unsuccessful reconquest attempt, attacked several Southern Tiwa villages including Isleta. He took hundreds of captives south to El Paso, where he settled them at a new village called Ysleta del Sur. Other Isletans fled to the safety of the Hopi pueblos, not returning until some 35 years later.

In 1880, a group of religious conservatives fleeing strife at their pueblo of Laguna were invited to settle at Isleta. Though many left a few years later, the religious leader stayed, along with the katsina masks and other religious objects.

Isleta was the only Rio Grande pueblo to adopt the Spanish custom of electing a governor. This caused a certain amount of confusion in leadership since it usurped the power of the cacique who ordinarily selected secular officials. By the late 1800s factionalism developed over the issues of leadership in village affairs and election procedures. It reached a peak in the early 1940s. A constitution and council form of government, adopted in 1947, did not solve the question.

Problems continued and in 1971 women were enfranchised as part of an effort to resolve these issues. Despite its factionalism, Isleta maintains a full and active ceremonial life, and is now moving forward on economic development for the community and dealing with the pressures brought on by the steady southward expansion of the city of Albuquerque. The urban encroachment and industrial development has created pollution problems downstream at Isleta, affecting water for drinking, farming, and several small fishing and recreational lakes owned by the pueblo.

Agriculture is a community enterprise, though many still maintain their own garden plots and raise stock. Profits from tribal gaming, a small industrial park, cattle grazing, and wage work are the primary sources of income. Some jewelry and pottery is produced. What is known as Isleta pottery is made by descendants of the Laguna colony who settled at Isleta in 1880.

Portions of the original structure, built after the Great Pueblo Revolt of 1680, are incorporated in the church of San Antonio de la Isleta. Of the 20 Tiwa Indian villages that existed in New Mexico before the revolt, only one, Isleta, remained by the late 1700s.

MARK BAHTI

YSLETA DEL SUR (iss-leh'-tah del sur) —
from the Spanish for "South Isleta." Language: Tiwa.
Reservation: 119 acres. Population: 1,473. Government:
Elected and appointed officials include cacique, cacique
teniente, alguacil, and war captain. The cacique and war
captain are appointed for life. The other positions are
filled by election each New Year's Eve. Dances: June 13 -
St. Anthony's Feast Day.

MARK BAHTI

Both the text and
the carved Indian
image are in
error. The Tiwa
who settled in El
Paso are generally
believed to have
been forced
to accompany
the Spanish.

Founded in 1681 by Tiwas from Isleta Pueblo,
most of whom were forced to accompany the
Spanish who fled the Great Pueblo Revolt, most
tribal members still recognize Isleta as the ancestral pueblo. Inhabitants also include Piro and
Manso Indians. The mission of Corpus Christi de
la Ysleta del Sur (dedicated to Our Lady of Mount
Carmel) was built in 1681, and remains the focal
point of the Tigua (Tiwa) Indian community.

The Tiwas helped defend El Paso against
Comanche and Apache raids, and for this service
were awarded a land grant from the King of
Spain in 1751. After the Americans assumed control of Texas, the Indians of Isleta found their
land steadily being lost to encroaching settlers
and speculators who used everything from the
state legislature to outright theft. The tribe was
recognized by the state of Texas in 1967 and by
the federal government in 1968, but was placed
under state jurisdiction for many years.

Tradition holds that katsina-like beings live
in the nearby Cerro Alto mountains. Called
*Awelo*s (from the Spanish word for grandpar-
ents—*abuelos*), they protect the tribe and punish
wrongdoers. They are represented by two dancers
who wear buffalo-hide masks. The masks, along
with the tribal drum, are kept in the *tusla*, a building used primarily for religious purposes. The
tribal drum has special significance for it is said to
have been brought from Isleta in 1680.

In 1971, virtually every family's income was
below the poverty level. In recent years, development of shops, a museum, a recreation area at
Hueco Tanks, a restaurant, and a casino operation
have greatly improved living conditions among
the Tiguas. There has been a modest revival of
some craftwork and the introduction of wheel-
thrown pottery.

Also associated with the Tigua of El Paso is
the Tiwa community of Tortugas in Las Cruces,
New Mexico, which does not have state or federal recognition. Run by a community corporation
(composed of Indians and non-Indians) founded
in 1914, they own 40 acres on which half of the
tribal members live. Many tribal members are
enrolled members of the tribe at Ysleta del Sur.

Since only a fraction
of the lands taken
from the Tigua of Ysleta
del Sur have been
returned, their
casino has been the
centerpiece of economic
revival efforts.

MARK BAHTI

The Catholic Mission at Laguna was built a few years after the pueblo was founded. The interior incorporates both Catholic and Indian motifs. A Presbyterian mission, built over a century and a half later, brought deep dissension. Bitter factionalism developed and, when an outsider was elected as the governor of the village, traditional Laguna religious leaders closed their kivas in protest and moved to the pueblo of Isleta.

LAGUNA (lah-goo'-nah) — Spanish word for "lake." Native name is *Kawaik*, from the word for "lake." Language: Keresan. Reservation: 528,684 acres. Population: 7,316. Government: Secular officers, with a tribal council headed by a governor. Constitution adopted in 1958. Dances: June 24 - San Juan's Day. Aug. 10 - Corn Dance. Sept. 19 - Harvest Dance. Dec. 24 - Christmas Eve Dance.

Laguna, founded in 1699, is the most recent of New Mexico's pueblos. It was built by rebels from Cochiti and Santo Domingo who survived de Vargas's attack on their stronghold at La Cieneguilla in 1694. Later they were joined by members of other pueblos—the clans at Laguna trace their origins to Acoma, Zuni, San Felipe, Zia, Oraibi, Sandia, and Jemez.

The population of Laguna, formerly concentrated at the mother village, now also occupies seven nearby settlements: Paguate, Encinal, Paraje, New Laguna, Mesita, Casa Blanca, and Seama. The latter community includes three "suburbs" named Harrisburg, Philadelphia, and New York.

Governor Cubero, who visited the pueblo in the year of its founding, named it San Jose de la Laguna. A mission was built at the village in 1706.

The introduction of Presbyterianism to Laguna in 1870, by two Anglos who had married Laguna women, resulted in bitter factionalism. A Presbyterian mission was built at the pueblo in 1875, and the new sect succeeded in electing an outsider to the position of village governor. In protest the conservatives closed their kivas, removed their religious objects, and left the pueblo. Most of them moved to Isleta where they founded the colony of Oraibi. A few took up residence at Mesita. The exodus left Laguna without traditional religious-based leadership.

The tribal government of Laguna was one of the first and most "progressive" of all the pueblos. For many years, beginning in the late 1950s, there was sizeable income from uranium leases which was invested in scholarship programs and local projects as well as individual disbursements. (Pollution from radioactive tailings is the other legacy from uranium mining, which ended in 1983.) Laguna Industries, located in a building previously occupied by an electronics plant initially underwritten by the tribe, continues to offer employment in the community. Among those who have contracts with the plant is the Department of Defense. Additionally, the tribe operates a construction company. For most tribal members, wage work combined with some farming and ranching are the primary sources of income. Sheepherding was once the major source of wealth for the pueblo, but overgrazing took its toll on the land and, in 1935, the federal government ordered the flocks reduced by over 70 percent.

Today, little craftwork is produced except for some embroidery and a limited amount of pottery and jewelry.

SANDIA (sahn-dee'-yah) — Spanish word for "watermelon" and for the nearby mountains. Native name is *Nafiat*, meaning "sandy place." Language: Tiwa. Reservation: 22,871 acres. Population: 368. Government: Cacique appoints secular officers. Dances: June 13 - Corn Dance and feast day. Dec. 31 - New Year's Eve Deer Dance.

The pueblo of Sandia dates from about A.D. 1300. Remains of the early village visited by Coronado in 1540 are still visible near the present church.

In the early 17th century, the Franciscans built the mission of San Francisco at the village. It was destroyed during the Great Pueblo Revolt in 1680. (The existing church was built in the early 1890s.)

Fearing Spanish reprisals the Sandia people abandoned their pueblo after the rebellion and took refuge with the Hopis. (Their fears were well founded as in 1681, during an unsuccessful reconquest attempt, the Spanish sacked and burned the pueblo.) On Second Mesa, north of the pueblo of Mishongnovi, they established the village of Payupki, where they lived until 1742 when two Spanish priests persuaded 500 of them to return to New Mexico. They reestablished their village on the site of the old one. The new pueblo was named Nuestra Señora de los Dolores y San Antonio de Sandia—the Hopis call it Payupki.

Despite its proximity to Albuquerque, Sandia has kept a low profile through this century, and little is known about its traditional beliefs and practices.

Farming has declined in importance, being supplanted by wage work. Tribal income and employment is derived from a successful arts and crafts enterprise, fishing fees, and a casino.

Sandia is a conservative pueblo where traditional Pueblo dress such as this manta is still generally worn during religious observances. They are very protective of their privacy. Though their land is virtually surrounded by development and they have built a casino and craft shop along the interstate, Sandia Pueblo does not encourage visitors and closes all access during ceremonies. There are no signs marking the way to Sandia Pueblo.

SANTA ANA (sahn'tah ahn'ah) — Spanish name for Saint Anne. Native name is *Tamaya*. Language: Keresan. Reservation: 61,931 acres. Population: 595. Government: Cacique selects secular officers annually. Council includes all adult male family heads. Dances: June 24 - San Juan's Day. July 26 - Green Corn Dance and Feast Day.

Oñate visited Tamaya, which he renamed Santa Ana, in 1598, and a mission was built there in the 17th century. In 1680, Santa Ana, San Felipe, and Santo Domingo joined forces during the Great Pueblo Revolt.

The governor of El Paso led an attack on Santa Ana in 1687 during a reconquest attempt, and burned the village. Those who escaped joined with survivors from Zia to establish a village on Red Mesa near Jemez as a defense against the Spanish. In 1692, de Vargas persuaded them to return to Santa Ana and rebuild the village. After this they remained loyal to Spanish rule and, as a result, suffered periodic raids by the Jemez people who wanted all pueblos to continue to resist Spanish rule. The present church at Santa Ana dates from 1734, but may include portions of the earlier mission.

A lack of agricultural land and water for irrigation has forced virtual abandonment of the pueblo of Santa Ana. Most of the tribe now lives at Ranchitos (also known as Ranchos de Santa Ana), a farming community on the Rio Grande near Bernalillo. The pueblo began buying farming land in this area in the early 1700s. Only a few people remain behind year-round to take care of the pueblo.

One of the seven Keresan-speaking pueblos, Santa Ana remains active ceremonially, and the people return to their village to perform their ceremonies. At all other times the pueblo remains closed to non-tribal members. After a series of devastating epidemics in the early 1900s, the population has recovered and is growing. Agriculture remains important, though the tribe has also developed a restaurant, golf course, and casino which provide revenue as well as employment.

Traditional pottery, revived twice since the 1940s, is not currently being made.

Most of the people of Santa Ana live east of the pueblo, in Ranchitos, along the Rio Grande. They return to the pueblo for traditional ceremonies, but only a few live there year-round. For this reason, it is closed to outsiders for all but a few days annually; hence, the very permanent-looking sign.

Without forgetting their past, many pueblos near urban areas are creating a new economic future. The country club and golf resort developed by Santa Ana overlooks an ancient pueblo past while providing an income for the tribe's present and future.

SAN FELIPE (sahn feh-lee'-pay) — Spanish
name for Saint Philip. Native name is *Katishtya*.
Language: Keresan. Reservation: 48,930 acres. Population:
2,516. Government: Religious leader selects secular officers
and council. Dances: Feb. 2 - Buffalo Dance. May 1 - Feast
Day and Corn Dance. June 29 - San Pedro's Day celebration. Dec. 24 - Christmas Eve Dance.

Tradition holds that the people of San Felipe and
Cochiti once were one, living in a pueblo known
as Kuapa. The aggressive expansion of the Tewa
people to the north eventually forced abandonment of the pueblo, with the group splitting and
going on to found separate villages.

The present pueblo of San Felipe, which
was established by 1706, is the fourth village to
bear the native name Katishtya. The first, located farther south, was abandoned before the
Spaniards arrived. The second, named San
Felipe by the Spanish in 1591, was on the east
bank of the Rio Grande at the foot of La Mesita,
across the river from a second village belonging
to these Keresan people. Here, in the early
1600s, a mission was established and maintained until the Great Pueblo Revolt of 1680
when the villagers destroyed the church and
abandoned their pueblo.

Fearful of Spanish reprisals, the people of San
Felipe joined forces with refugees from several
other pueblos at La Cieneguilla, a fortified site
north of Cochiti.

In 1693, General de Vargas persuaded the
residents to leave their fortress. The third village
of Katishtya was then established in a defensive
position on the top of Black Mesa on the west
side of the Rio Grande. San Felipe remained
obedient to the Spanish thereafter and provided
warriors to aid the Spaniards in subduing the
other pueblo tribes. This village was abandoned
in 1700, and the present town built below the
mesa along the Rio Grande.

San Felipe shares with Santo Domingo a
reputation for being a very conservative village.
The cacique, aided by a war captain and his
assistant, annually appoints all secular officers
and council members. This form of government
precludes elections and limits participation in
village affairs by its younger members. The
number of young people who leave the pueblo
to seek outside employment has risen steadily
for years.

Farming, which has declined in importance as
an economic pursuit, may improve if present plans
for land and water distribution are carried out.

*What is thought of as traditional San Felipe pottery has
disappeared. New traditions, based in part on the old,
and using traditional clays and paints, have emerged. As
in most pueblos, pottery art is replacing pottery utensils.*

San Felipe has always been noted among
the Rio Grande pueblos for its beautiful ceremonial dances and, in recent years, a number of old
rituals have been revived.

Traditional pottery has disappeared, but a
limited amount of very innovative pottery is
made. Other than that, no significant amount of
craftwork is produced.

The plaza in front of the present church (built in 1890) at Santo Domingo Pueblo is the site of many traditional religious observances during the year. For this reason, photographs of the church are no longer permitted.

SANTO DOMINGO (sahn'-toh dohming'-oh) — Spanish for Saint Dominic. Native name is *Giuwa*. Language: Keresan. Reservation: 71,093 acres. Population: 4,949. Government: Council made up of former governors chooses secular officers annually. Strong control exerted over village government by religious leaders. Dances: June 29 - San Pedro's Day celebration. Aug. 4 - Corn Dance and Feast Day. Dec. 24 - Christmas Eve Dance.

Santo Domingo has long been regarded as one of the most conservative of all the pueblos. The people are friendly but independent, maintaining a high degree of tribal unity in government and religious affairs despite outside pressures to change.

The present pueblo of Santo Domingo dates to about 1700. A disastrous flood in 1886 destroyed much of the town and its church. It was soon rebuilt and a new church (the present one) constructed in 1890. Floods have always been a particular menace to the villagers—at least three of their earlier towns and two Spanish missions have been destroyed by Rio Grande floodwaters.

Oñate visited Santo Domingo in 1598 and met there with the leaders of more than 30 pueblos. Whether they fully understood that the Spaniards were claiming their land is not known

(and not likely), but Oñate claimed that he had received pledges of allegiance to both the Crown and the Church from all those assembled.

Alonza Catiti, an interpreter from Santo Domingo, was one of the three leaders of the Great Pueblo Revolt of 1680. The village was abandoned at that time and the people moved to a fortified position, La Cieneguilla, in anticipation of a Spanish counterattack. In 1683, most of them returned to their village.

The Santo Domingans resisted reconquest by the Spaniards—they destroyed their pueblo in 1692 and joined forces with the Indians of Jemez. Their new village near Jemez was destroyed by de Vargas two years later, and many of the people were taken captive. Some who escaped fled to the Hopi villages, and others who had remained with the rebels at La Cieneguilla moved to Acoma country with some Cochiti refugees where they established the new pueblo of Laguna.

While there are Santo Domingo ceramists creating art pottery, traditional forms remain strong. Water jars, storage vessels, and stew bowls—both individual and communal—are regularly made, and the stew bowls are often used during feast days.

K. C. DEN DOOVEN

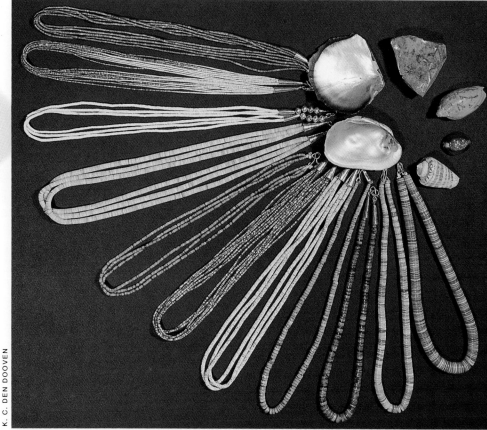

At one time stone and shell bead necklaces were made in all the pueblos, but by the latter half of the 1900s most were being made at Santo Domingo Pueblo. A number of silversmiths are also active at Santo Domingo.

Santo Domingo was later resettled by de Vargas's captives and those who returned from Hopi country. A number of Tano Indians from the Galisteo Basin—refugees from the Comanche raids—also joined the pueblo.

As far as was possible the people followed a policy of passive resistance toward the Spanish. Native ceremonies were carried on in secrecy in defiance of the Catholic church. Their present dislike for those who would pry into native rituals is probably a direct carry-over from those times.

Modern conveniences and technology, from running water to computers, are much in evidence at the pueblo, but the people resist any change that would alter their fundamental way of life and religion.

The economy of the pueblo is based on subsistence farming, cattle raising, wage work, and fire fighting. An outlet mall and other economic development programs are broadening and strengthening the tribe's economic base.

Many villagers supplement their incomes with craftwork. Pottery and silver jewelry are produced, but the best-known crafts are beads of shell and turquoise. These necklaces (erroneously called "wampum" by some) are known as *heishe*, from the word in their language for shell. Their work is much in demand by Indians of other tribes—as a result many Santo Domingan craftspeople have become something of itinerant salespeople. (As early as 1850 they were reported trading with tribes in Oklahoma.) It is not uncommon to find these Indians selling their work throughout the United States.

It is difficult not to admire the Santo Domingans—and other Indians—who resist the pressures which would change their distinctive life to that uniformly gray existence of the "average citizen."

This Corn Maiden from Jemez is an expression of the fundamental importance of corn in Pueblo Indian life.

JEMEZ (hay'-mez) — Spanish spelling of the native word *Hemish*, meaning "the people." Native name for the pueblo is *Walatowa*, which means "village of the canyon." Language: Towa. Reservation: 89,624 acres. Population: 2,588. Government: Cacique selects secular officers, including governor and lieutenant governor. Tribal council composed of former governors. Dances: June 24 - San Juan's Day. Aug. 2 - Old Pecos Feast Day and Dance. Nov. 12 - Harvest Dance and Feast Day.

This Towa-speaking tribe inhabited a number of villages on the tributaries of the Jemez River before moving into the main Jemez Valley. At the time of Spanish contact in 1541, they were living in 11 small villages in the Agua Caliente region.

In accordance with the Spanish policy of consolidating Indian populations wherever possible, the Jemez people were persuaded to abandon most of their pueblos so that by 1625 they were concentrated in only two villages. In each of these the Spaniards established a mission.

From their earliest contacts the tribe maintained a hostile attitude toward the Spanish invaders. Two unsuccessful uprisings against Spanish authority occurred at Jemez before the Great Pueblo Revolt of 1680.

Spanish efforts to reconquer Jemez were thwarted as villagers retreated to fortified positions on the nearby mesa whenever soldiers appeared. From this stronghold they sent out raiding parties to harass Santa Ana and the Zia for siding with the Spaniards.

In 1694, de Vargas, with the help of Indian allies from Santa Ana, Zia, and San Felipe, attacked and destroyed their mesa village. The survivors of this battle resettled one of their villages in the valley. Women and children who were taken captive were allowed to return only after the Jemez warriors helped the Spanish defeat the Tewas living at Black Mesa.

Before long, however, the Jemez had enlisted military aid from the Zuni, Acoma, and Navajo tribes and resumed their hostilities against pueblos to the south who had sided with the Spanish. The Jemez Rebellion was finally crushed, and those who escaped found refuge among the Navajo and the Hopi. (The *Hemis* katsina, a popular figure at the Niman ceremony of the Hopi, was introduced to them by the Jemez people at that time.)

In 1703, most of the people returned to the Jemez Valley and built their present village at the site of an earlier settlement.

In 1838, they were joined by the remaining 17 inhabitants of Pecos, another Towa-speaking pueblo located further to the east, near the edge of the plains. (Disease, warfare, and constant raiding had decimated their numbers, forcing abandonment.) Even today their individuality is still acknowledged—through the creation of the position of second lieutenant governor, filled by the governor of the Pecos immigrants.

Although many families farm small garden plots, agriculture is becoming less important to the pueblo's economy. Cattle raising, seasonal wage work, and a renaissance in pottery work provide income, but unemployment remains high at Jemez because of its distance from urban areas.

Plaited bowl-shaped baskets of yucca, pottery, storyteller figurines, and sculpture as well as some embroidery and jewelry are the arts and crafts presently produced at the pueblo.

The tribal fair at Jemez Pueblo is a continuation of the intertribal trade that has characterized Pueblo life for centuries. While trade goes on throughout the year, it is at its most intense during ceremonial events.

ZIA (tsee'-ah) — from the native name *Tseya*. Language: Keresan. Reservation: 121,600 acres. Population: 736 (resident 613). Government: Cacique selects governor who appoints committee to handle secular affairs. Council is made up of all adult males. Dances: Aug. 15 - Corn Dance and Feast Day of Our Lady of Asuncion.

Early Spanish accounts refer to Zia as the most populous (2,500+) and most important town in a province containing five pueblos. Oñate visited the pueblo in 1598, and shortly thereafter the mission of Nuestra Senora de la Asuncion de Sia was established.

Zia took an active part in the Great Pueblo Revolt and defied Spanish attempts at reconquest. In 1689, Governor Domingo de Cruzate attacked Zia, and in a bloody battle killed more than 600 Indians, destroyed the town, and sold the captives into slavery. Those who escaped built a new pueblo near Jemez where they stayed until 1692 when de Vargas induced them to return to Zia and rebuild the pueblo and its church. From this time on they remained friendly to the Spaniards and often served as allies in attacks on other pueblos. This loyalty to the Spanish did not endear them to other tribes, and Zia frequently found itself the target of punitive raids by neighboring pueblos. Even today that alliance with the Spanish is unfavorably remembered by some from the other pueblos.

Because of inadequate land and water, Zia has been a poor pueblo in historic times. Limited cattle raising and farming goes on, but wage work in nearby communities accounts for most of the pueblo's income.

Internal strife has plagued Zia. In the 1930s, a group of Zias living in Albuquerque joined an evangelical sect of faith healers. The converts returned to the pueblo seeking new members, but after much controversy they returned to Albuquerque. Other factionalism resulted in the burning of a kiva belonging to a rival group.

Faced by a shortage of land, an increasing population, and continuing unrest, the future of Zia is unclear.

Zia potters are widely known for their fine polychrome ware, which is traded to Indians and non-Indians alike. New Mexico's state flag is derived from a Zia pottery design. Zia artists almost lost the right to the Zia sun symbol design when a large corporation nearly succeeded in obtaining the copyright to it.

Traditional Zia pottery often incorporates bird designs. The Zia sun symbol is their most famous pottery motif and it graces the New Mexico state flag.

Classic Zia pottery is a black and red on a cream- or sand-colored slip with a red base, with bird, plant, and cloud motifs.

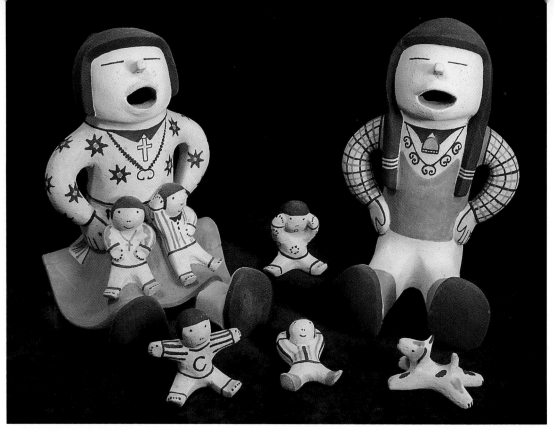

Storytelling is one of the most ancient of traditions, but making storyteller figurines only dates back to 1964 when Helen Cordero made one in memory of her grandfather. Cochiti Pueblo is famous for its figurines generally and its storyteller figurines specifically, which have almost completely replaced traditional Cochiti pottery. These were made by a granddaughter of the woman who began this figurative style.

COCHITI (ko'-chi-tee) — Spanish version of the native name *Kotyete*. Language: Keresan. Reservation: 50,681 acres. Population: 1,057. Government: Religious hierarchy selects secular officers annually. The Tribal Council is made up of former officers. Dances: June 13 - San Antonio's Day Dance. June 24 - San Juan's Day celebration. July 14 - Corn Dance and San Buenaventura Feast Day.

Before the arrival of the Spanish, the people of Cochiti and San Felipe had formed a single tribe. Warfare with their Tewa neighbors caused a split, and the two groups established separate villages in A.D. 1250. The present pueblo of Cochiti dates from this period.

Oñate visited Cochiti in 1598. The mission of San Buenaventura was built there in 1628. Although extensively remodeled many times since it was rebuilt in the 18th century, the present church still contains sections of the original.

The Cochiti people abandoned their pueblo after the 1680 Revolt, and retreated to the fortified village of La Cieneguilla with Indians from Santo Domingo, Taos, San Felipe, and Picuris.

In 1692, this band of insurgents promised de Vargas that they would return to their villages peacefully. Only San Felipe kept its promise—the others decided to continue their resistance. Under cover of darkness, de Vargas's soldiers and their Indian allies attacked the rebels, destroyed the village, and took many prisoners. Cochiti was not resettled until 1694.

During the late 1700s and early 1800s, Cochiti served as a refuge for Spanish and Mexican colonists from Navajo and Apache raids. As a result there has been considerable intermarriage between the two groups. Even today a few families of Spanish-American descent still live in the pueblo.

Conservative and progressive groups are present in Cochiti with control of village affairs in the hands of the conservatives for many years. Serious factionalism was avoided by urging progressive members to participate in the council discussions even though many did not take part in ceremonial affairs. In recent years the division between the two groups has faded, and there has been increased participation in the traditional religious life of the pueblo. Cochiti maintains a full ceremonial calendar which includes a number of katsina dances not open to the public.

Agriculture was an important economic activity at Cochiti, but is now limited to garden plots and alfalfa fields. The completion of Cochiti Dam provided a new development base that includes fishing, boating, housing, and golfing. These activities are the major sources of revenue for the tribe.

Drums and pottery—primarily the storyteller figurines, which originated here—are the best-known Cochiti crafts. Though not widespread, there is a long tradition of fine silverwork from this pueblo. Cochiti drums, noted for their superior workmanship and fine tone, are very popular with other tribes.

Cochiti is famous among all the pueblos for its excellent drums, used during religious dances held in the plazas as well as ceremonies in the kivas—and sold to the non-Indian trade. It is not unusual for a fine drum to be used for decades. Ysleta del Sur has one that dates back to the late 1600s. Making a fine, durable drum with a good "voice" is an art—generally passed down through the generations—and involves an extended apprenticeship. This gentleman learned from his father, a very well-respected drum maker—and is in turn teaching his sons.

Traditional foods are an important part of any culture, and the pueblos are no exception. Anyone who has visited Cochiti or any other pueblo when a ceremony was being held knows why they are often referred to as Feast Days. Pueblo bread, baked in an earthen oven called an horno, is a staple of such meals.

85

TESUQUE (teh-soo'-kay) — Spanish pronunciation of the native name *Te-tsu-geh*, meaning "cottonwood tree place." Language: Tewa. Reservation: 16,811 acres. Population: 400. Government: Religious leaders choose secular officers annually. Dances: Nov. 12 - San Diego Feast Day and Dance. Dec. 24 - Christmas Eve Dance.

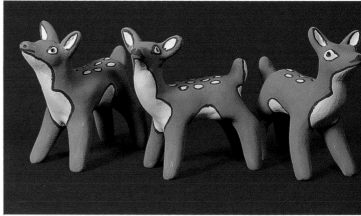

Blue deer by a Tesuque potter reflect the blue deer often seen in Indian paintings of an earlier era—from the 1930s until the early 1970s.

Tesuque has probably occupied two separate sites in historic times. Their first village was located three miles west of the present pueblo. It was abandoned, and its 17th-century mission destroyed during the Great Pueblo Revolt of 1680. Tesuque struck the first blow of the rebellion and took part in the general attack on Santa Fe—after this the villagers scattered to join other rebel Tewas at Black Mesa and La Cieneguilla, and did not return to reestablish their village until the early 1700s.

The pueblo of Tesuque has kept much of its old way of life—religious and political leadership remain in the hands of the two caciques, the heads of the village's Winter and Summer moieties. Nevertheless, they maintain a practical and progressive attitude by appointing capable young men to those secular offices that handle business affairs outside the pueblo.

Tesuque produced a very creditable pottery, but the craft disappeared in the early 1900s and the potters began to cater to the American tourist by turning out clay knickknacks decorated with poster paints. The most infamous of these was the so-called Tesuque Rain God, which was originally produced as a giveaway for a Midwestern candy manufacturer. Probably patterned after a figurine from Old Mexico, it had no connection with rain, Tesuque, or their religion. Traditional pottery, made from a micaceous clay, has been revived in recent years. Stock raising, wage work, some farming, gaming, and tourism are currently the primary sources of tribal income.

Figurines known as "rain gods" are still made at Tesuque. They are not rain gods, however. The first ones were made roughly a century ago—commissioned by a Santa Fe curio dealer for a Midwestern candy manufacturer who used them in a promotional scheme. The candy is no longer made, but the figures still are.

POJOAQUE (po-hwah'-key) — Spanish pronunciation of the native name *Posunwage*, meaning "drinking water place." Language: Tewa. Reservation: 11,601 acres. Population: 285. Government: Governor and lieutenant governor elected annually along with two other officials. Council is made up of past tribal officials. Dances: Dec. 12 - Feast of Guadalupe, fiesta and dance.

Currently the smallest of the six Tewa pueblos, Pojoaque was a very large pueblo in the 1300s. Its population suffered greatly after the Great Pueblo Revolt and during the reconquest. The tribe was decimated and the pueblo abandoned. Five families reestablished it in 1706, but the population never rose past 100. It was almost destroyed by a smallpox epidemic in 1890 and, combined with steady encroachment on their best farmland by non-Indians, the pueblo was again abandoned by about 1912. Traditional Pojoaque culture virtually disappeared. In 1933, some of the land was restored. At that time fewer than 40 descendants could be found, and only 14 were willing to move back.

The reservation was established in 1934 for the descendants of the original pueblo. This group forms the unit which handles the leasing of its commercial holdings on the highway between Santa Fe and Española, and development of the gaming enterprises as well as a travel agency, a construction company, and a visitor complex that includes a gift shop, museum, and restaurant.

At one time there was nothing in the appearance of this village to distinguish it from any other rural community in northern New Mexico. As part of an effort to revitalize traditional Pojoaque culture, a new kiva has been built. Several painters and silversmiths are active, and pottery making is enjoying a resurgence.

Some of Pojoaque's inhabitants participate in the dances of neighboring Tewa-speaking pueblos. No photography, sketching, or recording of any sort is allowed.

Pojoaque pottery, made from a mica-flecked clay, has been widely traded for centuries. This durable, thin-walled pottery is sought after by both Indians and non-Indians. It is prized for its utilitarian qualities as well as for its aesthetic merits.

Santa Clara pottery, which is indistinguishable from that produced by the neighboring San Ildefonso pueblo, is an important aspect of the economy of the pueblo. Over 300 potters are active at Santa Clara. Both carved and painted polished redware and blackware are made, along with some open-fired pieces which have a brownish-black appearance. Some polychrome work is made, and the sgraffito technique—which involves shallow carving after firing—is also employed.

SANTA CLARA (sahn'-ta clar'-a) —

Spanish for Saint Claire. Native name is *Kah'P'o*, meaning "wild rose place." Language: Tewa. Reservation: 45,744 acres. Population: 1,742. Government: Officers and council elected annually by adult tribal members. Tribal constitution adopted in 1935—the first pueblo to do so. Dances: June 8 - Buffalo Dance. June 13 - San Antonio Feast Day and dances. Late July - Puye' Ruins Fiesta. Aug. 12 - Corn Dance and Feast Day. ▪▪▪▪▪▪▪▪▪▪▪▪▪▪▪▪▪▪▪▪▪▪▪

According to their tradition the Tewas emerged from the underworld through Sip-ophe, a small lake in the sand dune country near Alamosa, Colorado. Before they settled in their present locations, the Tewas occupied several villages in the Ojo Caliente area in addition to the cliff dwellings at Puye'. Santa Clara, one of six Tewa-speaking pueblos in New Mexico, was built in the 14th century.

The Spaniards established a church at the village in the 1620s. The present church, which dates from 1918, occupies the site of the original structure.

At the time of the Great Pueblo Revolt the people of Santa Clara attacked a small party of Spanish soldiers at the pueblo, fortified the village against possible attack, and joined their allies to lay siege to Santa Fe. Later they joined other Tewas in the pueblo fortress atop Black Mesa. Some moved west to take up residence with the Zuni and Hopi. After the reconquest of New Mexico many moved back to reoccupy their village.

In the late 1800s, Santa Clara split into opposing factions over a controversy involving the acceptance of federal programs. Those who wished to cooperate with the government were accused of abandoning the old ways, and charges of witchcraft were common.

The adoption of a tribal constitution in 1935 did much to heal this factionalism. Today, the traditional religious hierarchy directs the ceremonial life of the village, and secular affairs are left in the hands of the progressive, educated young. The arrangement has been so successful that many of the disenfranchised young people of neighboring villages point to Santa Clara as an example of how things could be if the religious leaders of their villages would relinquish control over secular affairs.

Santa Clara, like San Ildefonso, is famous for its polished black pottery. Over 300 potters produce large numbers of bowls, jars, plates, figurines, and miniatures. Polished redware and a red polychrome are also made.

As with most pueblos, agriculture has been superseded by wage work as the most important source of income. Many people from the pueblo are employed at Los Alamos National Laboratory. Pottery making is a significant source of income for many.

Tribal income is derived from commercial property leases near Española, fishing and picnicking fees at the Santa Clara Canyon recreational area, a touring company, and admission fees charged visitors to the Puye' Ruins. A conference center has been built near Puye' which is available for non-Indian use.

SAN ILDEFONSO (san il'-deh-fon-so) —

Spanish for Saint Ildefonsus. Native name is *Po-ho-ge-Oweenge*, meaning "village where the river cuts down through." Language: Tewa. Reservation: 26,191 acres. Population: 575. Government: Governor, lieutenant governor, and council elected by adult male members of tribe. Dances: Jan. 6 - Eagle Dance. Jan. 23 - Feast Day and Buffalo-Deer Dance and Comanche Dance. June 13 - Corn Dance. Sept. 8 - Harvest Dance. ▬▬▬▬▬▬

According to tradition at San Ildefonso, the cliff dwellings of Mesa Verde are the ancient homes of this tribe. Around A.D. 1300 their ancestors moved into the upper Rio Grande Valley. Archaeological evidence indicates that the Indians of San Ildefonso had also occupied three villages on the Pajarito Plateau along with other Tewa-speaking groups before they settled in their present location.

The actual village site has been shifted a number of times. The village that Oñate visited in 1598 was located about one mile from the present pueblo. In the late 1800s, San Ildefonso was moved north of its old location, which meant that the kiva was no longer in the plaza. Problems that afflicted the pueblo afterwards were attributed to the move, and some years later a portion of the residents moved back to what became known as the South Plaza. The split and resultant factionalism affected both the religious and civil organization of the pueblo, with the North Plaza retaining civil authority. Since the mid-1970s, changes to the tribal council have caused the factionalism to subside.

A small pueblo, San Ildefonso not only suffered losses during the Great Pueblo Revolt and two subsequent revolts, but endured two smallpox epidemics in the late 1700s that reduced their population by more than half. An influenza epidemic in 1918 further dropped their numbers to less than 100. (During the first quarter of this century most Rio Grande pueblos had a death rate higher than their birth rate.) Wage work and craftwork are the major sources of income currently, though they also do some farming and stock raising. Tribal income is derived from fishing permits.

San Ildefonso shares a concern with other nearby pueblos over outside pollution threats to their lands, and is working with Los Alamos National Laboratory and nearby communities to resolve the problems.

There is a tribally owned lake where fishing is allowed by permit. Like most pueblos, photography is regulated and by permit only. Additionally, no early morning photography is allowed under any circumstances. There is also an admission fee to enter the pueblo.

The Comanche Dance is one of the dances that may be given at San Ildefonso Pueblo on their feast day, observed each year on January 23. It is a time when many people from surrounding pueblos come to take part in the celebration.

NAMBE (nahm-bay') — from the native word meaning "mound of earth." Language: Tewa. Reservation: 19,124 acres. Population: 630. Government: Governor and four officials elected annually by members of the pueblo. A council of past governors does the decision-making. Dances: Oct. 4 - St. Francis Day, Feast Day and dances.

The Spanish established a church in Nambe in the early 1600s. Revolts, decay, and fire destroyed each of the churches built between then and 1975, at which time the current one was constructed. There are remains of an older pueblo nearby, dating from around 1300, but there is also speculation that the current pueblo of Nambe was founded in 1598 by Tewas from other nearby pueblos. Very little is known of its history—either from Spanish records or archaeological work.

Only their kiva immediately distinguishes Nambe from other small rural settlements in the Rio Grande Valley, identifying it as an Indian community. The extensive outlines of old walls show that Nambe has declined considerably in size since its founding.

Intermarriage with the local Spanish-American population has been responsible for a weakening of tribal authority, and a gradual breakdown of traditional native life. A revival of ceremonialism—typical of a general trend in many Rio Grande pueblos during the past decade—has reversed the loss of native traditions that had caused many to predict the complete end of native culture here and at Pojoaque.

Craftwork is limited to some weaving, a little jewelry, and pottery work—some of which utilizes a micaceous clay found in the area, and the rest of which is typical Tewa red and black polished ware. Wage work—mostly off-reservation—some farming, and stock raising are the major

Traditional Tewa ceremonies had begun to disappear at Nambe Pueblo. In a reversal of this trend, the older ways have been revived to help reach a strong future.

components of the tribe's economy, along with income from recreational activities which center around Nambe Falls, a picturesque area developed by the pueblo. The tribe also owns and operates a tour company in northern New Mexico. Fees are charged for fishing, camping, picnicking, and sightseeing.

Kivas have been the heart of pueblo religious activity for over a thousand years. Beginning in the 1980s, there has been a resurgence of traditional ceremonialism among many Rio Grande pueblos.

SAN JUAN (san hwan') — Spanish for Saint John.

Native name is *Okeh*. Language: Tewa. Reservation: 12,236 acres. Population: 2,358. Government: Religious leaders of the summer and winter people alternate in selection of secular officers. Council is made up of all former *Tuuyon* or Governors. Dances: June 24 - San Juan Feast Day and Corn, Buffalo, or Comanche dances.

San Juan is the northernmost and largest of the six Tewa-speaking pueblos. It has been continuously inhabited since A.D. 1300.

Coronado's expedition visited San Juan in 1541, but the expedition's reputation preceded it—they found the pueblo abandoned and promptly plundered it. In 1598, Oñate named the village San Juan Bautista and established the first capital of New Mexico at a village just across the river from San Juan called *Yunque Owingeh Yunque* (Mockingbird Place, renamed San Gabriel by the Spanish), whose people relinquished their pueblo to the Spanish and moved over to San Juan. The hospitality of San Juan in receiving these new residents so impressed the Spaniards that they amended the name to San Juan de los Caballeros (gentlemen).

The initial period of goodwill soon gave way to feelings of discontent and hostility as the Indians experienced the harshness of Spanish rule. Suppression of native religion reached a peak in 1675 when 47 Indian leaders from a number of pueblos were convicted of practicing witchcraft and whipped. Among them was Popay, a religious leader from San Juan, who later conceived, organized, and led the Great Pueblo Revolt of 1680 which drove the Spanish colonists from the Rio Grande Valley. This was the only time that the pueblos had ever united to achieve a common goal.

Popay then attempted to purge the country of all Spanish influence and to return the pueblos to the old way of life, but he became so tyrannical in his methods that he soon lost the support of the people. The pueblos withdrew to their own village authorities, and the spirit of intertribal cooperation

The Deer Dance is part of a hunting ritual that seeks to ensure there will always be enough deer to hunt, and also honors the spirit of the deer for it is generally believed that a successful hunt requires the cooperation of the animal itself.

disappeared. This lack of unity helped make possible the reconquest by de Vargas.

San Juan was considered a major trading center, linking the two larger centers, Taos and Santa Fe. Crops, primarily corn, hay, and alfalfa, were the major source of income and employment well into the middle of the 20th century, with nearly half of their small reservation being cultivated.

Today farming has dwindled, but San Juan is expanding its economic base to provide both tribal income and employment for individual members. Current sources of tribal revenue include fishing and camping fees, a tribal arts and crafts cooperative (Oke Oweenge, begun in 1968), gas station, convenience store, restaurant, RV campground, and gaming.

The potters of San Juan Pueblo use a mica-flecked clay. The surface may then be incised, carved, or painted or slipped and polished. Stylized cloud symbols frequently grace their work.

TAOS (tah'-os) — from the Spanish version of a native word, *Tua-tah*, meaning "in the village." The native name for the pueblo translates as "at red willow canyon mouth." Language: Tiwa. Reservation: 95,341 acres. Population: 2,170. Government: Religious hierarchy made up of four kiva headmen and hereditary cacique who select secular officers. Dances: Jan 1 - Turtle Dance. Jan. 6 - Animal Dance. June 13 - Corn Dance. June 24 - San Juan's Day. July 25 - Corn Dance. Sept. 29 - Sundown Dance. Sept. 30 - San Geronimo Feast Day. Dec. 24 - Christmas Eve Procession. Dec. 25 - Matachines Dance.

The northernmost pueblo, Taos reflects Plains Indian influence in the dress, customs, and physical makeup of its people. The Ute, Apache, and Comanche met here to trade meat and hides for Pueblo foodstuffs and textiles. The multistoried construction of the pueblo was originally designed for defense, with no ground-level doors or windows and a surrounding adobe wall, giving evidence that not all contacts were peaceful.

The present village was built about 1700 after the old one, located a few hundred yards to the northeast, was destroyed by fire in the 1690s. It closely duplicates the original pueblo, consisting of two house groups: *Hlauuma* (North House) and *Hlaukwima* (South House) located on either side of Taos Creek.

Alvarado first visited Taos in 1540. In 1598 Oñate, following the Spanish custom of assigning saints' names to the pueblos, named it San Miguel. No trace remains of the original mission of San Geronimo which was established in the early 17th century. The church ruins (also called San Geronimo) inside the wall date from 1706. The present church was built in 1847.

Dissatisfaction with Spanish rule led to the abandonment of the village in 1639, and the people moved onto the plains with the Jicarilla Apache. They built a new pueblo in what is now Scott County, Kansas, remaining there for two years before they were brought back to the old pueblo by the Spaniards.

Trouble with Spanish authority continued, and Taos served as the base of operations for the planners of the Great Pueblo Revolt of 1680. On August 10 of that year, Taos warriors killed the resident priests and Spanish settlers and joined the other pueblos in attacking Santa Fe. The move was a military success, and Governor Otermin was forced to flee south to El Paso with all the surviving colonists.

Taos Pueblo is divided into two house groups, one on each side of Taos Creek. It is the most-photographed of all pueblos due to heavy visitation. The constant presence of a growing number of tourists in their village—designated a World Heritage Site by the United Nations—has caused an exodus to new housing outside the pueblo.

MURRAE HAYNES

Intertribal powwows are not new at Taos. For hundreds of years Taos Pueblo has been the site of intertribal trade. Being on the very edge of the Pueblo region, they had contact with the Ute, Apache, and even Plains Indian tribes like the Comanche.

In 1692, the Spaniards under de Vargas began to retake the province. An uneasy truce followed, marked by a number of small revolts and temporary abandonment of Taos when the people fled to nearby mountain canyons to escape Spanish reprisals.

The only major uprising at Taos after the United States assumed control of the territory occurred in 1847. The Taos Rebellion, instigated in part by Mexican pioneer settlers who harbored ill feelings toward the new American authorities, resulted in the deaths of Governor Charles Bent and 7 Americans. Troops from Santa Fe attacked and killed 150 rebels who sought refuge inside the church (the ruins of which are still visible) and later executed 15 more.

Encroachment on pueblo land by white squatters led to a threatened uprising in 1910, but the appearance of troops prevented bloodshed. Land-related controversies continued, however, with the most important regarding the traditional use and religious significance of Blue Lake, high on Taos Mountain.

Since the turn of the century Taos attempted to have the lake included as part of tribal lands in order to protect it. While ranchers were given ten-year grazing permits, Taos Indians were given only three days in August for exclusive use. Even then they had to notify the appropriate government agency in writing ten days in advance of their intention to hold their ancient ceremonies. The Taos people remained firm in their demand for the land—not money for the land—and the government finally capitulated.

In 1970, Taos Blue Lake was officially returned to them. (The current reservation contains less than one-third of the land they once used.)

The adoption of the peyote cult by some members in the 1890s led to 50 years of bitter factionalism within the pueblo. Factionalism over the control of village affairs and limited economic opportunities have led many younger members to leave the pueblo in search of employment and different living conditions. (Electricity and running water are not available in the oldest portions of the pueblo, which is also visited daily by large numbers of tourists. Lack of amenities and privacy have caused a number of tribal members to leave the pueblo.)

Nevertheless, Taos continues to function as a Pueblo society, held together by the strong ties of a common language, culture, and religion.

Crafts produced include drums, moccasins, jewelry, and pottery made from the distinctive mica-flecked clay found in the area. Tourist-related activities (including a casino) are the major source of tribal income. The tribe recently opened its own health clinic, and has been active in encouraging and providing for educational opportunities for tribal members. Current water-rights negotiations with the state of New Mexico may hold the key to greater self-sufficiency for this tribe.

The church at Picuris was built in the 1770s after the tribe returned from seeking refuge with the Jicarilla Apache in what is now western Kansas. The building restoration is one aspect of their economic development plans.

PICURIS (pee-kuu-rees') — probably a Spanish version of the Keresan name *Pikuria*, meaning "those who paint." Native name is *Piwwetha*, meaning "pass in the mountains." Language: Tiwa. Reservation: 14,980 acres. Population: 233. Government: Tribal officers elected by adult men. Dances: Aug. 10 - San Lorenzo Feast Day and Corn Dance.

Picuris and Taos are descended from a common ancestral group which settled in this general area about A.D. 900. Sometime during the 12th century these people split to form two separate tribes. Picuris, like Taos, has had considerable contact with Plains tribes in general and the Jicarilla Apache in particular, with whom they frequently intermarried.

The Tiwa Indians of Picuris are related to those of Taos Pueblo. Like Taos, with whom they have close ties, they produce a micaceous clay pottery. Pottery making is a craft passed down from one generation to the next within a family.

The original pueblo, now partially excavated, lies on the north edge of the present village. It dates from about A.D. 1250, and was first visited by the Spaniards in the early 1540s. They named the village San Lorenzo, and established a mission there in 1621.

Luis Tapato, one of the leaders of the Great Pueblo Revolt, was a governor of Picuris. The pueblo, which at that time had a population estimated at between 2,000 and 3,000, played an important role in the rebellion by providing a large force of fighting men for the campaign against the Spanish.

In 1692, they once again swore allegiance to Spanish authority, but followed this with three more revolts in less than five years. After the last uprising, in 1696, they abandoned their village to seek refuge at the Jicarilla Apache settlement of El Cuartelejo in western Kansas. In 1706, greatly decimated by disease and warfare, 300 people returned to their pueblo. The present church was built in the 1770s following their resettlement.

In the 1930s, traditional life at Picuris suffered as the tiny population (fewer than 100) faced a court decision that deprived them of most of their irrigated farmland. Several governors elected by the tribal council were impeached during this time—at the request of the Bureau of Indian Affairs, not tribal members. The pueblo was renamed San Lorenzo in 1947 but changed back in 1955.

Since the late 1960s, there has been a revival of traditional religious activities. Most recently, a buffalo bull provided by the Governor of Taos from that pueblo's herd, has prompted the tribe to consider building a herd of its own.

The isolation of the tiny pueblo has hindered development, forcing many to seek employment off-reservation. Fewer than half of all tribal members live on the reservation.

Two small lakes, Pu-na and Tu-tah, provide revenue from fishing and camping permits. A shop and restaurant also provide some income, as does a tribally owned hotel located in Santa Fe.

There is a fee for photography on the reservation. Crafts are limited to some jewelry and a little pottery—some of which is painted, while the rest is left with a finish created by the mica-flecked clay they use.

PICURIS

UTE (yoot) — from *Yuta*, the Shoshone and Comanche name for this tribe. Native name is *Nooche*, meaning "the people." Language: Shoshonean. Reservations: Southern Ute Reservation (Colorado) - 302,000 acres, Ute Mountain Reservation (Colorado and New Mexico) - 555,000 acres, and Uintah and Ouray Reservation (Utah) - 852,411 acres. Population: Southern Ute - 1,316, Ute Mountain - 1,911, and Uintah and Ouray - 3,154. Government (Southern Ute): Constitutional form of government provides for election of a six-member tribal council. ▬▬

Though they produce other items, such as flutes, the Ute are best-known for their buckskin and beadwork crafts. Ranching and farming, however, produce most of their income.

The Utes today occupy reservations in three states—Utah, Colorado, and New Mexico. This distribution is indicative of the tremendous area that was once claimed by the ten or more bands that make up this tribe. Their territory stretched from the Great Salt Lake southeast to the Four Corners region, and included most of Colorado and portions of northern New Mexico.

Originally these people lived in small family groups and subsisted in the manner of most Great Basin tribes—by hunting and gathering. Linguistically they are related to the Chemehuevi and Paiute. Culturally they were closely related to the Southern Paiute until they acquired horses from the Spaniards in the early 1800s. They then extended their hunting range onto the buffalo plains where they picked up traits typical of the Plains Indian cultures. This new mobility also allowed the family groups to unite into bands as political and social units. A single Ute "tribe" did not exist although bands might occasionally join forces to meet a common enemy.

The Ute maintained friendly relations with the Jicarilla Apache, Shoshone, and Paiute; traded with the northern Rio Grande Pueblos; and warred with the Navajo, Kiowa, Cheyenne, Comanche, and Sioux. At one time they even joined with the Spanish in a temporary alliance against the Comanche.

Although contact with Europeans began in 1776 with a visit from Father Escalante, the Ute felt little effect from white contact until the mid-1800s when American settlers began to arrive.

From 1849 through the end of the 1800s, the Americans made and broke a series of treaties with the Ute. After Colorado became a state in 1876, a public clamor was raised to remove the Ute in order to provide more land for settlers. Each demand resulted in a new treaty and less land for the Ute until one chief was led to sarcastically ask if the U.S. lacked the power to enforce its own treaties. (The land originally allotted to the Ute in 1868 was about 16,000,000 acres—it was reduced by more than 14,000,000 acres in less

than 30 years.) That the displacement of the Ute took place with a minimum of bloodshed is a tribute to Ouray, a leader of the Southern Utes, who recognized the futility of warring against overwhelming odds.

With the loss of their best hunting grounds, the Ute became dependent upon government rations during their early reservation years.

Today the Southern Utes, made up of the Weeminuche, Capote, and Moache bands, occupy two reservations in southwestern Colorado and a small part of New Mexico. Farming, stock raising, and sheepherding provide their main livelihood. Tribal income from gas and oil leases, gaming, and money obtained from a land claim settlement with the U.S. government is being used to develop and improve rangelands and purchase off-reservation ranches to better the economic standard of the people.

Little remains of the native culture—the Bear Dance, an annual spring ceremony, and the Sun Dance (derived from the Plains tribes) are still held, but are regarded by many as more of a social occasion than a religious one. A number of Ute Mountain groups are members of the Native American Church.

Crafts are becoming increasingly scarce, but beaded buckskin bags, belts, and moccasins are still being made along with some coiled basketry and hand-painted greenware pottery.

ZUNI

ZUNI (zoo'-nee) — Spanish pronunciation of the Keresan name for this pueblo, *Sunyi*. The Zuni name for themselves is *Ahshiwi*. Language: Zunian. Reservation: 421,481 acres, including a 10,085 - acre religious site in Arizona. Population: 8,996. Government: Tribal officers elected biennially by adult members. Dances: Late November or early December - Shalako. Spring and summer months - Koko (katsina) dances. ▬▬▬▬▬▬

The Zuni are the best-known fetish carvers, but other tribes make them as well—and in increasing numbers. Represented here are Zuni, Hualapai, Navajo, and Santa Clara artists.

Archaeological evidence indicates that the distinctive culture of the Zuni is the result of a blending of at least two diverse cultural groups in prehistoric times. This "melting pot" situation continued well into historic times as the Zuni absorbed into their population Indians from other areas, including a number of Tlascalans from central Mexico who had formed a part of Coronado's expedition. Linguistically, Zuni is unrelated to any other tribe in the Southwest.

At the beginning of the historic period the Zuni, numbering well over 3,000, occupied six villages in the broad Zuni Valley—the largest of these was Hawikuh. The present pueblo is built on the old site of Halona, one of the original towns that made up the province of Shiwona.

In 1529, Fray Marcos de Niza set out from Mexico to determine if this settlement could be the fabled Seven Cities of Cibola, which reportedly held the treasure of Montezuma. His advance scouting party was led by Estevan, a Moorish slave who had explored the Gulf of Mexico and Texas with Cabeza de Vaca. Estevan's earlier successes in dealing with Indian tribes failed him at Zuni. The Indians found his lordly attitude offensive, and cured his bad manners by killing him shortly after he reached Hawikuh and began making demands upon the people.

After receiving news of Estevan's death, de Niza traveled only far enough to get a glimpse of Hawikuh before retracing his steps to Mexico. There, in a report unbecoming a man of the cloth, he announced that he had found the Kingdom of Cibola.

The following year Francisco Coronado mounted an expedition to Zuni. He attacked and captured Hawikuh only to discover that de Niza's glowing report was a hoax.

The Franciscans built a mission at Hawikuh in 1629. The presence of the missionaries caused dissension among the Zuni and resulted in the death of two friars in 1632. Three Zunis then fled to a fortified village on Dowa Yalane (Corn Mountain), a mesa southeast of Zuni.

The Zuni outwardly appeared to accept Spanish rule, but actually followed a course of

A number of Zuni katsinas have been adopted and adapted by the Hopi. These Wakashi Koko *appear in a very similar form at Hopi where they are known as* Wakas Katsinas. *Sullivan Shebola*

The Zuni have been working silver since the late 1800s. The techniques we now think of as typically Zuni began to develop about 1930. Styles continue to evolve, but still have their roots in the prehistoric tradition of stone and shell mosaic work.

These figurines represent dancers in the Zuni Shalako ceremony. This ceremony, held in early winter, is usually thought of as a house-blessing ceremony, but is actually a 49-day ritual re-creation of Zuni emergence and migration legends. Called katsinas *by the Hopi, the Zuni name for these figures is* koko. *While carving such figures is common at Hopi, it is infrequent at Zuni.*

passive (and sometimes not so passive) resistance to this new authority.

Apache raids increased in intensity during the late 1600s, and finally led to the abandonment of Hawikuh in 1672.

The Zuni supported the Great Pueblo Revolt of 1680, but were less involved in it because they were remote from the Spanish settlements. Once again they retreated to Corn Mountain and remained there until 1692, when de Vargas persuaded them to return to the valley and resettle Halona. A new church was built in the village in 1699. (It was abandoned in the early 1800s.)

Because of its prosperous appearance, Zuni gives the impression of being a very "progressive" pueblo. However, it maintains much of its traditional life, especially its religious activities. Perhaps the best known and most spectacular of its many ceremonies is the Shalako, a house-blessing ritual that occurs in November or December. It includes huge, bird-like figures called Shalakos, who are the couriers of the rainmakers.

Subsistence farming and stock raising, supplemented by wage work, some seasonal employment (such as fire fighting), and jewelry making form the economic base of the tribe. Over 1,000 silversmiths, stonecutters, and fetish carvers work full or part time at their craft. Pottery making has been revived in recent years, but weaving and basketry have disappeared.

NAVAJO (nah'-vah-ho) —from a Tewa word
Navahu, meaning "cultivated fields." (Also spelled Navaho, though Navajo has been adopted as the preferred spelling by the tribal government.) Native name *Dine'* (din-neh') means "the people." Language: Athabascan. Reservations: Navajo, Alamo, Canoncito, and Ramah totaling 17,500,815 acres. Population: 219,198. Government: Constitution adopted in 1938 provides for tribal council delegates elected by adult members of the tribe. Headed by a chair and vice-chair elected at large.

The common ancestors of the Navajo and Apache reached the northernmost fringes of the Southwest some time after A.D. 1200 as small nomadic bands of hunters and gatherers. Linguistically, they are related to the Athabascan-speaking tribes of northwestern Canada. The way of life of each band was modified by its contact with other tribes. The Navajo were particularly influenced by the Pueblo Indians—weaving, agriculture, sandpainting, and certain ceremonial rituals were some of the customs they are believed to have adopted. As agriculture grew in economic importance, the Navajo became less nomadic and began to settle in small communities near their fields.

A Spanish reference to "Apaches de Navajo" (generally regarded as being a composite Pueblo name meaning "enemies of the cultivated fields") as a semi-sedentary agricultural people appears in 1626. It is the first mention of the Navajo that distinguished them from the Apache. Contact with the Spanish had far-reaching effects on both the Navajo and the Spaniards. With the acquisition of sheep and goats, the Indians began to lead a life that was more pastoral than agricultural.

Monument Valley, near the northern edge of the Navajo Reservation, is known the world over for its scenic beauty, often featured in movies. Called Tse'Bii'Nidzisgai—Plain Rocks—by the Navajo, it is a hard land in which to make a living, supporting only five people per square mile.

The use of the horse allowed them to increase their raiding activities, much to the sorrow of Indian and Spanish communities along the Rio Grande Valley. (They expanded westward as well, forcing the Havasupai out of the Little Colorado River region by 1686.) The Navajo considered their forays not as war but as an economic pursuit that yielded livestock, food, booty, women, and slaves. (The great use of Indian slaves by the Spanish probably stimulated this practice.) For this reason the Navajo were never as interested in driving the Spanish out of the Southwest as were the Pueblo tribes.

In 1745, the Franciscans made an attempt to establish missions among the Navajo of the Mount Taylor region. After two years the Indians rejected the new religion, but remained friendly to the Spanish. Because of this peaceful coexistence the Navajo of Canoncito and Alamo are still sometimes known by their fellow tribesmen by an old name meaning "the people who are enemies."

When the Americans assumed jurisdiction of New Mexico in 1846, they sought to control the

Football games on an irrigated field in the arid Monument Valley are a measure of the influence non-Navajo culture and technology are beginning to have on Navajos. The Navajo have thus far managed to adapt elements from other cultures without losing their own identity.

Navajo pictographs often portray actual historical events. This one records a raid by Utes in Navajo country in January, 1858.

The Navajo have moved back into Canyon de Chelly and rebuilt the homes, fields, and orchards that were destroyed during the scorched earth campaign led by Kit Carson in 1863.

Navajo by establishing military posts in their country. Without understanding the political makeup of the tribe, the U.S. military signed peace treaties with several "chiefs." The chiefs were actually merely headmen whose authority did not extend beyond their own small bands. Naturally, raiding by other bands continued since they had not been a part of the negotiations.

In 1863, Navajo depredations became so serious that a military force under Kit Carson was dispatched to subdue the tribe. Carson accomplished this objective not through military engagements, but by wiping out the economic basis of Navajo life. Livestock was slaughtered, crops and fruit trees were destroyed, and hogans were leveled.

By March of 1864, 2,400 Navajos had been rounded up to begin the 300-mile journey to their place of confinement at Fort Sumner on the Pecos River in southeastern New Mexico. Eventually some 8,000 men, women, and children made "The Long Walk" to captivity. An estimated 1,800 avoided capture by hiding out in the more inaccessible areas of their country.

Conditions at the Bosque Redondo reservation were miserable. Drought problems were aggravated by government contractors who cheated the Navajos out of much of their food

NAVAJO

Trading posts were the first contact points between Navajos and the American government, which claimed jurisdiction over the various sovereign Navajo bands. While Americans often found the customs of the Navajo puzzling and odd, the actions of the American government were every bit as strange and puzzling to the Navajo. One of the services traders often provided was to try and explain the new laws and regulations. The early trading post acted as a bank, post office, meeting place, livestock buyer, and general store. Redwing Nez

and supplies, and what was sent was generally of inferior quality. More than 2,000 Navajos died from disease before the government decided the relocation plan was a failure.

In 1868, the Navajos were allowed to return home. Sadly, this move was prompted not so much by humanitarian motives as by economic motives—it would be cheaper to allow them to become self-supporting in their homeland than to support them in confinement. But their troubles were not over—the white man had not yet lost his taste for Indian land, and clashes occurred. The schools promised in the treaty of 1868 were run like reformatories, and did much to maintain a hostile attitude toward whites.

Despite these problems the Navajo did make a comeback and became self-sufficient. Sheep and cattle became the basis of the Navajo economy, and a lively trade was maintained in wool and hides. Navajo weaving and silver found ready markets. The Navajo prospered, and their flocks of sheep increased to more than 300,000 by 1878.

By the 1930s, the basis of Navajo life, sheep, had increased to the point where the land was seriously overgrazed—erosion had become a major problem and land productivity plummeted. Sheep herds had grown to over 1,000,000 by 1933, leaving only one possible solution—drastic stock reduction. This was another critical blow to Navajo life, and the controversial manner in which it was administered is still bitterly remembered.

Navajo hogans or homes are low, round buildings built with whatever materials are available in that area of Navajoland. The doorway always faces east, a custom observed even in many modern Navajo homes.

Despite its size (roughly the area of West Virginia) the reservation has limited resources and much of the land, however scenic, is virtually worthless from the standpoint of economic development. Thousands of Navajos leave the reservation to seek employment. Craftwork, while providing an income, primarily for silver-

KENJI KAWANO

The Navajo suffered greatly at the hands of the U.S. military under the scorched earth campaign conducted to force them from their homes—lands they were returned to when the relocation effort failed. Yet even given that history, and incidents like the stock reductions of the 1930s that impoverished many Navajo, when the U.S. was attacked December 7, 1942, Navajo young men joined their counterparts across the country in signing up for military service. The Navajo Codetalkers, using a code developed in their own language, were instrumental in helping defeat the Japanese military, which was never able to break the code. U.S. military service continues to be a source of pride among the Navajo, and a special memorial to Navajo veterans was established at Window Rock in 1995.

Raising livestock is a major source of income for many Navajo families and has been since the Spanish introduced sheep, goats, horses, and cattle to the Southwest over 300 years ago.

smiths, is of minor importance in the overall economy.

The first Navajo council began with three Navajos, hand-picked by the Secretary of the Interior, and its first meeting was held for the purpose of ratifying gas and oil leases in a rapidly declining market.

Considerable tribal income is currently derived from gas, oil, and coal leases. Much of this income is being invested in tribal enterprises which in turn are providing jobs for Indians on the reservation. Not all of these ventures have been economically or environmentally sound, causing some—notably the tribal lumber industry—to

People who played cowboys and Indians as children probably never realized that sometimes cowboys are Indians or vice versa. The Navajo have their own rodeo circuit, and many belong to the national American Indian Rodeo Cowboy Association.

NAVAJO

Navajo culture seems to be able to absorb many outside influences without losing its identity. A Pioneer Day parade at Navajo Mountain led by a baton-twirling majorette is still an unmistakably Navajo event. At the head of the parade, in a position of honor, are the Navajo elders in traditional dress.

Work by Navajo painters has been avidly collected for three quarters of a century. While non-Navajo art critics argue about what is traditional or authentically Indian in paintings, Navajos continue to develop their own visions and styles. Shonto Begay

come under fire from tribal members. Serious problems still face the tribe, but for the Navajo adversity has long been a constant condition.

A long-simmering land use conflict with the Hopi, which resulted in additions to the Navajo reservation from land originally set aside for the Hopi and a declaration of a Joint Use Area, is still a sensitive issue. Aggravated by the need to clear title for a coal-mining lease (and by subsequent water problems), the land was partitioned in 1974, with both Hopi and Navajo relocations required. The Navajo tribe received 400,000 acres to accommodate the relocatees, but some have chosen to remain.

A historic agreement between the tribes, mediated by the federal government in 1992, promised to finally resolve the issue. It was undermined by the non-Indian majority of the state of Arizona, so the problem remains unresolved into the second century of its existence.

The tribe, in addition to forming an economic development authority, has built hospitals, airports, a museum and zoo, and an accredited tribal community college system, and is planning a resort. They voted down gaming in 1995. Unemployment is estimated to be roughly 30 percent.

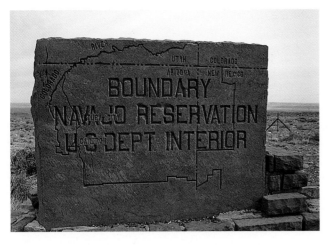

Indian reservation boundary markers are almost never carved in stone anymore—and with good reason. Rare is the tribe that has not had its boundaries changed at least a couple of times since their reservation was established. The Navajo Reservation boundary has been changed nearly 50 times since it was established in 1868.

NEVADA

UTAH

ARIZONA

NAVAJO

PAIUTE

Las Vegas

Colorado River

NAVAJO

HAVASUPAI

HOPI

NAVAJO

HUALAPAI

Navajo

Flagstaff

MOHAVE

HUALAPAI

YAVAPAI
& APACHE

ZUNI

Mohave

CHEMEHUEVI

Bill Williams River

CALIFORNIA

Colorado
River
Reservation
(NAVAJO, HOPI,
MOHAVE &
CHEMEHUEVI)

WHITE MOUNTAIN
APACHE

YAVAPAI
& APACHE

Chemehuevi

Salt River

SAN CARLOS
APACHE

Phoenix

PIMA &
MARICOPA

YUMA

PIMA

Gila River

COCOPA

TOHONO
O'ODHAM

Western
Apache

YAQUI

Tucson

TOHONO
O'ODHAM

TOHONO
O'ODHAM

Tohono
O'odham

Tohono
O'odham

COLORADO

NEW MEXICO

UTE

UTE

NAVAJO

JICARILLA
APACHE

Rio Chama

TAOS

PICURIS

SAN JUAN
POJOAQUE
SANTA CLARA   NAMBE
SAN ILDEFONSO   TESUQUE

JEMEZ   ● *Santa Fe*

● *Gallup*   COCHITI

ZIA   SANTO DOMINGO
SAN FELIPE
SANTA ANA
SANDIA

RAMAH-NAVAJO
ACOMA   ● *Albuquerque*

UNI   CANONCITO-NAVAJO

ISLETA

LAGUNA

Zuni

ALAMO-NAVAJO

San Juan

MESCALERO
APACHE

Rio Grande

Jicarilla
Apache

Jicarilla
Apache

INDIAN RESERVATIONS
OF THE SOUTHWEST

Each tribe in the Southwest has its
own distinct traditions which have
evolved over time. The clothing they
wear has also evolved over time
and reflects the climate, way of life,
and their beliefs, as well as influences
from other groups—Indian and
non-Indian. As examples: Some of the
northern Pueblo tribes have forms of
dress borrowed from the westernmost
Plains tribes, while the current
"traditional" style of dress among the
Navajo was influenced by Anglo
fashions from the post-Civil War era.

The katsina—here emerging from a kiva—plays a major role in Hopi life.

environment. Tiny springs at the mesa edge, fed by the drainage of Black Mesa, have sustained the villages for centuries. Because of their expertness at dry farming they have been able to grow crops of corn, squash, beans, and cotton on land that would give nightmares to a Midwestern farmer.

A short growing season (133 days) and limited rainfall (12 inches per year) made it imperative to obtain the help of supernatural forces to ensure adequate moisture and bountiful harvests. It was only natural that this would be the focus of Hopi religious activities. Much time was spent in performing complex and beautiful rituals designed

Corn is still important at Hopi, where it may be prepared in countless ways—boiled, parched, baked, and roasted—or even ground for use as a prayer offering.

HOPI (hoe'-pih) — a contraction of *Hopituh*, their tribal name, which is generally translated as "the peaceful ones." Language: Shoshonean. Reservation: 1,561,213 acres. Population: 9,199. Government: Constitution adopted 1936. Hopi tribal council made up of 15 members, most of whom are elected by villages according to population, but several are appointed by the *kikmongwi* (priest-chief) of their village. Chair and vice-chair are elected at large. Ceremonials: Katsina dances performed from January until late July. Unmasked dances begin in August and continue through December.

Hopi tradition tells of the people inhabiting three underworlds before emerging into the present world. The settlement of land is explained in terms of individual clans who wandered about and occupied many sites prior to settling in their present villages. There is no doubt that the Hopi tribe is made up of numerous groups of diverse origins.

At first appearance the arid mesa country of the Hopi appears incapable of supporting a permanent population. Yet, this agricultural tribe has not only existed but often thrived in a hostile

to bring about the desired results. Today, the Hopi still maintain one of the most active religious calendars of the Southwestern tribes.

At the time of the Spanish contact in 1540, the Hopi occupied seven independent villages. The Hopi submitted to Spanish rule after Pedro de Tovar attacked and defeated the pueblo of Kawaikuh. Oñate, in 1598, received formal promises of loyalty from the Hopi, but because they remained on the Spanish frontier no civil authority was established among them, nor were they required to pay tribute to the Crown.

Walpi, founded over 300 years ago, was moved to its current site to protect the village from Spanish attack. The narrow path leading to the village has also protected it from the onslaught of modern technology. This village still does without electricity or running water, a fact of life viewed by the residents with mixed emotions. Bottled gas is generally used for lighting and cooking, while wood and coal-fired stoves are the primary source of heat. Without power poles to give it away, at a distance the village blends with the rocky mesa.

The Hopi were subjected to missionary activities in the 1600s when the Franciscans established missions in several of the villages, but Spanish influence was much less intensive than among the Rio Grande pueblos. New crops, fruit trees, livestock, and metal tools were acquired, but religious and political life were virtually untouched. The Spanish system of selecting governors for secular offices was never adopted.

Nevertheless, the Hopi were anxious to rid themselves of any Spanish control, and joined the eastern pueblos in the Great Pueblo Revolt of

Hopi weaving is done by the men, who also embroider the kilts, sashes, belts, leggings, mantas, and shirts used in their religious ceremonies. Because there are few Hopi weavers today, many Hopi have to trade for woven goods with other pueblos—or improvise.

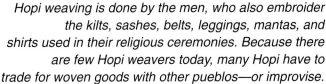

1680. Resident Spanish priests were killed and the missions destroyed, and the Hopi remained hostile to all subsequent attempts to reestablish Spanish authority. Awatobi, which was friendly to the Spanish and their priests, was attacked and destroyed by warriors from the other Hopi pueblos and the survivors absorbed into the villages of the attackers.

Hopis maintained friendly relations with most tribes, and traveled great distances to trade with other people. (Hopi weaving is still much sought after by the Rio Grande pueblos.) Occasionally, in times of drought, they left their villages to take up temporary residence with the Havasupai or Zuni. The Navajo and Ute, who harassed the Hopi with their constant raiding, were regarded as traditional enemies.

During some ceremonies, children not yet initiated into the Katsina Society are given katsina dolls that they are told have been carved for them by the katsinas themselves.

Hopi overlay jewelry, first developed in the 1930s, involves cutting the design out of one sheet of silver and overlaying it on a second, solid sheet.

The first Hopi-owned and operated store opened in the 1930s. The Hopi Cooperative Arts and Crafts Guild formed shortly after World War II. In recent years, a number of Hopi—many of them artists—have opened their own shops and galleries. Currently there are more than a dozen Hopi-owned and operated enterprises on the reservation. These shops provide visitors and collectors with an opportunity to meet some of the artists whose work they prize.

Hopi pottery comes in many forms and styles, but the polychrome ware produced at the villages on First Mesa (Hano, Sichomovi, and Walpi) is the best-known.

Anglo contact, which began in 1826, has had a much greater effect on Hopi life. Policies of the Bureau of Indian Affairs and the influence of Christian missionaries have resulted in considerable factionalism among the Hopi villages and disruption of their way of life. Nevertheless, it is apparent that the Hopi have retained much of their native culture.

Not all villages completely accept the authority of the Hopi tribal council—established in its present form in 1951—recognizing instead the traditional form of village government which accepts the *kikmongwi* (village priest-chief) as the authority. Much factionalism has resulted from the insistence of the U.S. government that the Hopi be dealt with as a single tribe rather than as separate autonomous pueblos in the manner of the Rio Grande pueblos.

Mining leases for the coal on Black Mesa provide some income (early estimates were that the state of Arizona was collecting more in related taxes than the Hopi and Navajo combined were receiving in royalties), and enormous problems. The need for clear title to the land in order to contract with a mining company sharpened the long unresolved and festering dispute over land assigned originally to the Hopi and then later designated for use (and occupied) by both Hopi and Navajo. (In a remarkable deviation from normal legal procedures, the BIA approved

a contract with a firm that represented both the Hopi and the mining company.)

Farming and stock raising are still important economic pursuits among the Hopi, although they are jeopardized by a plummeting water table (causing important and sacred springs to dry up) which many blame on the daily pumping of several million gallons of water needed for the mining operation at Black Mesa.

Wage work provides the bulk of individual income. Gaming was proposed as a source of revenue, but tribal members decisively voted it down. In recent years craftwork has provided a growing source of earnings for many individuals. No other tribe produces a greater variety of crafts than the Hopi—pottery, katsinas, silverwork, weaving, and three types of basketry.

Hopi dances, certainly as beautiful and impressive as any in the world, are dramatized prayers for rain, the growth of crops, renewal of the cycle of life, and the health and well-being of not only the Hopi but all people and all living beings. Unlike the Rio Grande pueblos, Hopi dances—both masked and unmasked—were usually open to the public, but repeated attempts by individuals to photograph and videotape religious observances in open violation of Hopi law has caused many villages to close their ceremonies to non-Hopi in recent years.

First Mesa

WALPI (wal'-pih) — "place of the gap." The people of Walpi occupied two earlier sites on the lower terrace of First Mesa before moving to their present location in 1680. Fear of a Spanish reprisal for their part in the Great Pueblo Revolt prompted them to change to a more defensive position. The move worked well, for neither of two punitive expeditions sent by the Spanish attacked the village because of its impregnable appearance.

POLACCA (po-lah'-kah) — This community at the foot of the mesa was settled in the late 1800s by First Mesa people who wished to live near the trading post and day school.

SICHOMOVI (si-cho'-mo-vee) — meaning "place of the mound where wild currants grow"—was founded about 1750 as a colony of Walpi. It is also referred to as "Middle Village" because it is flanked by Walpi and Hano.

Hopi pottery styles continue to evolve as potters experiment with different clays, forms, and styles. Some styles are inspired by other pueblo pottery or prehistoric forms—like the melon bowl in this group.

Looking across Hopiland to the Second Mesa villages of Shipaulovi and Mishongnovi, one can better see the rock formations referred to as mesas—from the Spanish word for table. First, Second, and Third Mesa received their rather dull names from Anglo visitors who named them in the order they found them.

Nuva'tukya'ovi—Snow Mountain. Known to non-Hopi as the San Francisco Peaks, they are sacred to the Hopi, whose katsina spirits are believed to inhabit their highest reaches. In a losing battle, the Hopi and the Navajo—who also revere them as a sacred place—have sought to keep skiers and mountain climbers from reaching and possibly desecrating those high sacred places. At the base of the mountains lie several ancestral villages of the Hopi.

HANO (hah'-no) — The Hopi name for this Tewa village may be derived from *anopi* which means "eastern people" or it may be a mispronunciation of the Spanish name for the Tewas, which was *Los Tanos*. (A popular Hopi story claims Hano is a nickname derived from the frequent use of the syllable "ha" in Tewa speech.) Hano was settled by Tewa refugees from the Rio Grande Valley after the Great Pueblo Revolt. The Hopi claim the Tewa sought refuge from the Spanish, while the Tewa claim the Hopi asked them to help protect Walpi. The argument is as old as the village. Despite their long association with the Hopi, the Tewa people retain their own language and religious customs. Nampeyo, the potter credited with the revival of Hopi pottery beginning in 1890, was a Tewa from Hano.

Second Mesa

SHUNGOPAVY (pronounced in Hopi: Tsi-mo'-pah-vee)—"place by the spring where the tall reeds grow"—is the most important of the villages on Second Mesa. Two earlier pueblos were located at the base of the mesa near Gray Spring. The Franciscan mission of San Bartolome was built at Old Shungopavy in 1629. It was destroyed during the 1680 revolt, and the village was abandoned in favor of the present mesa-top location.

MISHONGNOVI (mih-shong'-no-vee) — "Mishong's place"—named for Mishong, the leader of the Crow Clan, who brought his people to Hopi from the San Francisco Peaks region in A.D. 1200. The people of Shungopavy allowed them to settle at Corn Rock, a Shungopavy

OWEN SEUMPTEWA

shrine, with the understanding that they would protect it against the First Mesa people. In 1629, the Franciscans built the chapel of San Buenaventura at Mishongnovi. It was destroyed and the village abandoned in 1680. The present pueblo was established shortly thereafter.

SHIPAULOVI (shih-pau'-lo-vee) — "the mosquitoes"—was, according to tradition, settled by people from Homolovi, a prehistoric pueblo on the Little Colorado River (near the present-day town of Winslow) which they say was abandoned because of the swarms of mosquitoes that infested the area. A more likely explanation is that Shipaulovi was established after the Great Pueblo Revolt by people from Shungopavy so that in the event that the Spaniards returned and destroyed their village, Shipaulovi would be able to carry on its ceremonies and religious traditions.

Third Mesa

ORAIBI (o-rye'-bih) — "place of Orai rock"—claims (along with Acoma) to be the oldest continually inhabited town in the United States. It dates from about A.D. 1150. According to tradition, Oraibi was founded by a dissident group from Old Shungopavy. In 1629, the mission of San Francisco was established at Oraibi—the ruins of this church are north of the village. An abandoned Mennonite church, struck by lightning, stands on the mesa edge. Oraibi, with a population of 1,200, was the largest Hopi village until 1906 when a split occurred over ceremonial prerogatives, and whether or not to comply with the Bureau of Indian Affairs' policies. The problem was settled bloodlessly with a "push of war." The losers, led by Yukioma, left Oraibi and built a new village, Hotevilla. An inscription that commemorates the Oraibi split is carved into the bedrock north of the village. It reads: *Well, it have to be this way now, that when you pass me over this line it will "be done." Sept. 8th, 1906.* The clan symbols of the two leaders are included.

KYKOTSMOVI (kee-kots'-mo-vee) — "place of the hills of ruins" (also called Lower Oraibi or New Oraibi)—was settled in 1890 by people from Oraibi who wanted to live near the school and trading post. It is also the site of most Hopi tribal government offices.

The Hopi are expert dry farmers. Hopi men often had to travel considerable distances to suitable sites for planting. The village of Moencopi began as a farming outpost of Oraibi village over 40 miles to the southeast. At the very edge of the current boundary for Hopiland, it is the most reliable source of water on the reservation.

Factionalism within villages is probably nothing new. In 1906 push literally came to shove as two competing factions found a bloodless way to end their feuding. Two groups—one friendly to the Americans and their new ways, the other opposed to them—agreed to a "push of war." The conservative element lost and had to vacate the village in the weeks before what proved to be a bitter winter.

OWEN SEUMPTEWA

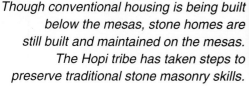

Though conventional housing is being built below the mesas, stone homes are still built and maintained on the mesas. The Hopi tribe has taken steps to preserve traditional stone masonry skills.

HOTEVILLA (hote'-vil-lah) — "skinned back"—derives its name from a village spring which is located in the back of a cave with a low overhang. The village was settled in 1906 by the conservative faction from Oraibi. Hotevilla has a long history of non-cooperation with the federal government, and is still regarded as the most conservative Hopi village.

BAKAVI (bah'-kah-vee) — "place of the reeds"—was settled in 1907 by a group who left the newly founded village of Hotevilla and attempted to return to Oraibi. They were refused admittance so they established their own village rather than return to Hotevilla.

MOENCOPI (mun'-ko-pih) — "place of running water"—is the westernmost of the Hopi villages. It was originally a farming settlement of Oraibi, but was established as a separate village in the 1870s by Tuvi, an Oraibi leader. Because its traditions are related to Oraibi, it is included here as a Third Mesa village even though it is located over 40 miles to the northwest. Moencopi is the only Hopi village with irrigated fields. Factionalism is beginning to result in a split, with some residents considering themselves members of either Upper Moencopi or Lower Moencopi.

APACHE (ah-pah'-chee) — from the Zuni name *Apachu*, meaning "enemy," a name they used for the Navajo. Native name varies with each band, but is usually a variation of *Nde, Indeh* or *Tinneh*, meaning "the people." *Inde'* (pronounced in-deh') is the most widely accepted. Language: Athabascan — related linguistically to the Athabascan tribes in Canada. (For reservations and populations, see individual listings.) ▬▬▬▬▬

The Apache still regularly hold Nah'ih'es—*coming-of-age ceremonies—for their daughters. It is a time when the entire community gathers together.*

KENJI KAWANO

The Apache, an Athabascan people, were comprised of many independent bands. They were hunters, warriors, and raiders who entered the Southwest sometime after A.D. 1200, and spread into northern Mexico by the 1500s. At the time of Spanish contact the division into separate tribal groups was still taking place. The name Apache was applied to all of these people, and is still used today as a general term for the individual tribes or bands.

Although contact with other tribes modified the culture of each group, they all remained largely dependent on hunting and gathering for subsistence. What could not be obtained by hunting, gathering, and some farming was stolen in raids on the villages of agricultural tribes.

With the acquisition of horses the range and frequency of their depredations increased until the raiding of Indian, Spanish and, later, Mexican and American settlements became a way of life. The Apaches ranged over an area that extended from southern Colorado to northern Mexico, and from central Arizona to western Texas.

Numerous unsuccessful attempts were made by the Spaniards, Mexicans, and Americans to eliminate the Apache. Military campaigns were launched against them, bounties were paid for scalps, captives were kept as slaves, and treacheries of the worst kind were perpetrated in ruthless efforts to put an end to the Apache raiders. (Because the history of this period is largely recorded by non-Apaches, the

The Gaan *or Mountain Spirit Dancers of the Apache appear during the Nah'ih'es ceremony. During this four-day celebration, the young woman coming of age is believed to have the power to bring rain and even heal with her touch. But the Gaan have other responsibilities as well. The Apache, like most tribes, mark their boundaries by sacred mountains. Those mountains and all the other mountains of their home are sacred to them and protect the Apache people. The spirits of those mountains are the Gaan. Oliver Enjady*

atrocities committed by the Apache are better known than those committed against them.) But the Apache refused to die or surrender—what they lacked in numbers they made up in ferocity and cunning. As guerrilla fighters the Apaches were unparalleled.

After the Civil War, attempts were made to confine the tribes to reservations so that the settlement of the Southwest by Anglos could proceed. Problems continued as corrupt officials cheated the Indians out of promised rations, and turned over large areas of Indian land to Anglos for mining and agricultural development. Distrust and discontent resulted and new uprisings occurred.

The last outbreak was led by Geronimo. His small band of Chiricahua renegades terrorized

Arizona, New Mexico, and northern Mexico from 1884 until their surrender in 1886. This ended the Apache wars, but not the mistreatment. The renegades were sent to Florida as prisoners of war as were *all* the Chiricahuas, men, women, and children, who had remained peaceably on the reservation—even the Apache scouts who had aided the U.S. Army in Geronimo's capture!

They were kept imprisoned far longer than any other POWs in American history—28 years. After their release in 1914 they were allowed to go home, but no land was set aside for them in their traditional homeland. Most settled on the Mescalero Reservation. Those that chose to remain in Oklahoma are known as the Fort Sill

The Apache one-string violin, crafted from an agave stalk, is still made and played by a few Apache musicians.

An Apache war cap, decorated with owl feathers in hopes the wearer would be as silent and swift as the owl. These were worn in dances and only rarely on actual raids.

Apache. Just over 100 members live on 3,568 acres of allotted land. They are distinct from the much larger Oklahoma Apache tribe, the Kiowa-Apache, a group who prefer to be known as the Plains Apache.

Western Apache

The Athabascan group known as the Western Apache originally consisted of a number of independent subtribes. The present San Carlos and White Mountain "tribes" are comprised of a number of early bands: the Mogollon, Pinaleno, Tonto, Aravaipa, Coyotero, and Chiricahua are represented in the San Carlos division, and the White Mountain "tribe" is made up of members of the Mimbreno, Mogollon, Pinaleno, Chiricahua, and Aravaipa bands.

SAN CARLOS — Reservation: 1,826,641 acres. Population: 10,120. Government: Constitution adopted 1936. Tribal corporate charter 1940. Tribal council consists of seven members elected at large, with chair and vice-chair.

WHITE MOUNTAIN — Reservation: 1,686,872 acres. Population: 10,147. Government: Constitution adopted 1938. Ten-member council elected at large, with chair and vice-chair.

CAMP VERDE (shared with Yavapai) — Reservation: 640 acres. Population: 650 (total).

TONTO — Reservation: 85 acres. Population: 92.

FORT MCDOWELL (shared with Mohave and Yavapai) — Reservation: 24,680 acres. Population: 816 (total).

The nomadic bands of hunters who were to be later known as the Apache settled in what is now southwestern New Mexico, northern Mexico, and southeastern Arizona during the 1400s and early 1500s.

By the latter part of the 16th century, they had begun to raid Spanish settlements in northern Sonora and Chihuahua. Early Spanish accounts do not refer to these people as Apaches, but it is possible that the raiders, whom they called

Sumas, Jocomes, and Janos were either these Athabascan-speaking bands or were later absorbed by the Apache (probably the Chiricahua and Mimbreno Apache). After 1700 they are referred to merely as Apaches.

Attempts to missionize these people ended in a full-scale rebellion in 1684. To protect their settlements from renewed Apache attacks the Spanish established a line of presidios or fortified outposts across northern Mexico, but the tactic proved useless against the hit-and-run warfare of the Apache. Besides, the Indians were not interested in driving out the Spaniards, but merely in raiding them for horses, cattle, and booty. Expeditions against the Apaches in their own territory were equally unsuccessful since pitched battles were avoided by the Indians whenever possible.

Warfare became more intense and widespread as bands pillaged as far south as Hermosillo, Sonora, and west into Tohono O'odham country past present-day Tucson. In 1848, Tubac was abandoned along with many other settlements, and the Mexicans were pushed south. The Apaches were in control.

Conflicts with Americans began in the 1820s when beaver trappers, bounty hunters, and prospectors began to invade the Apache domain. Nevertheless, many of the Apache groups seemed interested in maintaining peaceful relations with the Americans when the U.S. assumed control of Apache country in 1853. Exactly how the Americans could lay claim to Apache territory simply because they had defeated the Mexicans mystified the Apaches—after all, neither the Spaniards nor the Mexicans had ever succeeded in defeating the Apache. The greatest problem, however, resulted from the Americans' insistence that the Indians cease raiding the Mexican settlements across the border.

Attempts to confine the Apache to reservations were largely unsuccessful because of the prevailing atmosphere of mutual distrust. The period between 1853 and 1889 was marked by constant unrest. Disagreements between civil and military authorities on how best to handle the Indians prevented formulation of a consistent and constructive policy. White settlers and miners appropriated Apache lands with the help of corrupt administrators, and then demanded military

The Gaan *dancers of the Apache represent mountain spirits who live in caves near the tops of mountains in Apacheland. They are the guardians and protectors of the Apache people. At one time, they would appear among the Apache during times of great need or difficulty, such as famines and epidemics.*

TAD NICHOLS

Apache homes tended to be fairly simple affairs that could be quickly built from materials available in the immediate area. This type of brush shelter provided shade from the summer sun and yet allowed cooling breezes to pass through. The Apache were constantly on the move, following the game they hunted as well as the foods that ripened at different times in various areas. Because of this, their dwellings were quite different from the more permanent stone or wood and mud homes of more sedentary tribes.

protection or revenge when the Apache tried to defend their land. Dissident Apache bands frequently left their reservations to pillage Mexican and American settlements, and the peaceable Apaches who stayed on the reservation were often targets for vengeful Anglo raiding parties.

It was not until 1890, after 70 bloody years, that the Apache abandoned their old way of life for more peaceful pursuits.

Today, the Western Apache operate a number of successful tribal enterprises including livestock, lumber mills, recreational areas, resorts, gaming, stores, and service stations. The White Mountain Apache Reservation even supports a public radio station.

Beadwork, cradleboards, and some basketry (primarily burden baskets) are still being produced.

The scenic and sacred mountainous homeland of the Apache has provided the tribe with timber resources which they carefully manage. It also provides recreational opportunities for Arizona's non-Apache population. Hunting, hiking, fishing, and camping (with permits) are very popular, and the tribe has developed a ski resort as well.

JICARILLA (hee-kah-ree'-yah) — Spanish for "small basket," derived from their production and use of small baskets. Native name is *Tinde*, meaning "the people." Language: Athabascan. Reservation: 823,580 acres. Population: 2,764. Government: Constitution adopted in 1937. Tribal council, chair, and vice-chair elected at large. Ceremonials: Sept. 14-15 - Long Life Ceremony and race (inquire locally for location).

At the time of Spanish contact the Jicarilla occupied the mountainous region in the vicinity of Taos and Picuris. Their range extended across northern New Mexico and southern Colorado. They had roamed the buffalo plains to the southeast earlier but were driven out, along with the Mescalero, by the Comanche.

From their contact with Pueblo tribes, the Jicarilla learned to supplement their hunting economy with some agriculture. They maintained friendly relations with Picuris and Taos, but did not hesitate to raid the pueblos between peaceful trading visits. Spanish settlements, however, became the primary targets for they provided the Apaches with a source of horses and other livestock. From the Utes, with whom they allied themselves against the Navajo, they acquired a number of Plains Indian traits including buckskin clothing, beadwork, and tipis.

In 1733, the Spaniards established a mission near Taos in an effort to missionize the Jicarilla, who were actually two groups—the *Olleros* (from the Spanish for pottery makers) and the *Llaneros* (Spanish for Plainsmen). It was soon abandoned when the Indians refused to accept a sedentary life under Spanish rule.

Attempts to confine the Jicarilla included a treaty in 1851, which required them to stay at least 50 miles from any settlement. The U.S. government in 1853 attempted to settle several hundred Jicarillas on a reservation on the Rio Puerco. It was unsuccessful, and the Indians continued their forays against the Americans. Between 1853 and 1887, the Jicarilla were moved no less than eight times before the government made up its mind where the tribe should be settled. The boundaries of their new reservation—west of their heartland—were carefully drawn, giving the springs and best land to non-Indians. Schools were set up in 1903, causing an outbreak of tuberculosis to spread to epidemic proportions. An estimated nine in ten Jicarillas suffered from the disease.

Remaining traditional Jicarilla culture is represented by ceremonies like the "Bear Dance" (a long-life ceremony), a girls' puberty rite, and an annual race that re-creates a legendary race between the sun and moon. There has been some revival of older crafts—buckskin, beadwork, and a limited number of coiled baskets are still made.

The Jicarilla derive considerable income from oil and gas leases as well as the sale of timber. This income is invested in education and tribal enterprises that provide jobs for tribal members. A recently opened gaming facility is expected to add to tribal income.

Sheep and cattle raising along with wage work are the primary sources of individual income. Additional tribal income is derived from those who come to camp, hunt, and fish.

Jicarilla Apache baskets with bright aniline dye colors are still woven, though not in the quantity they were made earlier in this century when you could even buy a Jicarilla basketry fishing creel.

MESCALERO (mes-kah-ler'-o) — Spanish

meaning "mescal people" (for their extensive use of mescal cactus as food). Language: Athabascan. Reservation: 460,678 acres. Population: 3,585. Government: Tribal constitution and bylaws adopted in 1936. Tribe operates under federal charter as a corporation. A business committee of ten, elected biennially by tribal members, functions as a tribal council. Ceremonials: July 1-4 - rodeo and fiesta that includes the appearance of the Gaan (Mountain Spirit) dancers.

At the time the Spaniards entered the Southwest, the main band of the Mescalero tribe occupied the Sierra Blanca Mountains just north of their present reservation. Other bands inhabited the Big Bend country of Texas and the Guadalupe Mountains of the New Mexico-Texas border.

During the summers they lived in the mountains, moving from one campsite to another in search of game and wild plants. Occasionally they made buffalo hunting trips—using dogs as pack animals before the advent of the horse—onto the plains to the east. During these journeys they frequently fought Comanches who also claimed this territory as their own.

In winter they moved into warmer regions where they made great use of desert plants, par-

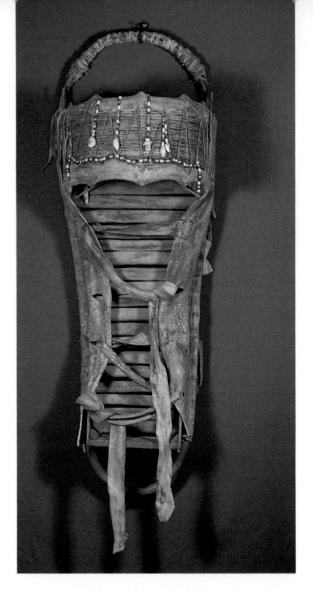

Apache buckskin and beadwork is a highly prized craft tradition—especially by the Apache themselves, who are probably the best customers for this type of work.
This detail is from a girl's Nah'ih'es dress.

ticularly the mescal cactus, the large tuberous root of which was roasted much like a sweet potato. In between they found time to raid the villages of the Pueblo Indians in the Rio Grande Valley.

Their first contacts with the Spanish explorers were friendly, but the occupation of their land by colonizers soon changed this. By the late 1680s, the Mescalero presented a serious threat to the Spanish settlements in the region.

In 1778-89, the Spanish launched a military campaign to subdue both the Mescalero and the Lipan Apache. Several defeats and the promise of free rations greatly reduced Apache depredations. Relative peace prevailed until 1831 when the Mexican government assumed control of the area. Financial troubles prevented continuance of the ration system, and the Apaches soon left the settlements to resume raiding as a livelihood.

Attempts to confine the Apache were made by the U.S. in the 1850s. Treaties providing "perpetual peace" and rations were made with the Mescalero, but never officially ratified. Raiding, quite naturally, followed and forts were estab-

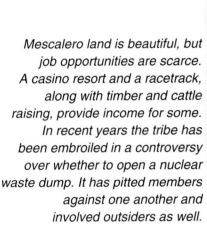

Apache cradleboards are made not only for collectors, but for use. When hung from a tree or a peg on the wall, infants get to see the world instead of just the ceiling or the treetops, and the snug wrapping makes them feel secure and safe.

Mescalero land is beautiful, but job opportunities are scarce. A casino resort and a racetrack, along with timber and cattle raising, provide income for some. In recent years the tribe has been embroiled in a controversy over whether to open a nuclear waste dump. It has pitted members against one another and involved outsiders as well.

lished in the lower Rio Grande Valley to protect the white settlers.

After a successful military campaign by U.S. troops in 1855, the Mescalero sued for peace and signed a treaty agreeing to settle at Fort Stanton. The experiment was short-lived as peaceful Mescaleros found themselves the victims of raids by revenge-seeking Mexican settlers.

General Carleton finally achieved a military victory over the Mescalero in 1862. In 1864, about 400 were confined to Bosque Redondo near Fort Sumner, New Mexico. The remainder escaped to Mexico or went to live with the Western Apache.

Those who remained at Bosque Redondo suffered greatly. Drought killed their crops and bad water, disease, and Navajo raids decimated their numbers. (In 1864, several thousand Navajos rounded up by Kit Carson were also confined on the 40-square-mile area with the Mescalero.) Once again the Mescalero drifted back to their land and old way of life.

A reservation was established near their home territory in early 1873, but "modified" (read: reduced) later to meet the demands of en-

croaching whites. Programs to "civilize" the Mescalero were designed to destroy the status and influence of the women elders, required the men to cut their hair, and attempted to stop traditional ceremonies and substitute the 4th of July, Thanksgiving, and Christmas for them. Farming was approved as an occupation.

The population of the Mescalero reservation includes members of other Apache tribes—Lipan, Mimbreno, and Chiricahua—the latter arriving in 1913 after their release from prison in Fort Sill, Oklahoma.

Today, most Mescaleros earn their living by wage work on and near the reservation. Tribal income is derived from timber, cattle, a sawmill, a racetrack, a casino, a resort, and recreational activities, which include skiing, hunting, and fishing. A proposal to bring jobs and income by locating a nuclear waste dump on Mescalero land was soundly defeated in 1995, but brought back for a second vote, in which it passed.

Traditional Mescalero crafts are largely limited to cradleboards, beadwork, and a few baskets.

TOHONO O'ODHAM (to'-ho-no ah'-ah-dahm) — native name meaning "desert people." (Formerly Papago, from the Pima name for them, *Papahvi-o-otam*, meaning "bean people.") Language: Piman. Reservations: Tohono O'odham - 2,855,874 acres, San Xavier - 71,095 acres, and Gila Bend - 10,404 acres. Total population: 18,751. Government: Constitution adopted in 1937. Three reservations constitute 11 districts. Adult members of each district elect two persons to tribal council. Tribal officers elected at large. Each district has a five-person council. Celebrations: June 24 - San Juan's Day celebration—dances and chicken pull in some villages. July (no specific dates) - saguaro wine festivals. Oct. 4 - annual pilgrimage to festival in Magdalena, Sonora. Late October - annual rodeo and craft fair.

Today, the Tohono O'odham occupy roughly the same area they inhabited at the time of Spanish contact. The members of this desert tribe are found in widely scattered villages in southern Arizona and northwestern Sonora.

Father Kino began his missionary work among the O'odham in 1687. In addition to a new religion, the Indians acquired European crops from the missions, including winter wheat that eliminated the hunger of the lean winter months. Additionally they gained horses and cattle, quickly becoming proficient cattlemen.

Catholicism, in a modified form which centered about the worship of Saint Francis Xavier as a source of magical power, did not replace native religion but was merely added to it.

ARIZONA STATE MUSEUM

Among the Tohono O'odham of the Sonoran Desert, the June saguaro harvest signaled the beginning of the new year.

Many Tohono O'odham have adobe or contemporary frame or masonry homes, but partially enclosed ramadas are still a feature of most homes. They provide shade during the blistering heat of summer, yet permit cooling breezes to pass through.

The Round Dance of the Tohono O'odham is often called a Friendship Dance because anyone—tribal member or not, Indian or non-Indian—may join in the circling dance. The singers in the foreground are using traditional instruments—the rattle and basket drum. Catholic missionary efforts are visible in every village, but many traditional values and customs remain, thriving side by side with newer beliefs and customs. Mike Chiago

Each O'odham village was politically autonomous, led by a headman called "The Keeper of the Smoke." A council of old men discussed village affairs, but took no action until agreement was unanimous. Leaders for hunting and war gained their positions through personal ability and knowledge of rituals (obtained from dreams) necessary for success.

TOHONO O'ODHAM

Traditional Tohono O'odham crafts include pottery and basketry. The pottery originally made was for cooking and storing water. Basketry was used for carrying loads, parching, and storage. Today most pottery and basketry is made for purely decorative purposes. Only a small amount of pottery is made, but the O'odham weave more baskets than all the other tribes combined.

All villages had two locations. From spring until the fall harvest the O'odham lived near the mouth of an arroyo where flash floods supplied moisture for their fields. Cultivating floodplains provides, at best, a precarious livelihood so great use was made of desert plants, particularly the saguaro fruit and mesquite bean. The winter villages were located near mountain springs where the O'odham hunted deer. In time of famine whole families moved north to the Pima villages where they earned their keep by helping the Pimas with their river-irrigated crops.

Tohono O'odham territory came under American control with the Gadsden Purchase in 1853. The Indians lived peacefully under the new government despite occasional skirmishes with white cattlemen who appropriated O'odham grazing land and water holes. For mutual protection against Apache raids they allied themselves with the Anglo settlers.

Because the Tohono O'odham had never fought against the U.S., they had no treaty that would protect them against encroachment by American miners, ranchers, and settlers. They

also did not receive the right to vote until 1948. (There's a moral in here somewhere.) In 1874 and 1882, two small reservations were finally set aside for the O'odham at San Xavier and Gila Bend.

In 1917, what is now known as the main reservation—the second-largest reservation in the U.S.—was established. O'odham were forced to leave other areas where they had lived for generations and move to the new reservation. The land they had to leave was among the most productive.

Until 1959, it had the dubious distinction of being the only Indian reservation in which the mineral resources did not belong to the tribe—a testimonial to the power of Arizona's mining industry.

Like the Pima, they also suffered the loss of their water—both surface and underground. The water-hungry growing metropolis of nearby Tucson had wells that began draining the aquifer under Indian land as early as 1881. In 1982, the federal courts awarded them water rights to 76,000 acre-feet, but as of 1995 no water had been delivered.

Many O'odham still weave, due in large part to a bleak employment situation on the reservation. As that improves, weaving will decline—but never disappear, for it is an important aspect of the culture. The apprentice spending long hours with an elder learns more than just basketry.

Today, less than one-third of the O'odham live on their reservation year-round. Many leave to find work in nearby towns—others find seasonal jobs in agriculture. Cattle raising and limited farming are the main sources of income for those on the reservation who are not employed by tribal or government agencies, but estimates of the unemployment rate on the reservation range to over 60 percent.

Income from mining leases was once the primary source of revenue for the tribe, but the recent construction of a gaming establishment on the San Xavier reservation near Tucson is proving to be an economic boon for the entire tribe. Plans are being made for further economic development that will provide jobs and housing, and fund social programs and educational opportunities.

The O'odham produce more basketry today than all other tribes combined. Coiled baskets in a variety of shapes and sizes, made of bear grass stitched with yucca and devil's claw, are the most popular. Horsehair miniature baskets are also made, along with some pottery.

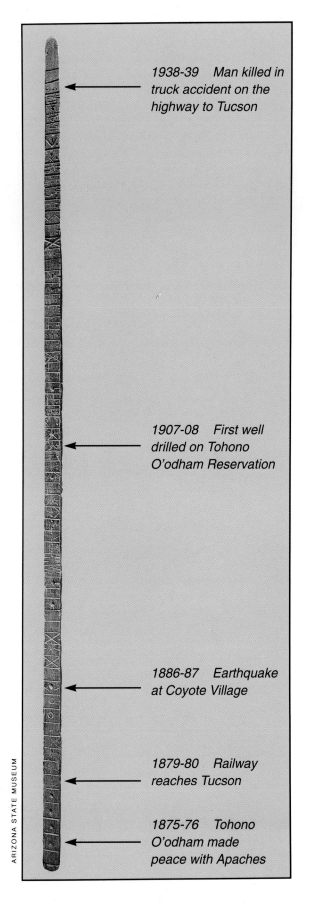

1938-39   Man killed in truck accident on the highway to Tucson

1907-08   First well drilled on Tohono O'odham Reservation

1886-87   Earthquake at Coyote Village

1879-80   Railway reaches Tucson

1875-76   Tohono O'odham made peace with Apaches

ARIZONA STATE MUSEUM

At one time most villages had a calendar stick to mark the significant events that happened over the years. The keeper of such a stick was charged with remembering what each symbol or mark commemorated, and the stick was handed down from one generation to the next. The practice has died out.

YAQUI (yah'-kee) — origin unknown. Native name is *Yoeme*. Language: Piman. Reservation: 995 acres, known as New Pascua, southwest of Tucson. In addition, they occupy four small villages or barrios—two in Tucson, and one each in Marana and Tempe. Population: (Arizona only) 6,227. Government: (New Pascua) tribal council elected by the adult population. Old Pascua village—not a part of the reservation—community buildings owned by the city of Tucson, but controlled by a council consisting of between 30 and 40 village members. Ceremonies: Christmas, Saints' days, and Easter week (which includes deer dancers, *pahkolas, chapayekas*, and *matachines*).

In addition to wearing cocoon rattles and bells, and carrying metal and wood rattles, Yaqui Pahkola dancers are accompanied by a combination flute-player and drummer along with men playing gourd drums and using rasps.

The Yaqui, who occupy five small villages in southern Arizona, are political refugees from Sonora, Mexico, where they originally occupied eight villages.

This tribe of agriculturists numbered about 30,000 at the time of Spanish contact in 1533. Their rancherias were strung out along the full length of the Rio Yaqui. Formidable in battle and fiercely independent, they successfully resisted Spanish efforts to subdue them. Nevertheless, they preferred to live in peace and signed a treaty with the Spaniards in 1610. At the request of the Yaqui, the Jesuits established scattered missions in their settlements and the dispersed population was eventually concentrated into eight towns.

Under the Jesuit program agricultural practices were improved, and livestock and new crops were introduced. The Yaqui were surprisingly receptive to Catholicism and eagerly embraced the new religion. They also accepted the Spanish system of village government, but considered themselves independent of Spanish authority. The Spaniards, reluctant to challenge this powerful tribe, were content to allow the Yaqui to remain autonomous and exempted them from paying tribute. Except for one revolt in 1740, caused by an influx of settlers and a conflict of interest between the Jesuits' program and civil authorities, the Yaqui remained at peace with the Spanish.

After Mexico gained its independence in 1821, it declared the Yaqui to be full citizens of the country. As a practical matter, the change in status meant that the Yaqui lost their sovereignty and had to pay taxes, something they strongly objected to. Combined with new pressures on Yaqui land and water from Mexican settlers and ranchers, it began a period of conflict which continued for over 100 years and ranged from extended guerrilla warfare to full-scale battles. Attempted solutions to the situation included peace offers, wholesale deportation of Yaquis to distant parts of Mexico, and military campaigns to exterminate Yaqui men, women, and children. The last skirmish occurred in 1927. It was during the last 40 years of this period that many Yaquis sought asylum in Arizona.

Because of their political status as refugees, the Yaquis in Arizona were not treated as wards of the U.S. or as a sovereign nation, and so were not entitled to any of the services of the Bureau of Indian Affairs until 1978, when federal legislation gave them recognition as a tribe and a reservation. In 1994 they were finally recognized as a "historic tribe," which then finally gave them the same rights and privileges as other American Indian tribes.

The development of a casino, which draws customers from nearby Tucson, has provided the tribe with employment as well as income to provide better housing and educational opportunities, and to begin planning new economic developments and address the social ills their tribe has endured.

Yaqui religious life, a combination of native and Catholic beliefs and ceremonies, is still very strong. Public performances occur on Saints' days, Easter, and Christmas.

Yaqui beliefs are a mixture of their native religion and Catholicism. Here a Yaqui Pahkola and Deer Dancer genuflect before a very Indian-looking Virgin of Guadalupe. The Maaso or Deer Dancer appears with several Pahkolas during Yaqui Easter observances. A hunt scene is symbolically reenacted with Pahkolas playing the part of hunters. Arturo Montoya

PIMA (pee'-mah) — from the phrase *pi nyi match*, meaning "I don't know"—the answer given to the Spanish explorers who asked questions in a language they had never heard. The native name is *Akimel O'odham*, meaning "river people." Language: Piman. Reservations: Gila River (shared with the Maricopa) - 371,929 acres, Salt River (shared with the Maricopa) - 66,802 acres, and Ak Chin—meaning "flood plain" (shared with the Tohono O'odham) - 21,840 acres. Population total including Maricopa: 17,091. Government (Ak Chin): Five-member council that elects its own chair and vice-chair. ▬▬▬▬

The desert tribes are some of the most impoverished in the Southwest. Recent opportunities to open gambling facilities on the reservations have provided a desperately needed source of income to provide fundamental services like housing, law enforcement, and educational opportunities. The need has deepened with severe cuts in many federal funding sources and services. Many tribes are reinvesting the proceeds in scholarships and economic development.

Hohokam, a Pima word meaning "those who have gone," is the name given to a remarkable agricultural people who occupied southern and central Arizona for about 1,500 years. Sometime after A.D. 1400 this culture, who had constructed elaborate irrigation systems in the Gila and Salt River valleys, declined and disappeared. Soon afterward they were replaced by Piman-speaking tribes—the Pima and Tohono O'odham, who are possibly descended from the ancient Hohokam.

At the time of Spanish contact the Pima occupied the Gila River Valley. These people were agriculturists who irrigated their farmlands with water diverted from the river. Their population,

estimated at 2,500 in 1775, was concentrated in a number of permanent villages along the river valley. Although they had a strong sense of tribal unity, particularly in time of war, each village was politically independent.

The introduction of livestock and new crops were the only important Spanish contributions to Pima life. Lack of church funds prevented Father Eusebio Kino's mission system from extending to their territory. The impact of a foreign religion was not felt until the late 1800s, when Presbyterian missionaries began working to convert them.

Intensive contact with Anglos began during the Gold Rush when thousands of migrants to California passed through Pima territory. The

The Pima once produced large numbers
of very durable willow baskets
like this one with a whirlwind pattern
called sivalik in Pima.

Pima weavers use willow, a more difficult
material than the yucca of the Tohono
O'odham. As a result, there are far fewer
weavers, but the craft is being kept alive.

Indians provided food and supplies for many of the travelers, and relations were consistently friendly.

After the Gadsden Purchase, Anglos began to settle in the rich farmlands of the Gila. Pima's land rights were not recognized until 1859, when a reservation—much smaller than the territory they previously used—was established for them on the Gila. Serious problems began for the Pima when the settlers upstream began to divert water from the Gila River for their own use. Formal protests to Congress proved useless. A tribe that had sold the U.S. Army and settlers an estimated 3 million bushels of surplus wheat in 1870, was so impoverished from water diversion and land theft that by 1895 they had to be issued rations.

A government proposal to relocate them to Oklahoma was rejected. Instead, many of the Pimas moved into the Salt River Valley. To solve the Pimas' water problem, Coolidge Dam was built on the Gila River. The project was a technical success, but once again the legal rights to the water wound up in the hands of non-Indians.

The government's early allotment program resulted in land holdings so fractionalized that, combined with lack of funds to drill wells and government restrictions that permitted only 600 acres to be irrigated, the Pimas were unable to operate successful farms. The Bureau of Indian Affairs, however, approved leasing of Pima land, without such restrictions, to non-Indians.

In 1962, the Ak Chin reservation began to regain control of its farmland. In recent years the tribal farming operation supplied more than 90 percent of the tribal budget, and employed 80 percent of the enrolled populace. The water table, however, drained by nearby Phoenix, began to drop limiting the amount of land they could farm, and prompting Ak Chin to go to Congress to force the government to deliver the water they had promised back in 1912. It finally arrived in 1987.

A casino was opened at Ak Chin in 1994, further enhancing their economic stability and future, and enabling them to begin meeting critical housing needs. An industrial park has opened, and a museum is planned.

The Gila River Reservation was the site of the third-largest internment camp during World War II. The BIA offered the Gila River Reservation as a site for relocating the Japanese without first consulting the tribe, who opposed the arrangement. Intensive negotiations and threats from both the Bureau of Indian Affairs and the War Relocation Authority finally pressured the tribal council into agreement.

Today, the reservation (immediately south of the mushrooming Phoenix metropolitan area) offers a museum, restaurant, and shop complex, which also serves as a job-training site.

The Salt River Reservation (west of Phoenix), home to both Pima and Maricopa, has leased a major discount shopping center—one of the largest in the country—on their land.

MARICOPA (mah-rih-ko'-pah) — derived from the Yuma name for this tribe. The native name is *Piipaash*, meaning "the people." Language: Yuman. Reservations: Gila River (shared with the Pima) - 371,932 acres, and Salt River (shared with the Pima) - 46,619 acres. Population: included in Pima population total. Government: The tribe has no separate tribal government, but participates with the Pima in tribal council organizations on their respective reservations.

The Maricopa tribe originally occupied an area on the lower Colorado River, but was driven out in pre-Spanish times by incessant intertribal warfare and gradually drifted eastward along the Gila River. In 1774, an estimated 1,500 Maricopas inhabited the middle Gila east of the present

Agriculture is still an important source of income for the Pima. This is highly-prized long-staple Pima cotton, domesticated by Indian farmers centuries ago. At one time the Pima produced enormous crop surpluses. In 1870 alone they sold 3 million bushels of wheat to the U.S. Army and settlers. But then their water, and later their best lands were taken from them. By 1895 they had been so impoverished by these thefts that they had to be issued rations to avoid starvation.

town of Gila Bend to the mouth of the Salt River. Under pressure from their traditional enemies, the Mohave and Yuma, they migrated farther east into Pima country.

During the 1800s, they were joined by the remnants of other Yuman tribes who had been driven out of their lower Colorado River territory. These tribes were the Opa (they may have been the same group known as the Maricopa), Halchidhoma, Kahwan, Halyikawamai, Cocomaricopa, and the Kavelchadom (the latter two may have been one and the same). Former identities were submerged into a single group that was referred to collectively as Maricopa, though many on the Salt River Reservation still identify themselves as the Halchidhoma. They allied themselves with the Pima for protection against their common enemies. In 1857, the decisive defeat of a Yuma and Mohave raiding party by the Pima and Maricopa ended their troubles with those two tribes.

In spite of close contact with the Pima, the Maricopa maintained a way of life typical of Colorado River Yumans, among whom dreams were an important source of power. The weaving of cotton blankets on a horizontal loom, and the use of a calendar stick to record events were two of the few traits they did pick up from their neighbors. They produced pottery in quantity, but little basketry.

Little remains of the old culture today. A very small amount of finely polished red pottery, painted with black mesquite sap, is still produced. Native dances, curing rites, traditional tribal organization, and the great emphasis on dreaming for power are all things of the past.

Today, the Maricopa of the Salt River Pima-Maricopa Reservation (established in 1879) and the Gila River Reservation (set aside in 1895) earn their living by subsistence farming, growing cotton and alfalfa, wage work, and leasing land for non-Indian developments, including industrial parks and a motor-sport and recreation facility at Firebird Lake. Most individual land allotments are too small now to be farmed economically, placing the emphasis on tribal farming, overseen by the Maricopa Indian Cooperative Association.

The pottery of many Indian tribes has been influenced by the non-Indian market. This "wedding vase" form is not a traditional Maricopa shape, but was made to meet the demands of the market.

K. C. DEN DOOVEN

Maricopa pottery, which is very similar to that produced by the neighboring Pima, is usually red on black, but a cream-colored slip is sometimes applied to create a polychrome ware. Mesquite sap is used for the black paint.

Colorado River Tribes

The Yuma, Mohave, Cocopa, and Maricopa are the remaining tribes of a number of closely related groups who occupied the Colorado River and lower Gila River valleys. (Several merged into what are known as the Maricopa by the early 1800s.) They share a common language—Yuman—and a common culture.

These people were primarily agriculturists—crops of corn, beans, and pumpkins were raised on the fertile floodplains of the river. Wild desert plants (especially mesquite beans), small game, and fish supplemented their diet.

The groups maintained a strong sense of tribal identity although they lacked formal political organization. They lived in small, widely separated settlements strung out along the river bottoms. Leaders gained status through their demonstrated abilities, but had no formal authority. Religious ceremonies consisted of individuals singing song cycles that had been "dreamed." Great emphasis was placed on the acquisition of power through dreams. Success in gambling, curing, or war depended solely on this source.

Intertribal warfare was a common occurrence. The acquisition of new farmlands and scalps (a source of supernatural power) led to most fighting. Battles were conducted in a highly formalized manner—long lines of warriors faced each other and, after a warm-up period of shouted insults, engaged in hand-to-hand combat, the favorite weapon being a short, stout club of mesquite wood. Occasionally a champion from each side was selected to settle the dispute.

The dead were disposed of by cremation accompanied by the burning of personal property—a custom that appalled the early white settlers and which the Bureau of Indian Affairs suppressed in favor of a more "civilized" burial.

Contact with the Spanish was very limited and these tribes remained, for the most part, outside the Spanish sphere of influence.

The Treaty of Guadalupe Hidalgo in 1848, and the Gadsden Purchase in 1853, gave the U.S. jurisdiction over these tribes. The tribes objected to the encroachment on their lands by whites, but their mode of warfare was not effective against the tactics and weaponry of the U.S. Army.

Although none of these tribes had treaties with the U.S., reservations were established for them beginning in the 1860s. However, loss of tribal lands to squatters continued as late as 1940, when the Fort Mohave Reservation was opened to settlement by whites.

MOHAVE (mo-hah'-vee), also spelled Mojave. Mispronunciation of the native name *Aha mahkahve*, meaning "people along the water." Language: Yuman. Reservations: Fort Mohave - 32,697 acres, and Colorado River Indian Reservation (CRIT) (shared with other tribes) - 269,918 acres. Population: 836. Government (Fort Mohave): Tribal affairs are handled by a combination tribal council and business committee elected by tribal members. At CRIT, an intertribal council elected by adult members governs.

The Mohave occupy roughly the same territory today as they did in early times. Their settlements were scattered along the bottomlands on both sides of the Colorado River stretching from Cottonwood Island south to the peaks called "The Needles." According to Mohave tradition they were given the land by their creator, Mutiviyl, who spoke to them through his son Mastamho. At the time of Spanish contact in

Among Yuman tribes rattles were used to accompany a medicine man or shaman's songs. One's right to practice as a shaman came from dreams—the source of all power in Yuman religion.

1776, they numbered about 3,000 although other estimates range as high as 20,000.

Strongly nationalistic and warlike, the Mohave fought with neighboring tribes, and often traveled great distances to make war on other groups. Most of these military expeditions were conducted out of a sense of curiosity about new lands and people rather than to acquire territory or booty. They maintained friendly relations with the Yuma, Chemehuevi, Western Apache, and the Yavapai. They regarded the

Yuman pottery from the turn of the century varied from traditional forms still used by them to shapes designed to appeal to the Americans who came through on the train. The clays and paints are very similar to those used by the ancient Hohokam in this same general region.

Pima, Tohono O'odham, Maricopa, and Cocopa as traditional enemies.

The last major intertribal battle took place in 1857 along the Gila River where Maricopa Indians were attacked by over 100 Mohave and Quechan warriors. After the initial surprise attack, several hundred Pima warriors came to the aid of their Maricopa neighbors and together they nearly annihilated the attackers.

In the 1840s, a wagon trail to the California gold fields ran through Mohave territory. Friction with the immigrants culminated in a full-scale attack on a wagon train in 1858.

The following year Fort Mohave was built to maintain peace. Five Mohave headmen were held as hostages at Fort Yuma as insurance against any outbreak, and then later executed. (The official version of the story is that they were killed while trying to escape.) To impress the Mohave with the futility of further resistance, an important Mohave leader, Irrateba, was sent to Washington, D.C., to observe the great numbers and strength of the Americans. He returned duly impressed and used his influence to convince the Mohaves to remain at peace with the whites and settle on a reservation in the Colorado River Valley in 1858. The conservatives, comprising two-thirds of the tribe, remained behind in Mohave Valley and for decades regarded the Fort Mohave people as "the weak ones."

The Fort Mohave Reservation (which includes parts of California, Nevada, and Arizona) has fewer Mohaves residing there than the Colorado River Indian Reservation (CRIT), which was set aside by the War Department in 1870. During World War II the largest internment camp was established on the CRIT. For this purpose 25,000 acres of their land was appropriated—without tribal consent. After the war, the land was open to settlement by Hopi and Navajo families—many of whom spent their first years in barracks built for the Japanese-Americans imprisoned there. The Mohave and Chemehuevi, fearful of being overwhelmed, voted to stop the immigration in 1952—a move that Congress did not ratify until 12 years later. Increasingly, many descendants of

families that moved to CRIT are coming to think of themselves as primarily Mohave. (Current total population is 3001.)

Many Mohaves turned to farming. Others drifted to nearby Anglo communities, particularly Needles, California, to find work. With the development of tribal lands, stock raising and farming have become important economic pursuits. On CRIT the unemployment rate has plummeted due to agricultural jobs, but at Fort Mohave, where much of the farmland is leased to non-Indian agricultural enterprises, the unemployment rate remains staggeringly high. Long-term leasing of some land for non-Indian housing developments, recreation, commercial developments, and a casino promise a better economy for the Fort Mohave people.

Mohave pottery recently died out, but beadwork—including elaborate beaded capes—is still produced. Craftwork, however, has almost no economic importance.

Figurines were extremely popular with tourists and collectors from the late 1800s until well into the 1900s. Now exclusively regarded as collectors' items, they were made for the tourist trade and not for traditional purposes. The markings on the face and body reflect traditional Yuman tattoos.

COCOPA (ko'-ko-pah) — name derived from *Kwi-kah-pah*, the Mohave name for this tribe. Language: Yuman. Reservation total (East and West Cocopa): 6,009 acres. Population: 646 (approximately half reside in the Colorado River delta region of Mexico). Government: Tribal council consisting of five members. Constitution adopted in 1964.

The Cocopa, the southernmost of the Yuman tribes, occupied the delta region of the Colorado River. This tribe, divided into three bands, had a total population of 3,000 at the time of Spanish contact in 1540.

They were considered less warlike than the Yuma and Mohave, but often fought with these tribes over territorial disputes. They maintained friendly relations with other neighboring groups with whom they traded for pinyon nuts, acorns, hides, and tobacco. Occasionally captives taken in battle were traded to the Spanish for horses, though children were usually adopted by childless couples.

Dreams were of great importance in predicting the future, and as a source of power. To dream of water ensured success as a warrior; a mockingbird indicated a future as an orator; the appearance of an owl in a dream forebode death. No course of action was taken if a dream predicted anything other than success.

The Cocopa farmed areas of the rich, 50,000-acre Colorado River delta, but also relied heavily on wild desert foods. Fishing and hunting supplemented their diet. When land promoters diverted the Colorado River in 1905 (forming the Salton Sea in California), the delta Cocopa were forced to disperse. Although the river began to flow again after 1907, upstream diversions and polluted runoff from irrigated fields further north destroyed much of their delta land. A crackdown by the U.S. Immigration Service in the 1930s split the tribe into Mexican and American residents.

Today, the Cocopa raise cotton and do some subsistence farming. Land settlements in 1985, which added 4,000 acres to their tiny 500-acre reservation (which was established in 1917), enabled them to farm the land on a commercial basis. Beadwork is the primary craft produced.

Like most Yuman pottery traditions, that of the Mohave has died out or nearly died out several times in the last 40 years. During most of that time, when pottery was being produced, it was usually the work of a single artist. Currently there are no active potters among the Mohave.

YUMA (yoo'-mah) — derived from *Lum*, the Pima name for this tribe. Native name is *Quechan*, a reference to the trail they followed in leaving *Wi Kahme*, Spirit Mountain, from which all Yuman tribes are believed to have emerged. Language: Yuman. Reservation: Fort Yuma - 43,561 acres. Most of this reservation lies in California— only about 480 acres are in Arizona. Population: 2,234, of whom fewer than 100 live in Arizona. Government: Adult members elect a president, vice-president, and five-member council. ■■■■■■■■■■■■■■■■■■■■■■■■■■■■

The Yuma, or Quechan as they prefer to be known, occupied the Colorado River between the territories held by the Cocopa and Mohave.

Early Spanish contact was limited to a brief visit by Hernando de Alarcon, who sailed up the Colorado River to Yuma country in 1540. Kino paused in the Quechan villages during his trip to California in 1698 only long enough to distribute "canes of authority" to a few leaders.

In 1779, the Franciscans sent Padre Garces with a military escort to establish missions in Quechan territory. The Indians, who had proved to be friendly when treated as equals, resisted this attempt to subjugate them. They were unwilling to give up either land or independence in return for the dubious benefits of a new religion. In 1781, Quechans destroyed the mission (located near the present town of Yuma) and killed the priests and soldiers. Except for the introduction of new crops, Spanish contact had no influence on Quechan culture.

The discovery of gold in California resulted in an invasion of Quechan lands by thousands of "forty-niners" on their way to the goldfields. Despite raids on their farm plots by the migrants, and the pilfering from wagon trains by the Indians, the situation remained relatively peaceful.

Some enterprising Quechans even constructed rafts and provided ferry service to transport the white men across the Colorado River.

Any attempt to settle on Quechan lands, however, met with opposition. The earliest difficulties arose when Anglos tried to establish a ferry service in competition with the Quechans. By 1850, the Americans were demanding "protection" from the Indians, and a military outpost was established at Camp Yuma. The small detachment kept hostilities to a minimum, but failed to prevent the whites from taking Quechan land.

Hostilities soon broke out, and the army proceeded to subdue the Quechan. This was done not by military engagements, but through the destruction of Yuma fields and settlements, most of which were then regarded as "abandoned" and taken over by white settlers.

A reservation was established in 1883 but thrown open to settlement by non-Indians the following year, and a new reservation was set aside, with much of the land arid and unsuited for agriculture. Less than ten years later this reservation was severely cut in size. Finally, in 1978, the tribe regained control of nearly 25,000 acres of their land, though water rights to the land were not included and some of the choicest parcels remained in non-Indian hands. In 1914, tribal members living south of the border fled civil unrest to join their northern kin in what had become the U.S., avoiding the tribal separation many other border tribes endure.

A few women still produce beaded items ranging from belts and pendants to elaborate capes, but virtually no other traditional crafts survive.

CHEMEHUEVI (chem-eh-hway'-vee) — the
Yuman name for the Paiutes of southeastern California.
Native name is *Nuhwuh*, meaning "the people."
Language: Shoshonean. Reservation: Colorado River
(shared with several other tribes) - 265,850 acres, of which
225,995 are in Arizona and 39,855 in California.
Population: 95. Government: Constitution adopted in
1937. Tribal officers selected by a nine-member council.
Council members elected biennially for four-year terms.

The use of present-day political boundaries to
identify and locate Indian tribes in prehistoric
times does more to confuse than enlighten. State
lines are generally accepted as logical dividing
lines for closely related tribes, and little regard is
shown for natural geographic boundaries that
cross the neat but imaginary lines drawn on maps.

Thus it is that the Chemehuevi are usually
listed as a "California desert tribe," when in reali-
ty they are linguistically and culturally part of the
Great Basin culture which occupied the major
portion of what is now Nevada and Utah.

A small tribe of about 800, they led a semi-
nomadic life in the eastern half of the Mojave
Desert. Extensive use of wild plants supplemented by small game allowed the Chemehuevi to eke
out an existence in this inhospitable region. Small
bands, sometimes no more than an extended
family unit, ranged over wide areas to gather sufficient quantities of seeds, roots, and berries. It
was much more practical to move a camp to the
food supply than maintain permanent settlements. The necessity to roam did not permit the
development of strong tribal unity, complex social
organization, or elaborate rituals and ceremonies.

In the late 1700s, the Chemehuevi moved
into Mohave territory on the west side of the
Colorado River. This contact resulted in the acquisition of a number of Yuman traits including
mourning ceremonies, dreaming for power, and
much of Mohave mythology.

In 1867, hostilities disrupted their friendly
relations with the Mohave, and the Chemehuevi
withdrew to the desert country to the west. Later,
however, they drifted back to occupy the
Chemehuevi Valley.

A reservation was set aside for this tribe on
the California side of the Colorado River, but the
construction of Parker Dam in 1938 caused much
of the arable land to be flooded. Most of the
Chemehuevi then moved to the Colorado River
Indian Reservation.

A resort in California, reached by ferry from
Lake Havasu City, Arizona, is now an important
source of tribal income and employment, surpass-
ing that from the growing of alfalfa and cotton.

Once noted for fine coiled baskets of willow
and devil's claw, the craft has nearly disappeared.
Native ceremonies have also disappeared.

*Chemehuevi basketry
has long been admired
for its fine coils and tight stitching.
The number of weavers active in
this very demanding, time-intensive
craft has steadily and predictably
dwindled. At the moment there
is only one master weaver,
and she has a single apprentice.*

MARK BAHTI

Hualapai twined basketry was on the verge of disappearing in the late 1960s when there were only a few active weavers—mostly elderly— and no one in the younger generation seemed interested in learning the craft. A rebirth of interest beginning about 1970 resulted in a number of new weavers.

HUALAPAI (wah'-lah-pai), also spelled Walapai — derived from the native name *Hawwahlah pa'a*, meaning "pine mountain people." Language: Yuman. Reservations: Peach Springs and Big Sandy - 992,463 acres. Population: 1,498. Government: Constitution adopted in 1938. Tribal council made up of eight elected members and one hereditary chief chosen by subchiefs of each band. Tribal officers are selected by the council.

Originally 13 bands of the Pai, or *Pa'a* ("the people"), occupied the area north of the Mohave on the upper Colorado River in what is now northwestern Arizona. Long before the Spanish entered the Southwest they had moved eastward into the plateau region. From this original group there emerged three separate tribes—Hualapai, Yavapai, and Havasupai. Linguistically they are related to the Colorado River Yumans, and trace their migration back to the Yuman emergence from Spirit Mountain, but culturally they are closer to the Southern Paiute.

The territory of the Hualapai (who were comprised of two Pai bands) included the area between Bill Williams River and the Grand Canyon, and west almost to the Colorado River.

The Hualapai were a small tribe whose total population did not exceed 1,000. Their tiny settlements, usually consisting of two or three families, were scattered over the arid plateau wherever a permanent water supply was located. The Hualapai practiced a limited amount of agriculture, but were primarily dependent upon game and wild plants for food.

Although they were not particularly warlike, they occasionally fought with the Paiute and Yavapai. Friendly trade relations were maintained with the Mohave and the Hopi, with whom they exchanged buckskins for foodstuffs, and even with the Navajo, from whom they obtained blankets.

Contact with the Spanish was limited to one brief visit by Father Garces in 1776, so trouble with foreigners had to wait until the arrival of the Americans in 1852.

At first, relations with the Americans were peaceful, but in 1865 the Pai War (which included the Havasupai and the Yavapai) began when miners and cattlemen began to appropriate Hualapai springs and waterholes. The government was unwilling to defend Hualapai rights so, under the guise of avoiding bloodshed, the Indians were force-marched in 1874 to the Colorado River and placed on the Mohave Reservation near Parker, Arizona, thereby allowing whites to take over their land. Unaccustomed to the intense heat of the region they faced starvation, spoiled rations, and epidemics before the survivors moved back to their old homeland—which no longer belonged to them. Destitute, they were forced to accept government rations to survive. In 1883, a reservation was set aside for them in their native country, but it was made up of areas that the whites had found unsuitable.

Because the Hualapai were no longer at war and therefore not dangerous, they were regarded by the Americans merely as an intolerable nuisance. One newspaper, the *Mojave County Miner*, suggested editorially in 1887 that rations for the Indians be mixed with "a plentiful supply of arsenic" to solve the "problem." The army, which hired many Hualapais as scouts in their battles with the Apache, became concerned for the welfare of its valued scouts and recommended that the Hualapai be given a reservation. In 1884, nearly a million acres of rough country was set aside for them. Even so, much of their land was leased to non-Indian ranchers—with none of the revenue going to the Hualapai.

Under the circumstances it is little wonder that the Hualapai eagerly took part in the Ghost Dance—a messianic movement started by Wovoka, a Paiute medicine man. For two years the prescribed dances were performed in the belief that they would result in the return of Indian dead and the disappearance of the troublesome whites. Unfortunately (depending upon your point of view), they failed.

Stock raising is the main livelihood for the Hualapai today. Except for limited acreage on the Big Sandy Reservation, most of the tribal land is unsuited for farming. Tribal income is derived mainly from timber sales, with some also gained from the limited sale of bighorn sheep hunting permits ($20,000 each), and fees for river running, camping, and hiking. All travel off the state highway on Hualapai land requires a permit. Because of limited natural resources most Hualapais must leave the reservation to earn a living. The unemployment rate is estimated as high as 70 percent. The tribe hopes to build a major resort.

A casino was established to generate income to reinvest in an economic development program, but lack of visitation to their isolated reservation forced them to close it after less than a year in operation.

In 1976, in an effort to maintain Hualapai language and culture, the tribe instituted a bilingual, bicultural program for the tribe's children. Enormously successful, it has become a national model for other tribes.

Basketry, the only remaining craft, continues to be produced in limited quantity. All Hualapai basketry employs a diagonal twining technique; bands of simple geometric patterns in aniline dye colors are the only decoration.

YAVAPAI (yah'-vah-pai) — from *Enyava-pai*, meaning "people of the sun." Language: Yuman. Reservations: Yavapai - 1,559 acres, Camp Verde (shared with the Tonto Apache) - 653 acres, and Fort McDowell (shared with Apache) - 24,680 acres. Population total: 703. Government: (Yavapai) Community council with elected chair. (Camp Verde) Constitution adopted in 1938. Tribal members elect eight-person community council which in turn elects chair and vice-chair. (Fort McDowell) Constitution adopted in 1936. Tribal members elect a five-member community council.

The Yavapai claimed as their territory the area from the Verde Valley to the Colorado River between the Gila and Bill Williams rivers. The tribe, which probably numbered no more than 1,500, was divided into four subtribes, each comprised of a number of bands.

According to their tradition, the Yavapai once formed a single tribe with the Hualapai, but intratribal conflict brought about a split. After that time the Hualapai were regarded as enemies along with the Havasupai, Maricopa, and Pima. They maintained friendly relations with the Western Apache, particularly the Tonto band with whom they frequently intermarried. As a result, the Yavapai have often (and confusingly) been referred to as the Yavapai-Apache, as well as Mojave-Yavapai and Yuma-Apache. The fine coiled baskets they once produced and are famous for, were a craft they learned from the Apache.

Unlike their Yuman-speaking relatives on the Colorado River, the Yavapai did not practice agriculture but instead led a semi-nomadic existence, subsisting entirely by hunting and gathering wild foods. Dwellings were caves as well as brush shelters similar to Apache wickiups.

Contact with the Spanish was very slight, and the Yavapai managed to remain beyond the reach of both the Church and the Crown.

In the 1860s, their territory was invaded by Anglo prospectors and miners. Bloody feuds and massacres resulted, and continued until both the Yavapai and the Apache were defeated by General Crook in 1872. Settling on their new reservation, they managed to hand dig a five-mile canal to irrigate their 50 arable acres.

Their first harvest was such a success that the army contractors who had been supplying substandard (and often shortchanged) rations were afraid the Yavapai might become self-sufficient. Their complaints were heard, and the following year the 1,000 Yavapais gathered at Camp Verde were force-marched 150 miles to the San Carlos

Reservation. Many died along the way or were murdered by the soldiers—a few managed to escape. They remained there for 25 years before being allowed to return to their home country.

Some settled at Fort McDowell (established as a reservation in 1903) when they discovered that their traditional lands had been taken over by white settlers. Others returned to Camp Verde where a small reservation was established for them in 1914. In 1935, a third reservation, 75 acres in size, was set aside for them near Prescott. The town had now grown to the edges of the reservation, providing the Yavapai with badly needed income from the development and leasing of their lands. The westernmost subtribe were never given back any of their land.

The most famous member of the tribe was Wassaja, born in 1865, taken captive by the Pima as a young boy, and then bought by an Anglo who renamed him Carlos Montezuma. He earned a medical degree, published a newspaper, and was a tireless and eloquent advocate of the Indian. Montezuma argued for the abolishment of what was then known as the Indian Bureau, saying it worked against Indian rights, self-determination, and self-sufficiency.

Camp Verde (which includes land at the Middle Verde and in Clarkdale) relies upon agriculture for its income, while the Yavapai near Prescott have an industrial park, shopping center, resort hotel, and gaming operation.

The Fort McDowell Reservation has limited resources, with only a tiny amount of land suitable for farming and grazing. While their relatives in Camp Verde were having to fight for enough water to irrigate their land, the Fort McDowell people had to fight being inundated by it. Orme Dam threatened for decades to flood the last of their best land before the project was shelved.

The Yavapai and Apache people of Fort McDowell opened the first Indian gaming operation in Arizona. It is a good example of the effect gaming has had on tribes in the Southwest and how they have handled the income derived from it. Unemployment rates have dropped from a highly conservative 28 percent in 1989 to virtually zero by 1994. Differing from several other tribes, 34 percent of the casino's revenue is distributed directly to adult tribal members (or into savings for those under age 18, who must graduate from high school or obtain a GED before they have access to their account—otherwise they must wait until age 21). Tribal operations, including health, housing, and economic development projects split 60 percent, and 6 percent goes to support charitable causes off-reservation.

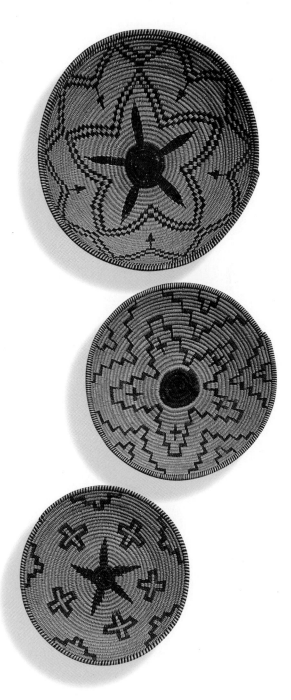

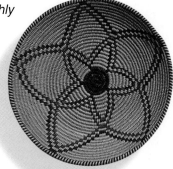

Yavapai Apache coiled basketry is highly sought after by collectors and prized for its design work which ranges from highly intricate to very simple yet elegant. Working with willow coiled basketry is a difficult and demanding craft that requires years to master. Unfortunately, it has died out among the Yavapai.

HAVASUPAI

HAVASUPAI (hah-vah-suu'-pai) — from the native name *Hawasuwaipaa*, which means "people of the blue-green water." (Also referred to as *Supai* and *Coconino*—the Hopi name for these people.) Language: Yuman. Reservation: 188,077 acres. Population: 591. Government: Constitution adopted in 1939. Tribal council made up of four elected council members and three hereditary chiefs selected by subchiefs. Tribal officers selected by council. Ceremonies: Harvest Dance in late summer.

The Havasupai, a branch of the Hualapai, separated from the main tribe during the 12th century to seek refuge from potential enemies, and moved to the very bottom of the Grand Canyon. Today, they are still the most isolated tribe in the U.S. Other than by helicopter, their reservation can be reached only on foot or by horseback over two long trails that lead down from the rim.

In early days the Havasupai occupied the canyon bottom only during the spring and summer months to farm their tiny gardens. In the fall, after the harvest, they moved to their winter dwellings on the plateau where they hunted deer, antelope, and mountain sheep. (The Navajo stopped their eastward expansion and drove them out of the Colorado River Basin area

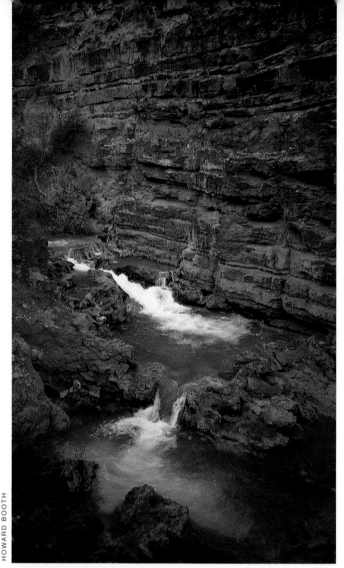

HOWARD BOOTH

Flooding in 1993 changed the appearance of many scenic areas in Havasu Canyon and caused considerable destruction on the reservation, requiring long-term restoration.

JEFF GNASS

after a final battle in 1638.) During the winter months the land along the river bottom becomes bitterly cold and damp as the steep canyon walls shut out the sunshine.

Life among the Havasupai was simple. Rigid social and political organization was hardly necessary for a group with a population of less than 300. Religious activities were in the hands of medicine men who controlled the weather, treated illnesses, and ensured success in hunting and farming. A fall harvest dance was more a social activity than a religious ceremony. Cremation of the dead and the destruction of the deceased's personal property (one of several customs this tribe has in common with other Yuman tribes)

The travertine pools of Havasu Canyon have long been a significant attraction for visitors from around the world. The blue-green color of the waters give the tribe their name— Hawasuwaipaa, *People of the Blue-Green Water.*

HAVASUPAI

was practiced until 1895, when the Bureau of Indian Affairs forbade this "uncivilized" practice.

Despite their isolation the Havasupai had considerable contact with the Hopi, trading buckskins, salt, mountain sheep horns, and red mineral paint for agricultural products, textiles, and pottery. Father Garces (in 1776) was the only Spaniard to visit this tribe. Plans to missionize the tribe failed to materialize. Contact with Americans, which began in the 1850s, was equally unimportant. No one, it seemed, coveted the isolated homeland of the Havasupai.

In 1882, a reservation of 512 acres was established for the tribe in Havasu Canyon. The Havasupai refrained from requesting a larger tract (which they had traditionally occupied and used) in the belief that holding title to a greater area would only invite trouble with the Americans—a tiny reservation would be no temptation to even the most land-hungry white man.

Much of their traditional land, including the area known as Indian Gardens, was taken away from them when Grand Canyon National Park was established. Though many continued to stay on, working for the National Park Service, their traditional homes were destroyed and they were forced to rent cabins. In 1975, they were given back 185,000 acres of their homeland, plus exclusive rights to use 95,300 acres in Grand Canyon National Park. There are, however, significant restrictions on how they may utilize their 185,000 acres, and even a limit on how much money they can make from its use! Ironically, the U.S. government has allowed a uranium mine to be developed upstream from the Havasupai by non-Indians on federal land—with no similar restrictions.

Although often referred to as a "Shangri-la" by the casual visitor, the reservation is considerably less idyllic to those who live there. Agriculture, once the main occupation of the tribe, today only supplements the income derived from outside wage work and some leasing of grazing land. A few Havasupai earn a livelihood by providing transportation (horses and mules) and accommodations to visitors to their canyon. Tourism is the major source of income for the tribe.

Baskets, in both twined and twilled techniques, are still produced by the Havasupai, but in very limited quantities.

Havasu Canyon, where the Havasupai Reservation is located, is a fraction of the land the Indians once used. In 1975 the Havasupai were officially given back much of their homeland and granted permission to use several thousand acres in the Grand Canyon—but in both cases, a limit was placed upon how much money they could make from its use!

JEFF GNASS

141

KAIBAB PAIUTE (pi'-yoot or pah'-yoot) —

which may come from the words *Pai-ute*, "true Ute," or *Pah-ute*, "water Ute." Also known as the *Nuwuvi*. Native name for this band (one of over 30) is *Kaivahn-eetseng*, "mountain lying down people." Language: Shoshonean. Reservation: 120,827 acres. Population: 205. Government: Constitution adopted 1951. Members elect a six-person tribal council. Council selects tribal officers who operate in conjunction with a committee of elders. Other bands of Paiute occupy reservations in Utah and Nevada. ▬▬▬▬▬

The Kaibab band, a branch of the Southern Paiute, originally ranged over portions of northwestern Arizona, southern Utah, and southeastern Nevada beginning about A.D. 1150. Their original territory covered approximately 5,000 square miles that varied from lush to barren.

The economy of the Paiute was based on food gathering. They led a semi-nomadic existence in order to make maximum use of whatever wild foods were available. Their extensive use of edible roots earned them the name of "Diggers" from contemptuous Anglos, but even the most ethnocentric settler had to admit that the Paiutes could exist in lands where a white man would quickly starve to death. Nothing was overlooked—pine nuts, wild grass seeds, even grasshoppers and caterpillars were eaten. Over 100 species of plants were utilized as food and still others for medicinal purposes. Big game was scarce so the Indians hunted rabbits, birds, gophers, prairie dogs, and mice.

Life for the Paiute was a constant search for food, and it left little time to develop elaborate crafts or social or religious organizations. The land would not support large concentrations of people, so most groups consisted of two or three families. Leaders had no formal authority over their followers, relying on the consensus of the group. Medicine men conducted brief hunting and curing rituals.

The Kaibab Paiute had some contact with Utes and learned from them the use of buckskin clothing, the horse, and the tipi, which replaced their earlier earth-covered lodges.

Encroachment by Mormon settlers began in the early 1860s. If land claimed and used by the semi-nomadic Paiute happened to be unoccupied at the time a settler arrived, it was claimed and fenced, and the Paiute prevented from ever using it again. In this manner they lost most of their land. Poor land management practices by the settlers started erosion that caused the once-lush Kaibab region with abundant surface water to dry up and rely heavily on ever-deeper wells.

Before Captain John Wesley Powell led his famous exploration of the Grand Canyon in 1869, he consulted with the Kaibab Paiute who were quite familiar with the canyon.

Permanent water sources on the Kaibab Plateau are few and far between. Pitch-covered basketry bottles were made to collect and store water.

ARIZONA STATE MUSEUM

By the time a reservation was finally established for them in 1909, European-introduced illnesses combined with the loss of their best lands had decimated the tribe, reducing their numbers by 90 percent.

The land set aside for their reservation is marginally suitable for some cattle raising and limited agriculture. A casino was established to generate income for an economic development program, but their remote isolated location resulted in its closure.

Buckskin and basketry were the two main crafts of the Kaibab band. Burden baskets, trays for winnowing, bowls for parching wild seeds,

and hats were made using a twining technique. Coiled baskets in bowl and bottle shapes are made of sumac.

The "wedding basket" (actually used in a variety of ceremonies) is made by the San Juan Paiute, a group of Southern Utes who moved into the San Juan area which is now a part of the Navajo reservation. The San Juan Utes are generally counted as Navajos by the government, and have been struggling for recognition (recently awarded) and autonomy. They now have a tribal headquarters in Tuba City, Arizona, but the land on which they live is still part of the Navajo reservation.

The extensive Kaibab Plateau was home to the Kaibab band of the Southern Paiute. Typical of the experience of most tribes, the best land was quickly taken by settlers. The land they now have supports a limited cattle operation and garden plots.

*I*tems such as corn, gourds, drums, feathers, and cloth
fulfill very significant roles in the culture of the
Southwestern tribes. Their ceremonies represent
their beliefs in the totality of life, both past and future.

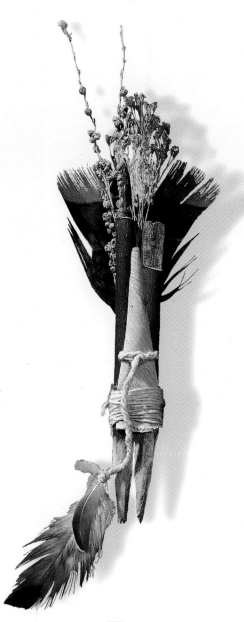

Chapter III

SOUTHWESTERN INDIAN CEREMONIALS

Religion lies at the heart of the identity of each tribe in the Southwest. Their beliefs, legends, and rituals are their strength. The creation, emergence, and migration legends are part of the common body of knowledge that knits one generation to the next.

As varied as their religious practices and beliefs are, and as different as they may be from those of the reader, they all stem from the same basic need to make sense of the world around us and to provide us with hope.

Hopi paho *or prayer stick.*

Introduction

Religion has been described as man's attempt to control those forces which lie beyond the glow of his campfire, and it matters little whether the reference is made to a small band of hunters huddled in a cave around a cooking fire or a modern city dweller who cringes before the prospect of a nuclear fireball destroying his modern metropolis. The basic need is identical.

When discussing religion, either one's own or someone else's, it is best not to be too concerned with logic, for all mythology, whether based on written or spoken traditions, is singularly illogical. A Christian, for example, may find no inconsistency in acceptance of the Commandment "thou shalt not kill," along with acceptance of capital punishment, armies (with the chaplains that serve them), biological and chemical warfare along with nuclear weapons, but rationalization for this is based not on logic but on an unquestioning belief in the myths of his own society. In examining the religion of another society, however, he may not be as tolerant or understanding and instead be either indignant or condescendingly amused if all beliefs cannot be neatly and logically pigeonholed into an instantly comprehensive concept.

Further complications arise with the tremendous variation in understanding and degree of belief among members of any religious sect. The range of belief extends from fanatically devout to passively indifferent in all groups. It is less accurate to say, "All Christians believe that..." than to say, "Most (or some) Christians believe that..."

Attempts to translate religious concepts from one language to another cause additional confusion; there is no equivalent in the English language vocabulary, for example, for the Zuni word koko, *or the Hopi word* katsina. *Conversely, the Zunis have no equivalent for the English word* religion; *they regard religion as being inseparable from life itself.*

The brief descriptions that follow are not intended to represent Southwestern Indian ceremonials as "peculiar" or "quaintly colorful," but simply as attempts by fellow human beings to meet a basic need in ways that are merely different from our own.

Superstition, it should be recalled, is the other man's religion.

— Tom Bahti, 1970.

Native Religions and Foreign Influences

That native ceremonies are still held by the Indians of the Southwest is a tribute to their way of life and the strength of their religious beliefs.

From prehistoric times to the present it has been customary for the various tribes in the Southwest to borrow from each other's religion. If one group performed a particularly effective ceremony, it could be learned from them and performed as one's own. Dances, songs, and rituals were shared freely and the practice continues today.

It was not uncommon even for traditional enemies to borrow each other's ceremonials. Much of Navajo mythology, for example, was adapted from Pueblo tribes, and the Hopi possess a number of katsinas they recognize as being of Navajo origin. The similarities in the emergence myths of many Southwestern tribes indicate a sharing of legends as well.

No group presumed its religion to be superior to that of another, and certainly no tribe ever conducted warfare against another for the purpose of forcing its religious beliefs upon them. It must have been bewildering, therefore, to find that the European invaders of the Southwest made a special effort to stamp out native beliefs in order to impose their own religious doctrines.

THE SPANIARDS

The Spaniards explored, conquered, and settled the Southwest to harvest gold for the Crown and souls for the Church. Civil and Church authorities regarded the native people as barbarians, completely devoid of civilization and Christianity. It was not a matter of replacing one culture with another since they did not believe the Indians *had* a culture.

In the name of "civilizing" and "Christianizing" the Indians, katsina masks along with any and all other religious objects were destroyed.

Preceding pages: Looking east to the Hopi villages of Second Mesa and Corn Rock. Photo by Owen Seumptewa.

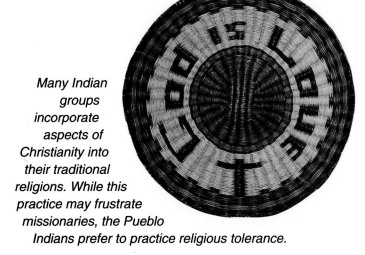

Many Indian groups incorporate aspects of Christianity into their traditional religions. While this practice may frustrate missionaries, the Pueblo Indians prefer to practice religious tolerance.

"Idolaters" were confined in stocks, and flogging was commonly used to enforce the Spanish prohibition against Indian religious observances. But instead of stamping out native religions, the Spaniards merely drove them underground. Several minor rebellions and the Great Pueblo Revolt of 1680 are directly traceable to the harsh punishment meted out to religious leaders.

The Church finally learned to live side by side with native religion, though it is doubtful whether it was—or is—as tolerant of Indian religions as the Indian is of Western religions.

The American invasion of the Southwest, which followed the 1848 Treaty of Guadalupe Hidalgo, had no immediate effect on native religions. Catholic missions continued to operate and the Pueblo Indians made nominal use of them while adhering to native beliefs.

In the 1870s and '80s, the U.S. government adopted a policy of turning over the task of "civilizing" Indians to the churches, and various Christian denominations were assigned to specific reservations. The practice was discontinued in the 1890s, but not before the influence of some 27 Christian sects became established among a number of tribes, particularly those whose native culture had been reduced to a state of disintegration.

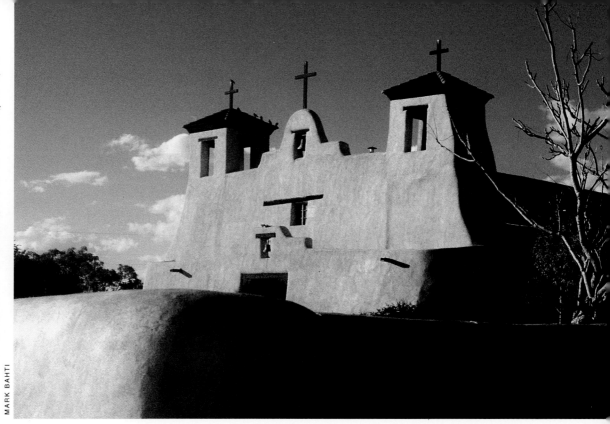

When European missionaries first arrived in the New World they attempted to suppress all forms of "heathen idolatry," refusing to recognize them as religions. Missions were established in most of the pueblos, and many still stand today. After the Great Pueblo Revolt of 1680, the Church developed a degree of tolerance toward Indian religious practices. It was not until 1934 that the U.S. government extended the concept of religious freedom to Indian religions.

MARK BAHTI

GOVERNMENT SUPPRESSION OF NATIVE RELIGION

About this same time, the Bureau of Indian Affairs, which was originally under the War Department, made a number of attempts to suppress native religions with a series of departmental regulations. It is ironic that the very people who took inordinate pride in the fact that their immigrant ancestors came to this country to escape religious persecution tolerated such a move. Begun as a frightened reaction to the Ghost Dance movement of the 1880s, which claimed to foretell the disappearance of the white man as well as the return of the buffalo and the old ways, the regulations were also directed against the Sun Dance of the Plains tribes and the rising strength of the Native American Church.

This anti-Indian movement culminated in 1889 with a set of regulations known as the Code of Religious Offenses. It was used as late as the 1920s in an attempt to crush Pueblo religion, restricting the time of year and days of the week for native religious observances. It even restricted the number of participants and set age limits—all in an attempt to deny younger Indians the opportunity to participate and learn.

In a specific campaign against Taos, the religious leaders were accused of being "half-animal" in their practice of "sadistic" and "obscene" pagan religion. And if that was not enough to swing public opinion against them, one U.S. senator declared them and their Anglo supporters to be un-American and agents of Moscow.

It was not until 1934 that this policy was reversed. Under John Collier's administration as Commissioner of Indian Affairs, the following directive was issued: "No interference with Indian religious life or ceremonial expression will hereafter be tolerated. The cultural liberty of Indians is in all respects to be considered equal to that of any non-Indian group." Freedom of religion, the goal of so many early white immigrants, was thereby finally extended to America's original inhabitants.

The impact of Christianity upon Southwestern Indian religions is difficult to summarize except in broad generalizations. A minority accepted the new religion to the complete abandonment of native practices. A majority merely accommodated the new doctrines by modifying them to fit with native beliefs (much as the tribes borrowed from each other's religions)—this was primarily the case with the Rio Grande pueblos. The Yaquis modified Catholicism into a form that was not recognized by the Roman Catholic Church, but which suited their needs. Others, such as the followers of the Native American Church (Peyote Cult) combined native and Christian beliefs to form an entirely new religious movement. And, of course, a surprising number, notably among the Hopi and Zuni, practice their native religions to the total exclusion of Christian beliefs.

Navajo

THE EMERGENCE MYTH

In the beginning, First Man and First Woman were transformed from an ear of corn. It was they who led the people during the Emergence.

The world today, by Navajo reckoning, is the fifth to be inhabited by the First People. (Other estimates vary from 4 to 16.) The four previous worlds were located underground, each one a different color, but none of them contained light. The First People lived in each of these worlds successively until they finally ascended to this world by making their way through a hollow reed. The "Place of Emergence" or "Center-of-the-Universe" is believed to be a badger hole in the mountains of southeastern Colorado.

At first the land was covered with water, a wet and disagreeable place, but in time the Holy People (another name for the First People) transformed the earth into a livable place, and defined the boundaries of Navajoland. Mount Taylor, in New Mexico, is the Southern or Turquoise Mountain; Mount Humphrey, in the San Francisco Peaks near Flagstaff, is the Western or Abalone Mountain. There is a difference of opinion over the exact identification of the Northern (Jet) and Eastern (White Shell) mountains. Light was created by First Man and First Woman who fashioned the moon, sun, and stars of precious stones. An orderly arrangement of the stars was upset when the ever-present trickster, Coyote, scattered them about the sky.

Evil existed in the form of monsters who had also come up from the underworlds and now began to kill many of the Earth People. At this time, a cradleboard containing a baby girl clothed in light magically appeared. She grew to become Changing Woman, sometimes identified as Earth with its constantly changing seasons, or as Nature itself. Changing Woman eventually married Sun and Water and gave birth to twin boys, Monster Slayer and Born-of-Water. (In some versions of the story Changing Woman—or Turquoise Woman—and her sister White Shell

Navajo sandpainting ceremonies are part of a healing ritual that includes songs, chants, prayers, and herbs. Recognizing the important role of the patient's frame of mind in the healing process, hospitals and clinics on the reservation often work with Navajo hatathli—*medicine men—in the treatment of patients. Andy Tsinajinnie*

Navajo oral tradition includes stories, legends, and religious practices that are interrelated, intricately detailed, and highly complex. According to Navajo belief, they must be preserved down to the smallest detail. To properly learn the oral traditions requires careful listening and begins in childhood. Harrison Begay

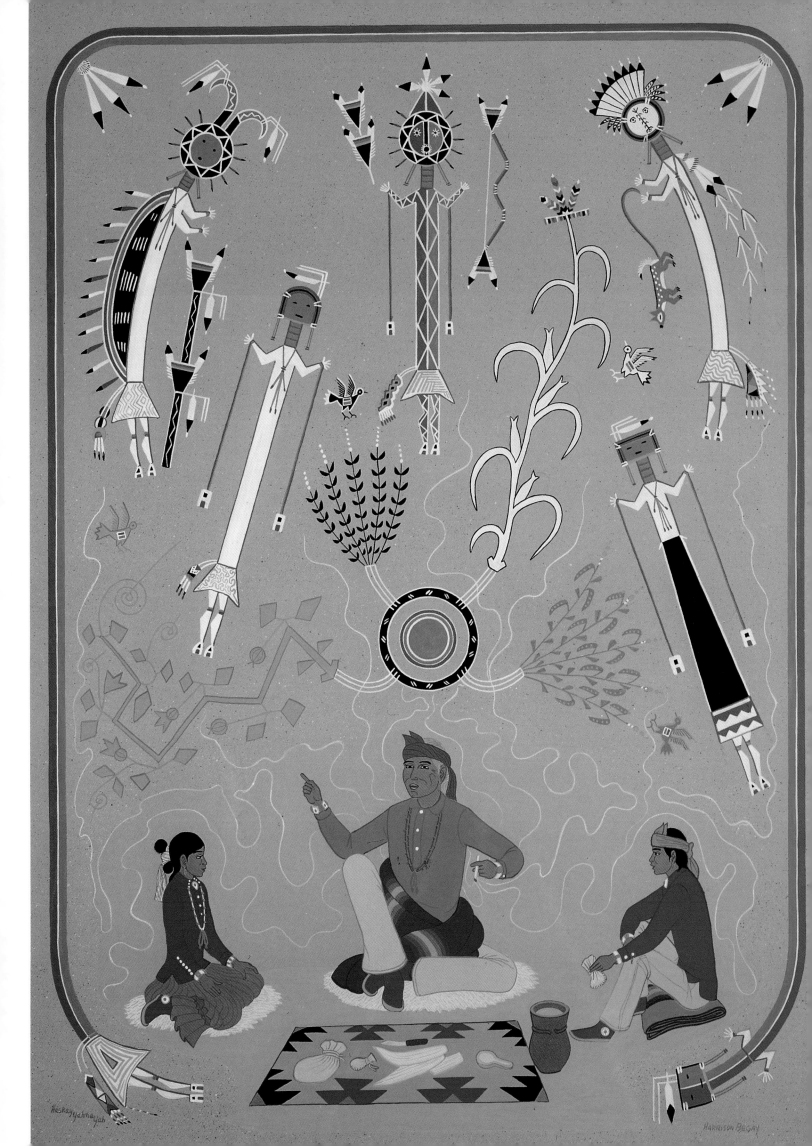

To become a hatathli *requires years of careful study and practice as an apprentice. This young Navajo sheepherder is beginning his lifelong study of the Navajo traditions and stories that are crucial to the success of a good medicine man. Harrison Begay*

Woman married, respectively, Sun and Water and gave birth to the Twin War Gods.)

The exploits of the Twin War Gods form a goodly part of Navajo mythology. In their journeys they encountered, and succeeded in slaying, many of the monsters that were bothering the Earth People. They failed only in dispatching Old Age, Poverty, Sickness, and Death. Throughout Navajo country is evidence of the Twins' battles. A lava flow east of Grants, New Mexico, is the dried blood of a slain monster. Shiprock is the remains of a man-eating eagle, and various volcanic peaks are the heads of monsters decapitated by the Twins.

It was Changing Woman who finally created human beings, using flakes of skin from her own body. She formed six groups of people, believed by some to represent the first Navajo clans. There is no supreme being in Navajo religion. The most powerful and most important deities include Changing Woman, Sun, and the Twin War Gods. Of these only Changing Woman is consistently helpful to people. Changing Woman lives on an island in the Western Sea where she is visited daily by her husband, the Sun. All other deities are capable of helping or harming, and are sometimes classified on the basis of how difficult they are to persuade to be helpful.

Lesser deities include *Yeis*—the male and female figures that are depicted in sandpaintings and represent forces found in nature such as wind, thunder, and lightning. Below them on the list of Holy People are the ancestors of animals and plants, and figures identified with specific geographical locations.

AFTERWORLD

The Anglo concept of an Indian's "Happy Hunting Ground" does not apply to the Navajo—nor to many Indian tribes, for that matter. *This* is the life that is important. It is not considered as mere preparation for another world. Neither is there a concept of another world for eternal punishment. The Afterworld is a shadowy and ill-defined, dull but not unpleasant place, an underground "to the north" which is reached by four days' travel after death.

Death is considered inevitable and therefore not so much feared as the dead themselves. Since the deceased are always a possible source of *chindi,* or malevolent ghosts, they are disposed of as quickly as possible and with strict performance of all required rituals. Any error may offend the deceased and cause the chindi to seek revenge.

The Twin War Gods, Born-of-Water and Monster Slayer, were given weapons by their father, the Sun, that enabled them to slay most of the monsters who plagued humankind. (A few, like poverty, sickness, and lice, managed to survive.) Here one of the Twins attacks the Monster Bird who used to attack and eat unwary travelers. His petrified remains are known in English as Shiprock, in northwestern New Mexico. Navajoland is dotted with evidence of the Twins' great battles.
Andy Tsinajinnie

In Navajo culture, as with most Indian cultures in the Southwest, corn pollen is gathered for religious purposes. A symbol of the promise of fertility and the renewal of the cycle of life, corn pollen is a vital part of any prayer or prayer offering. The Navajo believe that if a prayer is offered correctly, with a good heart, it will be answered. For some the yellow pollen also symbolizes the yellow light of the life-giving morning sun. A. C. Begay

JOSEF MUENCH

Most Navajo healing songs are accompanied by a rattle.

The sandpaintings or ikaah *used in Navajo healing rites are made of ground rocks and plant matter—all collected within the traditional boundaries of Navajoland. These images are begun after sunrise and must be completed by sunset. Their remains are then taken a safe distance away for a ceremonial burial.*

CURING CEREMONIES

The Navajo concept of the Universe in an ideal state is one in which all parts—each with its power for good and evil—are maintained in inter-related harmony—*hozhon*. The balance, at best, is precarious and may be upset intentionally by ghosts or witches, or unintentionally by persons who break a religious taboo or unwittingly come in contact with snakes, bears, or lightning. To cross the path of a bear or touch a piece of wood that came from a lightning-struck tree is enough to upset the balance.

Illness, whether physical or mental, results from upsetting the harmony. Conversely, the cure for illness is to restore the patient to harmony. It is to this end—the preservation or restoration of harmony or *hozhon*—that Navajo religious ceremonies are performed.

To determine the cause of a particular illness is the job of a diagnostician—*ndilniihii* or "hand trembler." Prayer, concentration, and the application of sacred pollen to the patient causes the priest-practitioner's hand to tremble—it is from these movements that the exact cause of the illness is determined.

The cause of the sickness determines the ceremony or "sing" needed to effect a cure. Also called "chants" or "ways," these sings are based on Navajo mythology. They consist of complicated ceremonies lasting from one to nine nights, and can include the use of chants, songs, prayers, dances, prayer sticks, herbs, emetics, sweat baths, and sandpaintings, all performed under the direction of a "singer," or priest-practitioner, known in Navajo as a *hatathli*.

There are six main groups of chants or song ceremonials, although some have become obsolete through disuse. The Blessingway rites are not curing rites, but are performed for general well-being, to ensure, as the Navajos put it, that one may "walk in beauty."

The curing ceremonials or chantways are concerned with specific illnesses. The Bead Chant cures skin disease. The Shooting Chant is used against disease attributable to lightning or snakes. Insanity and paralysis usually require the Night Chant, while nervousness can be alleviated with the Mountainway. The Windway cures disease caused by evil winds and covers a host of afflictions ranging from poor vision, insomnia, and hoarseness to tuberculosis, heart trouble, snakebite, and even alcoholism.

There are probably over 50 chants or ways, not counting the variations. Most singers or priest-practitioners know no more than two or three complete chants and specialize in those. It would be impossible for one man to know all of the complicated rituals for over a dozen curing rites. If a chant is not performed precisely it will not cure, and instead can cause harm to befall those present.

The performance of a lengthy curing rite is an expensive affair, and taxes the finances of the patient's entire extended family. Not only is the hatathli well paid, but tremendous quantities of

The Navajo Yeibichai Dance is part of a nine-day healing ceremony known as the Night Chant. A Navajo medicine man carrying a basket of sacred cornmeal for blessings, walks ahead of a yei known as Talking God, who is in turn followed by seven other yei.
Johnny Secatero

food must be provided for guests—and they arrive from far and wide to share the blessings derived from attending the ceremonies, and to take part in the related social activities.

The patient, through the rituals, becomes purified and eventually identified with the deity whose help is sought. From them he obtains power and overcomes the evil causing the illness, thereby restoring him to harmony with the Universe. Once again he "walks in beauty." The sense of security and well-being the patient derives from the host of friends, family, and fellow tribespeople who surround him during the ceremony is also conducive to his recovery.

This yeibichai dancer is known in Navajo as B'ganaskiddy. The name does not translate and consequently some bizarre names, like Camel God, have been given to this being who carries the seeds of living plants in his pack. Sometimes referred to as Harvest God, he is far more complex than such a simple name suggests. Bruce Watchman

155

Nahas'tsan Beh'assun *and* Yaa-diklith Beh'hasteen *are known in English as Mother Earth and Father Sky. In the center of Mother Earth are the four sacred plants—corn, beans, squash, and tobacco. (The latter is sometimes used in praying or purifying.) The night sky is symbolized in Father Sky, including the Milky Way (the zigzag lines across his shoulders) with key constellations and stars.*

Sandpaintings

Sandpaintings, probably the best-known portion of the lengthy, complex Navajo curing ceremonies, are used in various religious rites by most tribes in the Southwest. The Navajos, however, have developed them to the greatest degree and recognize between 600 and 1,000 separate designs.

Dry paintings, as they are sometimes called, use pulverized minerals to form the patterns although vegetal material such as pollen and corn-meal may also be used. They range in size from 1 to 20 feet across, and may require a dozen or more persons working most of a day to complete. The sandpainting is created, used, and destroyed between sunrise and sunset of a single day.

The sandpainting is a symbolic representation of some portion of Navajo mythology. The patient is seated on the sandpainting after it is completed, and parts of it are placed on the patient's body. By identifying in this way with the deities invoked, power is gained from them. The evil that has caused the sickness is absorbed by the sand and is then ceremonially buried.

The colors used in Navajo dry paintings are usually symbolic of direction. As a general rule white is east, blue (a female color) is south, yellow is west, and black (male) is north, while red represents sunshine.

The Night Chant or Nightway—more commonly referred to as the *Yeibichai*—is a major winter curing ceremony that can be held only after the snakes are asleep and there is no longer danger of lightning. The rite can be performed to cure patients of nervousness or insanity. It is a dangerous ritual, for mistakes made by either the patient or singer during its performance can cause crippling, facial paralysis, loss of sight, or loss of hearing.

The name Yeibichai is used for the Nightway because of the appearance of numerous *Yeis* (supernatural beings that possess great powers) during the last two nights of this nine-day annual ceremony.

On the eighth day the Yeibichais conduct an initiation rite to introduce Navajo children to the secret of the masked gods. The children first have their hair washed—a standard act of purification among most Southwestern tribes—and then white clay is daubed on their bodies.

The boys are blessed with sacred meal and then ceremonially whipped with yucca leaves by the masked figures. The girls are marked on the feet, hands, shoulders, and head with cornmeal and touched with ears of white and yellow corn wrapped in spruce twigs.

Shortly afterwards the Yeibichais remove their masks so that the children learn they are really ordinary human beings who only play the part of supernatural figures. *Hastseyalti*, the Talking God of the East, places his mask on each of the boys while the female *Hastse-baad* places hers on the girls so that each child may view the world through the eyes of the Yeibichais.

Adults often take part in this ritual for it is necessary for each Navajo to participate in the initiation ceremony four times during his lifetime.

Throughout the ninth night Yeibichai dance teams perform, each group singing in the falsetto voice for which these dancers are noted.

Unlike the katsinas of the Hopi, Navajo yeibichai are rarely carved. The very first set was probably made in the 1930s. There are, however, some similarities, ranging from the initiation of children into the secret of the masked dancers to the communal ownership of such masks, which forbids their ever being sold or otherwise removed from the tribe.

A central theme to well-being among the Navajo is the concept of hozhon. *There is no one-word equivalent in English. Symbolized here by the rainbow guardian, it has to do with balance, harmony, and the beauty that arises from them.*
James Wayne Yazzie

SQUAW DANCE

The *Entah* or Enemyway—mistakenly referred to as a Squaw Dance by non-Navajos—is a war ceremonial conducted only during the summer months. Formerly it was given as a purification rite for warriors who had been contaminated by contact with the enemy. Now it may be performed for persons whose sickness has been diagnosed as resulting from contact with whites or other non-Navajos.

The Entah is a three-day ritual that begins at the patient's hogan and moves to a new location on each succeeding day—usually a day's ride away by horseback. Much of the time between specific parts of the rite is spent in racing, gambling, and listening to informal talks by recognized leaders.

On the third day the Black Dancers—the clowns of the War Ceremony—perform a Mud ceremonial. Emerging from the smoke hole of a hogan, they seize the patient and toss him into the air. Afterwards they stretch him face down in a mudhole while they attempt to loosen the hold of the evil that is causing the sickness by running over the patient. After this ritual is completed, spectators are fair game and those caught are also given a mud bath.

The Round Dance is performed on the third night and is primarily a "coming out" event for eligible young females. The girls, with much encouragement from their mothers, invite young men to join them in a round dance. At the end of several rounds the man is required to make a token payment to the girl for the privilege of dancing with her. The Round Dance is an all-night affair performed to the accompaniment of a chorus and drummer.

The Mountain Chant or Mountainway is a winter ceremonial, to be given when there is the possibility that summer thunderstorms or spring windstorms might cause death by snakebite or lightning. The Mountain Chant gets its name from the dwelling place of the deities whose aid is invoked during the ceremony. The names Fire Dance or Corral Dance are derived from rituals performed as part of the nine-day ceremonial.

On the ninth day of the chant, a huge semicircular corral of evergreen is erected. It is here that medicine men perform magical feats: a yucca plant appears to grow and blossom in a matter of minutes; men swallow arrows; a feather dances unaided; or a sun symbol may climb out of a basket and up a pole and then return to its container.

Afterwards the Fire Dancers appear, daubed with white clay, and carrying torches of cedar bark that they light at the huge central fire. They dash in and out of the fire with impunity, lashing themselves and their fellow dancers with flaming torches. This is a purification ritual that completes the Mountain Chant. After the Fire Dance, spectators pick up bits of the charred cedar bark as a charm against fire.

The Fire Dance occurs on the ninth night of the Mountainway. After the hatathli present perform certain magical feats, men daubed in white clay appear within an enclosure made of evergreen. Brandishing cedar bark torches, they dash in and out of a bonfire without harm. After this purification ritual, spectators gather bits of the charred bark as a charm against fire. Andy Tsinajinnie

Rio Grande Pueblos

Corn Mother fetishes—which vary in appearance among tribes—are the most important fetish in most pueblo traditions. Roger Tsabetsaye

KERESAN EMERGENCE MYTH

The emergence myth varies somewhat in detail among the seven Keresan-speaking pueblos. The version given here relies primarily on accounts from Santa Ana and Santo Domingo pueblos.

In the beginning the people lived in the innermost of the Underworlds. Seeking light, they moved progressively upward through four worlds, each of a different color—white, red, blue, and yellow.

With the aid of various plants, animals, and birds an attempt was made to break through the crust of the present world. Finally a badger, standing on an eagle's nest built on top of a spruce tree, succeeded in enlarging a hole, made by a woodpecker, until it was big enough to allow people to pass through.

Assisted by *Iatiko*, Mother of All, they emerged at the *Sipapu*, the Place of Emergence or Center of the World. The world was wet and soft until the Sun, father of the Twin War Gods, dried it and made it habitable.

Sipapu was too sacred a place in which to dwell, so the people left to seek another location. Only Iatiko remained, but before the people left she gave them her heart—corn—and instructed the religious leaders to care for the people as she had done. She also told the people to return to Sipapu at death.

The people wandered about and finally settled at White House (an unidentified site "to the north" of their present villages). Here they dwelt with the deities who taught them all that was necessary for their life in this world. The katsinas appeared among them to dance for rain and the *Koshare* and *Kurena* came to help make the crops grow.

Although life was good at White House, eventually groups began to leave to seek new places—each became a new tribe in doing so. The Keresans also left and moved southward until

The Deer Dance of the Tewa pueblos reflects the belief that a hunter will be unsuccessful if he does not first gain the deer's cooperation through showing respect. After a deer is killed, further rituals ensure that the deer's spirit will be reborn as another deer. Animals disappear only when hunted disrespectfully.

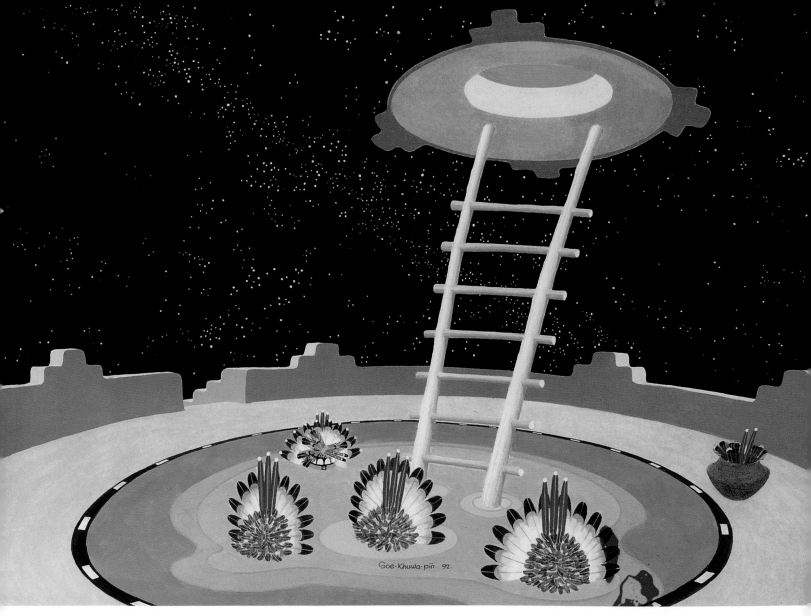

The Emergence stories of many tribes in the Southwest speak of entering this world through either a body of water or through an opening in the sky. Many tribes tell of occupying a succession of previous worlds before arriving in this one. Taos legend states that they emerged at Blue Lake. Soe Khuwa-pin

they reached their present locations. No longer do the masked gods live among the people, making it necessary now for the people themselves to impersonate the deities and perform the dances to ensure the well-being of the pueblos.

THE CREATION AND COSMOS

Thought Woman, the deity who created all things by thinking them into existence, is responsible for the world as it appears. She may also be the same figure as Spider Grandmother, another deity to whom the same role is attributed.

The Keresans envisage the earth as the center of the universe with all other planets functioning in order to make the earth livable. The sun is referred to as "Father" and is an important deity. The sky is "in charge" of the earth and its people, and the earth is referred to as "Mother." Corn is also called "Mother."

AFTERWORLD

At birth each person receives a soul and a guardian spirit from the Mother of All. At the time of death both the soul and the guardian leave the body but remain in the house of the deceased for four days before making the journey to Sipapu, the entrance to the Underworld. The guardian spirit carries a prayer stick, necessary for the admission of the soul to Sipapu. Depending on the virtue of the individual, the soul is assigned to one of the four Underworlds. Those qualified to enter the innermost world become *Shiwana* (Rainmakers) and return to the villages in the form of clouds.

Death is explained as a natural and necessary phenomenon for "if nobody died there would soon be no room left in the world."

Corn has always been the basis of Pueblo life. To maintain the precarious balance of an agricultural economy in this land of little rain requires the cooperation of all forces, natural and supernatural. It is not surprising, therefore, that all religious ceremonies (except for curing rites) revolve around the cultivation and propagation of corn.

Constant references to Earth Mother and Corn Mother indicate that agriculture is more than just a practical art; it goes far beyond to encompass the philosophy and religion of the Pueblo Indians.

The Corn Dance, commonly performed during the spring and summer months, may be given at any time. Although its purpose is always the propagation of corn, it may be performed to mark the annual installation of new secular officers of the pueblo, or the village's Catholic saint's day.

The dance, as with all Southwestern religious ceremonies, is a combination of song, drama, dance, and poetry which forms a prayer for rain, bountiful harvests, the propagation of animals and plants, and the well-being of the pueblo and all those who attend the ceremony.

All Rio Grande pueblos perform the Corn Dance. Perhaps the largest and most impressive is given at the village of Santo Domingo on the fourth of August—Saint Dominic's Day—the saint assigned to the village by the Catholic priests who accompanied the Spanish explorers.

Early in the morning of the fourth, Indians attend Mass at the church just outside the pueblo. On this day, baptisms and marriages are performed and recorded for the previous year. The statue of Saint Dominic is removed from the church, paraded through the village streets to

Feast Day at Santa Clara is held on the Saint's day for Saint Claire, but the ceremonies observed pre-date Catholicism at this pueblo.

the beating of a snare drum and the firing of guns, and then deposited in a temporary shelter of cottonwood branches in the dance plaza. The saint is guarded by the pueblo's officers, and the noise of guns and the snare drum continues while the dancers pay homage to Saint Dominic. After this, the day is devoted to the native ceremonial. Catholicism and Pueblo religion exist side by side, but there is no real mixing of the two.

The pueblo's population is divided into two moieties: the Squash or Winter People and the Turquoise or Summer People. (Each half is responsible for the village affairs during six months of the year.) The dancers of each moiety alternate performances during the day.

Because of the centuries-long importance of corn to pueblo life, the Corn Dance is a ritual that is shared—though in varying forms—by all pueblos. This is a Tewa Corn Dance. Tonita Peña

Corn must be cultivated; if left to reseed by itself, the crop quickly dies out. This special relationship between the farmer and the plant has led it to be personified as both Corn Mother and Corn Maiden. Stories remind people of the respect that must be shown in tending the crop lest the corn maidens leave and famine follow. The Blue Corn Maiden represents one of the many color varieties of pueblo corn. Gilbert Atencio

Each kiva, the Squash and the Turquoise, provides its own *Koshares,* chorus, drummer, standard bearer, and corn dancers—usually numbering over 200 persons. The bodies of the male Squash moiety dancers are painted with a yellow ochre, and those of the Turquoise are painted with a blue-gray clay.

The first figures to appear are the Koshares of the Turquoise moiety, with their bodies painted horizontally in black and white stripes and dressed in ragged black breechcloths. On their wrists and moccasins are worn strips of rabbit fur, and their hair is tied up in "horns" decorated with cornhusks. The *Kurena* of the Squash kiva are similarly attired except their bodies are divided vertically, with one half painted white with black spots and the other half yellow. Both wear deer-hoof rattles at the waist.

The dancers during a ceremony, such as this feast day at San Ildefonso Pueblo, are accompanied by a chorus of men with drums. Their deep voices and drumming fill the plaza with sound.

As invisible spirits of the deceased, the Koshare and Kurena possess much power to bring rain clouds and to influence the growth of crops. Related to the sun, their home is in the east. During the dance they magically protect the pueblo and its inhabitants from all enemies. They also perform many practical services for the dancers by making needed adjustments or repairs to the dancers' costumes during the ceremony.

As clowns they pantomime, with exaggerated gestures, the chorus or the dancers themselves. Between dances they indulge in ribald horseplay, much to the delight of the spectators and the chagrin of their victims.

The chorus, made up of 50 or more men and a drummer, are next to appear. They are dressed in loose-fitting, bright-colored shirts and trousers split at the ankle. Each carries sprigs of the evergreen—as a symbol of growing things and everlasting life. Although the chants follow a traditional rhythmic form, they are usually composed anew each year. The expressive movements of the chorus mimic the words that describe the gathering of the clouds from the four directions, the falling rain, and the growing plants.

The main procession of corn dancers is led by a man who bears the sun symbol. This consists of

Known by different names among the different pueblo tribes, the Koshare is a clown who performs in ways that are both humorous and sacred. Koshares live in the east, home of the sun, and are able to bring rain clouds and influence the growth of crops. Geraldine Gutierrez

a long pole (representing the fir tree that enabled the people to climb up from the Underworld) from which is suspended a dance kilt with eagle feathers and a fox pelt. Fastened to the end of the pole is a painted gourd (containing sacred seeds) and a dazzling cluster of macaw feathers. Under this banner the dancers perform. The waving of the sun symbol over the corn dancers constitutes both a blessing and a purification, and a request to the *Shiwana*—the Rainmakers or Rain Cloud People— to bless the pueblo with moisture.

The male corn dancers are dressed in white cotton kilts (this was formerly the ordinary attire of Pueblo men) embroidered with symbols of clouds and rain. Over this is tied the white, tasseled rain sash. From the back of the belt is suspended a fox skin, which some say is a reminder of man's common ancestry with animals, of a time when all had tails. Behind the right knee is tied a turtle-shell rattle with deer-hoof tinklers. In the right hand is a gourd rattle with which the sound of falling rain is imitated. Skunk fur worn over the moccasins protects the wearer from evil. A bandolier hung over the left shoulder is decorated with conus shells from the Pacific Ocean. A cluster of parrot feathers is worn on the top of the head—the plumage of this bird is believed to bring rain from the south. Personal jewelry and sprigs of evergreen complete their clothing.

The female dancers wear a black *manta*— blanket dress—tied at the waist with a red and green woven belt. In most pueblos the women dance barefoot. In each hand they carry evergreen boughs. Their hair hangs loose in imitation of the long wisps of summer rain that sweep the land. On their heads are worn *tablitas*, thin wooden boards cut in a terraced cloud pattern and either pierced or painted with sun, moon, or star designs.

The Corn Dancer carries in her hands prayer offerings of turkey feathers and evergreens from the mountains. Her white sash with its long fringe is called a rain sash. On her manta (dress) are the inverted triangles that symbolize rain clouds, and in her hair macaw tail feathers are symbolic of the south, where summer rains originate. Geraldine Gutierrez

Young women of San Ildefonso Pueblo prepare to participate in a Harvest Dance. "Dance" is the word most commonly used by Indian and non-Indian alike to describe a religious observance that includes rhythmic movement and music as part of an involved and complex prayer ritual. The public dance is the culmination of weeks of less visible activity.

The Buffalo Dance is a winter ceremonial. In many instances it ends with a ritual "hunting" when dancers are "shot" with arrows of straw and then carried off where they are honored as slain game. This ensures that when the actual hunt occurs, the animals will allow themselves to be caught, as they know they will be treated with respect and "sent home," thereby allowing them to be reborn. Paul Vigil

The casual observer often labels Indian dances and the accompanying music as "monotonous." It may well appear that way if one does not know the language and is unfamiliar with the music, but even a slightly alert visitor will soon realize that complicated rhythms and dance steps are employed and anyone who attempts to "keep the beat" will find himself confused by the frequent changes.

The moieties dance alternately during the day—both groups and their choruses then combine for a spectacular final performance at the end of the day.

HUNTING CEREMONIALS

Hunting was formerly an important activity. Deer was the most common game animal but antelope, elk, and mountain sheep were also hunted for meat and hides. The Rio Grande Pueblo people ventured onto the Great Plains occasionally to hunt buffalo, a dangerous journey that exposed them to attack from hostile tribes who jealously guarded their territories against trespassers.

To be successful in hunting, a man had to have more than just practical skills—he also needed the cooperation of the animals he hunted, and it was to this end that most hunting rituals were directed. This was not a matter of a superior being attempting to control a lower life form, but one in which two equals sought an understanding of their respective roles in the scheme of life. As the cloven-hoofed mammals must eat plants to survive, so must man rely partly on animals, in turn, to sustain himself.

The hunting dances not only honored the animals, but also ensured their propagation. Further, they gained the cooperation and permission of the game so the hunters could take those that were needed for food and clothing.

Even today hunting requires rites before, during, and after the hunt. Fetishes are used in an effort to obtain assistance from the beasts of prey—the expert hunters of the animal world. If a hunter is successful, he first removes the heart from the game and ceremonially feeds it to his fetish. Tobacco, cornmeal, and a prayer feather may be offered to the dead animal's spirit to appease it and ensure it will return, thereby guaranteeing a steady supply of game animals.

Upon returning to the village the game is taken to the home of the hunter, wrapped in a ceremonial robe, and greeted as a visitor by those who enter the house. Anything less than this ritual treatment would offend the animals and the deity who is in charge of all game.

Respect for the animal continues even after it has been consumed. The skulls of deer and elk are painted with clay, and prayer feathers are hung from the antlers before they are placed on the housetop. During the animal dances, the homes bearing skulls are visited by the dancers. The bones of the animals are never thrown to the dogs, but are blessed with cornmeal and ceremonially deposited in the Rio Grande.

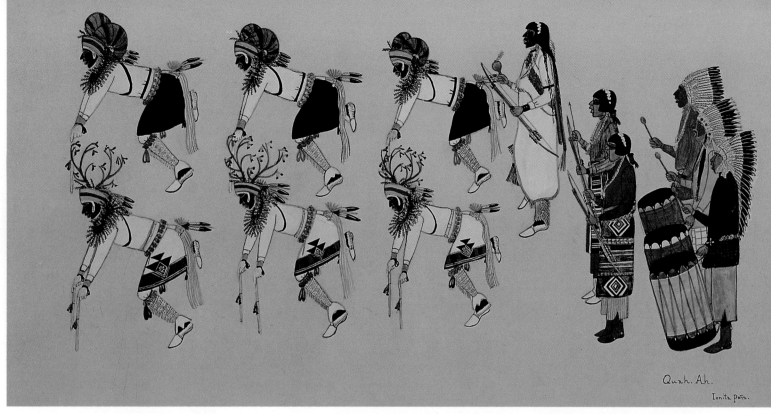

Quah. Ah.
Tonita peña.

A Pueblo animal dance with deer and mountain sheep. Tonita Peña

ANIMAL DANCES

Animal dances in the Rio Grande pueblos are usually winter ceremonials. The number of participants varies greatly and may include as few as a pair of Buffalo dancers and a Buffalo Woman, who represents the Mother of All Game, or a massed group of deer, elk, buffalo, antelope, and mountain sheep impersonators plus a hunt chief, hunters, a drummer, and a chorus.

A typical Tewa animal ceremonial begins the night preceding the dance. Small fires are built in the plaza and on the housetops to guide the animals to the village. At dawn the Hunt Chief calls in the animals from the surrounding hills and leads them along paths of sacred cornmeal into the plaza where they dance. The impersonators often carry two sticks with which they imitate the movements of the forefeet of the animals.

In Keresan pueblos a young female participant races into the hills in the early morning where she "captures" the animal dancers and leads them to the village. The dance plaza is planted with small evergreens, and in this artificial forest the animal impersonators dance. At the end of the performance the hunters shoot the dancers with arrows of straw, and carry them off to their houses where they are honored as slain game. This ritual assures the success of the hunters when they go out after real game.

In the Deer Dance, held at San Ildefonso Pueblo, the dancers use wooden staffs to represent the forelegs of the deer. The "legs" have evergreen attached to them to symbolize the deer's mountain home.

167

The eagle is the most powerful of birds—able to fly out of sight into the clouds and believed to have a close relationship with the sun. The Eagle Dance honors the eagle and its role as an intermediary between humans and the sky deities. Gilbert Atencio

EAGLE DANCE

The eagle plays an important role in Pueblo mythology. A powerful bird, it can soar out of sight so it is believed to have a close relationship with the sun. Its power is often sought in curing rites, and its plumage is an essential part of many costumes of both masked and unmasked dancers. The downy feathers represent the "breath of life" and are used as prayer plumes by all tribes.

A favorite performance at public exhibitions, the Eagle Dance is also given in the villages. The ritual, performed by young men who imitate the eagles' flight, depicts man's affinity with the sky deities through the eagle as an intermediary. The dancers often wear a decorated shield on their backs. To some this indicates that the eagle is the chief of birds—others refer to the shield as a "moisture tablet," an acknowledgment of the eagle's ability to bring rain from the clouds it can soar through.

Beginning at a very young age, children in many Rio Grande pueblos take part in Pueblo religious traditions, thereby learning their importance.

HOOP DANCE

The origin of the Hoop Dance is unknown, but there is some suggestion that it was originally a symbolic reenactment of man's emergence from the Underworld. Today it is staged at most public exhibitions and powwows as a spectacular acrobatic performance. The dancers are usually dressed in costumes of the Plains Indian variety.

The Hoop Dance is a staple of most powwows and public performances. Though costumes are usually styled after the Plains Indians, many believe the dance may have originally symbolized Pueblo emergence legends. Guy Nez Jr.

Exposed to television, videos, and computers, Pueblo children are also exposed to ancient Pueblo traditions, which form the core of their identity and a part of their expression of daily life. Gina Chavarria

RIO GRANDE PUEBLOS

Zuni

The Zuni have probably the most complex of all native religions in the Southwest. Every aspect of traditional Zuni life is completely integrated with their religion. Numerous religious organizations, through an intricate system of interlocking ceremonials, interrelate the whole of Zuni culture.

Six esoteric cults (in addition to the ancestor cult to which all Zuni belong) form the basis of Zuni ceremonialism. These are the cults of the Sun, Rainmakers (which is in charge of 12 priesthoods), *Koko* (or katsinas), Priests of the Koko, War Gods, and Prey Gods (representing the animal patrons of 12 related curing societies). Each cult has its own priests, fetishes, rituals, and ceremonial calendar.

Basic to the religious philosophy of the Zuni is the recognition of man's oneness with the universe and the absolute necessity of maintaining this harmony through the correct execution of prescribed rituals. If the ceremonies are properly performed, the rains *will* fall, the harvests *will* be bountiful, the life of the people *will* be long and happy, and the fertility of the plant and animal worlds *will* continue.

CREATION MYTH

In the beginning there was only fog and mists. "Above" existed three deities: *Awonawilona*—a bisexual supreme being (Creator of All); Sun, the giver of light, warmth, and life; and Moon, the deity responsible for dividing the year into 12 months and delineating the life span of man. "Below" existed two superhuman beings, *Shiwanni* and his wife *Shiwanokia*.

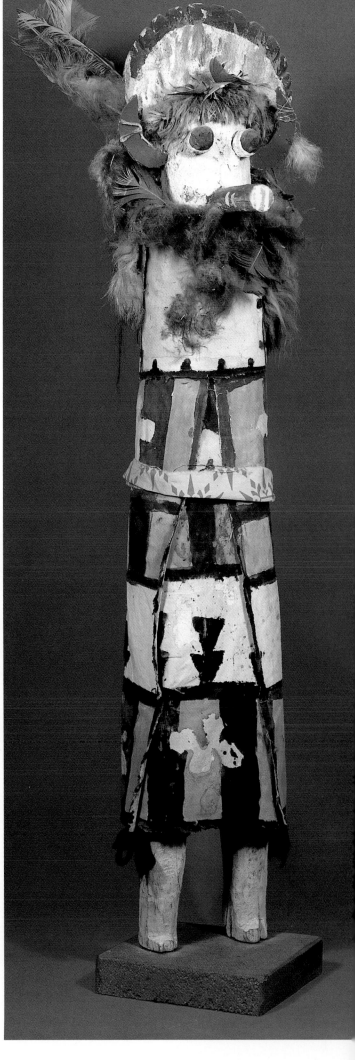

The Zuni Shalako is the most typically Zuni image— in the non-Zuni mind, at least. These kokos or spirit beings are not often carved at Zuni. One is more likely to see the image used in paintings or in their fine inlaid shell and turquoise jewelry.

The first part of the public portion of the Zuni Shalako ceremony begins with the sighting of them far to the south of the village. This is a re-enactment of the migrations of the Ahshiwi—*the Zuni people—that led them to their present home. Awa Tsireh*

Awonawilona created clouds and water with the breath of his heart. Shiwanni formed the constellations from bubbles of his saliva. Shiwanokia, using her saliva, created Mother Earth. The *Ahshiwi* (Zuni) are the children of Shiwanni and Shiwanokia—they were born in the innermost of the underworlds.

EMERGENCE AND MIGRATION MYTH

The Underworld which the Ahshiwi inhabited was totally dark—the people lived in holes and subsisted on wild grass seeds. They are said to have been peculiar creatures with tails, gigantic ears, webbed hands and feet, moss-covered bodies, and a foul odor.

Sun Father created two sons, *Kowituma* and *Wahtsusi*, out of bits of foam and sent them to the Underworld to bring the Ahshiwi into the Upperworld. The sons, known as the Divine Ones, made light for the people by kindling fire. Following a path marked with sacred meal, they led the Ahshiwi to the North where they planted a ponderosa pine. They climbed the tree to make their way into the Third or Water Moss World. The next trail led to the West—here a Douglas fir was grown to allow the Ahshiwi to enter the Second or Mud World. The third trail went South to an aspen which was used to reach the First World of Wings (Sun's Rays). The last journey was to the East, and the Ahshiwi climbed a silver spruce to emerge into the Upperworld. The actual entry was made through a spring or small lake whose waters parted to allow passage.

At the time of emergence the Divine Ones used their stone knives to transform the animal-like Ahshiwi into human form. They also taught the Zuni how to make fire and to cook their food. Corn was acquired from *Paiyatemu*, assistant to the Sun.

The Zuni then began their wanderings to seek the Middle Place (the middle of the world) where they were to settle. Many years were spent

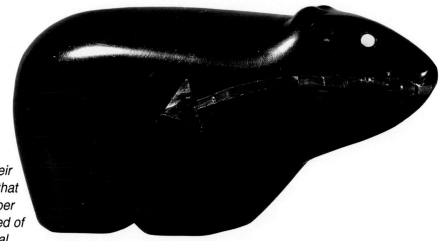

Fetishes are objects, carved or in their natural state, which have a spirit inside that can assist the owner if treated with proper respect and ritual. This Zuni bear, carved of jet (a type of coal), is inlaid with a coral heartline, a term perhaps better translated as a breathline or source of life, symbolizing the life force of the animal. It is a design convention used in pottery painting to show that the animal represented was living. To do otherwise might jeopardize the success of the hunters. Its use in fetishes and animal carvings is, with a very few exceptions, quite recent.

in the search and numerous villages were built only to be later abandoned. At one stage in the wanderings Shiwanni of the North sent his son and daughter to seek a village site. During their search the brother suddenly became enamored of his sister's beauty and possessed her. The same night ten offspring were born to them—the first was normal and became the ancestor of the *Kokokshi*, the Rainmakers. The other nine became the *Koyemshi* (Mudheads), the idiot offspring of this incestuous union.

The brother created the Zuni and Little Colorado rivers by marking the sands with his foot, and at their junction a lake (Listening Spring) was formed. Within the waters of this lake he created a village, *Kothluwalawa* (sometimes called *Wenima*), the home of the Council of the Gods.

The Council of the Gods came into being as the result of a river crossing by the Ahshiwi during their migration. The children of the Wood Fraternity were being carried across, but became panicky and fell into the rushing water. Immediately they were transformed into various water creatures—turtles, tadpoles, frogs, and snakes—which made their way to Kothluwalawa. Here they matured instantly and became the Council of the Gods.

In their migration to the Middle Place the Ahshiwi were stopped by a tribe known as *Kianakwe*, which was led by *Chakwena*, the Keeper of the Game. The Divine Ones grew weary of leading the Ahshiwi in fighting the Kianakwe, so they petitioned their Sun Father to send them two War Gods as replacements. The Sun impregnated a waterfall and the *Ahayuda* (as they are known in time of peace) or *Uyuyewi* and *Masailema* (as they are known in time of war) were created.

With the help of the War Gods the Ahshiwi defeated the Kianakwe in a four-day battle. They captured the village and released the wild game held captive by Chakwena. The ruins of the village are said to be some 50 miles south of the present town of Zuni.

The Ahshiwi continued to wander and lived in several villages (the ruins of which may still be seen) before they finally settled in the Middle Place, *Itiwanna*, the Zuni name for their pueblo.

AFTERWORLD

At death the corpse is bathed in yucca suds and rubbed with cornmeal before burial. The spirit of the dead lingers for four days, during which time the door of its former home is left ajar to permit its entry. On the morning of the fifth day the spirit goes to the Council of the Gods in the village of Kothluwalawa beneath the water of Listening Spring. Here the spirit becomes a member of the *Uwannami*—a Rainmaker. If the deceased was a member of the Bow Priesthood, he becomes

Fetishes can be owned by individuals, clans, religious societies, or the tribe itself. Many of the more important communally owned ones may be kept in special bowls. This is a replica of such a bowl.

Though Hopi katsina ceremonies may be better known than Zuni koko ceremonies, the Zuni's highly complex religious calendar is filled with rituals which involve some of the many Zuni koko or spirit beings. J. Cachini

a lightning maker who brings water from the "six great waters of the world." The water, in the form of rain, is poured through the clouds which are the masks worn by the Uwannami.

SHALAKO

The *Shalako*, a winter ceremony held in late November or early December, is the major ritual performed at the pueblo of Zuni. Usually referred to as a house-blessing ceremonial, it is a 49-day re-enactment of the Zuni emergence and migration myths. In addition, it is a prayer for rain, for the health and well-being of the people, and for the propagation of plants and animals. During the Shalako the spirits of the dead return to be honored and fed. As the final element of this lengthy ceremonial, a hunting rite is performed. The description that follows can do little more than touch the surface of this highly complex ceremonial.

Participants in the Shalako (both impersonators and the sponsors of the Shalako houses) are

chosen during the previous Winter Solstice ceremony. Preparations for the numerous and varied rites begin immediately afterward and occupy much of the participants' time for the intervening ten months. Long and complicated chants must be learned, prayer sticks must be placed each month at certain shrines that mark the migrations of the Zuni in ancient times, and minor rituals must be performed each month.

In addition to this, the houses that will honor the Shalakos must be built or extensively remodeled. (The floor is left unfinished and dug deep enough to accommodate the tall Shalakos.) Ideally, eight houses are used—six for the Shalakos, one for *Sayatasha* and the Council of the Gods (usually called the Long Horn House), and one for the *Koyemshi*. To sponsor a Shalako house is a tremendously expensive undertaking—added to the cost of construction is the expense of providing food for the participants and a myriad of visitors.

The principal masked figures that appear during the ceremony are:

Shalakos—the Giant Messengers of the Rainmakers—one to represent each of the six kivas. The masks and bodies of these ten-foot figures are carried on pole frames by the impersonators. Each Shalako has two impersonators who take turns dancing.

Sayatasha—the Rain God of the North—often called "Long Horn" for the projection from the right side of his mask which is said to symbolize long life for the people. Sayatasha oversees all the activities preceding the actual appearance of the Shalakos.

Hututu—the Rain God of the South—is the deputy of Sayatasha. Both carry rattles of deer scapulae, bows and arrows, and numerous prayer plumes.

Shulawitsi—the Fire God—is a representative of the sun. The part is always played by a young

The Shalako ceremony is usually thought of as a house blessing. However, the 49-day observance includes a number of other aspects—re-enactment of the emergence and migrations of the Zuni people, prayer offerings to ensure the well-being of the people and the propagation of plants and animals, and a hunting rite. Mac Schweitzer

ZUNI

boy from the Badger Clan. Shulawitsi carries a fawn skin filled with seeds.

Yamuhakto—Spirits of the Forest—these two figures are also called Warriors of the West and East. They have sticks of cottonwood tied to the tops of their masks that represent their authority over forests and trees. The antlers that they carry are symbolic of the deer that live in the forests.

Salimopya—are the warriors who carry yucca whips to guard the performers and keep spectators from coming too close. There are six—one for each of the six directions, with masks painted accordingly—but only two appear during the Shalako.

Koyemshi—the Mudheads—are led by *Awan Tachu*, Great Father. The others are called Deputy to the Great Father, Warrior, Bat, Small Horns, Old Grandfather, Old Youth, Water Drinker, Game Maker, and Small Mouth.

Members of the Council of the Gods taking part in this ceremony include Sayatasha, Hututu, two Yamuhakto, and Shulawitsi.

(continued on page 178)

A model of a Zuni temporary shrine (as opposed to the permanent ones that dot Zuniland) with the masks of Shulawitsi and two Salimopya—Zuni warriors. There are six Salimopya, each colored to represent a different direction. Only two appear during Shalako.

PHOTOS BY K. C. DEN DOOVEN

Deposits of prayer offerings are an important part of the
Shalako ceremony. On the final day the Shalako races
take place. As the Shalako dancers race away, young
men try to catch them to ensure luck in hunting deer.
Mac Schweitzer

Eight days before the arrival of the Shalakos,
Koyemshi appear in the village to exhort
the people to complete their preparations for the
coming of the gods.

Four days later Shulawitsi and Sayatasha arrive from the west, having retraced the migration
of the Ahshiwi. The Fire God lights fires on
the way to guide the Council of the Gods to the
Middle Place.

FORTY-EIGHTH DAY

Shulawitsi and Sayatasha appear in the village to inspect the six holes—one for each kiva—
that have been dug to receive prayer plumes.
Later in the day the Fire God and his ceremonial
father deposit their prayer sticks. They are followed by Sayatasha, Hututu, and the two

*Preceding pages: Navajo come from afar to attend the
summer Entah ceremony's Round Dance. Quincy Tahoma
Photo from the Amerind Foundation, Inc.*

Yamuhakto who bless the shrines in brief ceremonies and also leave prayer plumes. They then
retreat to their Shalako house to perform blessing
ceremonies for the building and the altar that has
been installed, and to place special prayer sticks
near the roof beams. After this they smoke cigarettes of native tobacco. The smoke, symbolic of
clouds, will bring rain to the land.

At dark the giant Shalakos arrive at the
south side of the river where they use a narrow
footbridge to cross over into the village. Upon
reaching the north side the impersonators briefly
leave their masks and go to the Shalako houses.
They return shortly and the bird-like creatures
rise and approach the houses with much clacking
of beaks and strange whistling sounds. Before
they enter, the houses must be properly blessed
in ceremonies similar to those conducted at the
Long Horn House.

After bringing the Shalako inside, the impersonator leaves his mask and enters into a lengthy
dialogue with the sponsor of the houses. This
recitation of the emergence and migration myth
consumes a great part of the evening. Food is
then taken by the Shalako impersonators to the

river where it is offered to the spirits of the dead who live at Kothluwalawa.

General feasting follows and the kitchens of the Shalako houses bring forth unbelievable quantities of food for performers, townspeople, and visitors.

Dancing by the Shakalos begins after midnight. The Salimopyas and Koyemshi also make the rounds to all of the Shalako houses to perform. A Zuni version of the Navajo Yeibichai is also staged—to the great delight of the Navajos who are present. It is said that this dance commemorates a time when the Navajos performed this ceremony at Zuni to cure the people of an epidemic that caused swellings.

FORTY-NINTH DAY

The dancing continues until sunrise, at which time Sayatasha climbs to a rooftop to offer prayers on behalf of the Zuni people. The dancers are purified with a hair-washing rite.

About noon on the final day, the Shalakos and their attendants leave the pueblo, crossing the river to an open field south of the old village. Here the Shalakos race, placing prayer plumes in six specially dug sites before returning to Kothluwalawa. The race depicts the manner in which the Shalakos, as couriers of the gods, deliver messages and prayers for rain throughout the year.

As the Shalakos disappear in the distance, the young men run to catch them. Those who succeed in "capturing" a Shalako believe they will have future success in hunting deer.

Zuni fetishes include a group called weh'mah'weh or prey beings, like this bear with an arrow tied to its back.

Hopi Pueblos

EMERGENCE MYTH

Each Hopi village has its own particular version of the emergence myth, and legends that trace the wanderings of the Hopis before they reached their present location vary with each clan.

Huru'ing Wuuhti (in some legends it is Spiderwoman) is credited with creating mankind out of saliva and colored sand. Four sets of male and female figures, black, red, yellow, and white, were made. Each was given a different language and the power to reproduce. Life began in the innermost of four Underworlds. Some legends depict life there as good, with animals and people living in harmony and amidst plenty. Others maintain the Underworlds were dark and overcrowded, and that the upward journey was an attempt to alleviate those unpleasant conditions.

Most of the stories allude to social disorder caused by the presence of *powaku* or witches. The dissension and fighting that followed caused the people to forget their ceremonies and life plan. In disgust, *Sotunangu* (God of the Sky) destroyed, in turn, each Underworld in an attempt to wipe out the witches and related failure to live right. Each time a few good people were saved to populate the new world only to repeat the mistakes of the previous one.

To escape the flood that was used to destroy the Third Underworld, the priests sought the aid of animals and birds. They had heard the footsteps of someone walking above and decided to ask permission to ascend to the next world.

After several attempts by different birds, the shrike found the opening that led to the Upperworld. To reach the *Sipapu*, the Place of Emergence, the help of the chipmunk was sought. Chipmunk planted a series of trees and sang magic songs over them in an effort to make them grow tall enough to reach the opening discovered by the shrike. Neither the spruce nor the pine trees grew tall enough, but a bamboo finally grew up through the hole. Chipmunk then chewed an opening at the base of the reed to admit the passage of the people.

The One Horned priests stayed below to prevent the witches from reaching the Upperworld. Before all the people had reached the Sipapu they cut down the reed. The joints in the bamboo were caused by the people who were trapped inside. Despite the precautions, some witches succeeded in reaching the new world. Another version describes a raft constructed of reeds that the people used to ride out the flood.

At the time of emergence this world was occupied only by *Masau'u,* a deity. According to some versions, Masau'u himself assisted the people through the Sipapu. In others, the first contact with Masau'u was made by the shrike, who acted as an intermediary. In any case, Masau'u gave the Hopis permission to settle in his land and marked off the boundaries of the territory they were to occupy.

For roughly six months out of the year, the katsinas visit the Hopi people and assist in the performance of religious ceremonies meant to ensure the renewal of the cycle of life for all living beings—plants, animals, and people. Ray Naha

AFTERWORLD

At death the hair of the deceased is washed in yucca suds, and prayer feathers are placed on the hands and feet, and in the hair. Over the face is placed a mask of cotton that represents the cloud mask the spirit will wear when it returns with the Cloud People to bring rain to the villages. Women are wrapped in their wedding robes, and men are buried in a special twill weave plaid blanket.

The ghosts of the dead are feared rather than death itself. To prevent the ghosts from returning to bother the living, *pahos,* or prayer offerings, are given to the parting spirit of the deceased and the trail back to the village is ceremonially closed with cornmeal. Those who did the actual burying are purified with juniper smoke.

Four days after the burial the spirit leaves the body and climbs out of the grave by means of a digging stick that was placed there to serve as a ladder. It then begins the journey to the land of the dead. The entrance to the Underworld is through the Sipapu, which is located in the Grand Canyon. *Kwanitaka,* the One Horned God who can read a person's thoughts by looking into his heart, guards the Underworld. He forces those who have caused harm to others to take a slow, difficult trail fraught with dangers to reach the Underworld where the dead live. Persons who have followed the Sun Trail hurry along the path of sacred corn-meal to reach the village of the Cloud People where their departed relatives wait for them.

The evil ones meet their ends in fire pits where they are thrown, later to emerge as black beetles.

The spirits of children who die before they are initiated into one of the Hopi religious societies are believed to return to the mother's house to be born again.

Hopi gourd rattles may be painted in a wide range of designs, but all have painted "stitching" around the perimeter, reminiscent of the ancient rawhide rattles that preceded them.

Principal Deities

The Hopi pantheon includes between 30 and 40 deities ranging in importance from culture heroes to major gods. There are often considerable differences in the functions and appearances of these deities among the various Hopi villages. The myths relating to the gods are sometimes vague, and may differ greatly from one mesa to the next.

Sotunangu, the God of the Sky, is considered by most Hopis to be the most important deity. Some refer to him as the Supreme Being, although he exercises no control over the other deities except for the Twin War Gods. Others call him Creator of the Earth for, according to one myth, he created a young maiden whom he later transformed into the earth. He is in charge of the heavens, lightning, and clouds, and can send rain to make the plants grow.

Masau'u is both the God of Earth and God of the Underworld. It was Masau'u who permitted the Hopi to settle in his domain. He is depicted as a giant of a man and black in color. Although believed to be handsome, he always wears a terrifying mask, covered with blood, whenever he has contact with people. He is thought of as a fertility god of man and animals and is also associated with fire.

Mui'ingwa or *Alosaka,* the God of Germination, is also called the Two-Horn or Germ God. Alosaka lives underground and is concerned primarily with the propagation of plant life. He is thought by some to be responsible for the fertility of the sky and earth. His female counterpart, Sand Altar Woman, is associated with childbirth. Both were created by Huru'ing Wuuhti.

Huru'ing Wuuhti is thought of as the Mother of the Universe. As Goddess of Hard Substances (turquoise, shell, and coral) she is associated with wealth. Ugly by day and beautiful by night, she is visited daily by the Sun in her kiva which is located in the western ocean. She is credited most frequently with being the Creator of the World, and is said to own the stars and the moon.

K. C. DEN DOOVEN

Sometimes mistakenly referred to as katsinas, unmasked dancers such as the White Buffalo Dancer are not katsinas in the traditional Hopi sense of the word.

Po'okang Hoya and *Palo'ngao Hoya* are the Twin War Gods created by Spiderwoman who is their grandmother. According to some legends they are responsible for keeping the world turning and preventing Palolokon from causing earthquakes. They are helpful to the Hopi people, but are not above playing tricks on them on occasion.

Palolokon, the Water Serpent, is probably related to the Plumed Serpent, *Quetzcoatl*, of the Aztecs. It is believed to inhabit the waters under the earth, and uses springs and lakes as windows to watch the people. When displeased it may cause floods and earthquakes, so this deity is one that must be placated. All moisture—sap, blood, and water—is in Palolokon's control.

Mu'yao, the Moon Deity, is seen as an old man who provides light at night. In the emergence legend Spiderwoman made the moon by weaving a white cotton robe and then placing it in the sky.

Ong Wuuhti, Salt Woman, inhabits the Salt Lake south of Zuni. Pahos are offered to her by Hopis who journey there to gather salt.

KATSINAS

Katsinas are not gods, but the symbolic representation, in humanlike form, of the spirits of plants, animals, birds, places, ancestors, or forces of nature.

Katsinas at one time lived with the Hopis after their emergence from the Underworld and brought them rain with their dances, but the people became disrespectful so the katsinas left them and went off to live by themselves. Before they departed, however, they agreed to teach the people how to perform their rituals.

A katsina impersonator is believed to receive the spirit of the katsina he depicts when he wears the mask. (The mask, though sacred, does not actually house the spirit.) In doing so he straddles the threshold between the world of the Hopi people and the katsina world, enabling him to act as an intermediary, conveying the prayers of the Hopi people to the deities.

Classifying katsinas is a pastime of students of Pueblo religion, but not of the Indians themselves. They find classifying and counting to be of

Kwanitaka is the One Horned God who guards the entrance to the Underworld, and determines which trail the spirits of the dead will follow to reach the land of the Cloud People.

Tawa, the Sun or Father Sun, is thought of as the Giver of Life who acts as a special emissary for Sotunangu. Tawa travels daily to visit Huru'ing Wuuhti. The Sun has special powers that may be sought in ceremonials relating to both war and fertility. A morning prayer and an offering of cornmeal are made to the Sun daily by traditional Hopis. Newborn children are "presented" to the sun on the eighth day. Tawa is especially honored at the Winter Solstice ceremony to bring him back from his northward journey.

Kokyang Wuuhti, Spiderwoman, is depicted as a wise, kind old woman who is always ready to help the Hopi people. Each village has a shrine to this deity who is believed to be present everywhere. She is the mother of the Twin War Gods. In some legends Spiderwoman plays a major role in creating mankind—in others she is thought of as the creator only of those who are not Hopi.

no more importance to the practice or understanding of their religion than Christians would find a similar pigeonholing of their numerous saints.

All Pueblo tribes have katsinas and related ceremonies, but the Hopi and the Zuni have the largest number. The Hopis have about 30 *mong* or "chief" katsinas who perform specific annual ceremonies. In addition to these there are over 200 other katsinas who may appear at various times during the katsina ceremonial year. Katsinas may be added or disappear depending upon need and effectiveness.

Katsina Dances

Katsina dances are held outdoors in village plazas after the weather becomes milder, usually in April. Permission to stage a dance is given by the village chief; the sponsor of the dance determines which katsina will be presented and the day of the performance. Much time is spent by the impersonators in learning the songs that will be sung in the day-long presentation, and in preparing the masks and other necessary equipment.

The purpose of a katsina dance is multifold—the bringing of clouds and rain is of prime importance, but a successful dance also promotes harmony in the universe and ensures health, long life, and happiness for the people. It is believed that the prayers of the people will be conveyed by the katsinas to the gods.

Major Ceremonies
Wuwutsim

Wuwutsim is an annual initiation ceremony in which the Emergence from the Underworld is reenacted. During the rites all trails and roads into the village are ceremonially closed with sacred cornmeal except the one leading from the burial ground. Lights and fires are extinguished and the spirits of the dead are invited to return to their villages. Masau'u officiates at the initiation and ceremonially kindles a new fire that is then distributed to all households in the village. No outside visitors are permitted to attend the Wuwutsim which is held in November.

Soyal

Shortly after the Wuwutsim the *Soyal* katsina appears in the village. His walk is unsteady and he sings in a quiet voice. Some believe this is because he has just awakened from a prolonged sleep. Others say the halting movements are childlike and symbolic of being reborn.

AMERIND FOUNDATION, INC.

Soyal is the Winter Solstice ceremony held in December. The main purpose of the ceremony is to bring back the sun from its northward journey. It is also a time for purification and blessing rites to mark the rebirth of another year. Numerous pahos are made during the Soyal for houses, animals, plants, people, and objects. It is during this time that the kivas are ritually opened to mark the beginning of the katsina ceremonial year.

POWAMU

Powamu, commonly called the Bean Dance, is the first major ceremony of the new year and includes the appearance of a number of *mong* katsinas. (Prior to this, night dances have been held in the kivas.) It is at this ceremony that the greatest variety and number of katsina dancers participate. Beans are planted in boxes of moist sand and forced to grow in the kivas where constant fires create a hothouse atmosphere.

An initiation for children into either the Powamu or Katsina society is also performed during the 16-day Powamu ceremony. The children are ritually whipped, and afterwards learn that the katsina dancers are impersonated by humans.

The Powamu dancers perform in the kiva to bless the bean sprouts. If the beans have grown tall, a good harvest is predicted for the coming summer. Early the following morning the bean sprouts are distributed throughout the village, and the children receive presents—basketry plaques, katsina dolls, bows and arrows, rattles, moccasins—from the katsinas.

Powamu is also a time for the *Soyoko* katsinas to visit the homes of naughty children. These ugly monsters threaten to carry off and eat the disobedient youngsters if their behavior does not improve. The parents often must ransom the children with food. The sight of these terrifying ogres is enough to make anyone, young or old, improve his conduct.

PACHAVU

Every four years *Pachavu* is held during Powamu. The observance includes a spectacular procession in which innumerable beautifully dressed katsinas appear, many carrying huge basketry plaques covered with bean sprouts. As the procession moves about the village it is joined by new katsinas, each singing his own song and dancing his particular steps.

PALOLOKONTI

Palolokonti or the Water Serpent Ceremony (not an annual occurrence) takes place at night in the kiva about the same time as Powamu. The light is extinguished as the impersonators approach the kiva—in a matter of minutes the room is once again illuminated to reveal an elaborate screen that stretches nearly wall to wall. On the floor, in front of sun shield covers on the screen, are placed tiny corn shoots set in cones of clay. To the accompaniment of roaring sounds the sun shields lift and the heads of huge plumed and horned serpents appear. Snake-like, they sway farther and farther into the room while the Koyemsi (Mudheads) sing. With violent motions they sweep away the miniature cornfield.

Hahai Wuuhti, the Mother of all Katsinas, approaches the serpents with a tray of cornmeal and "nurses" each serpent. The Mudheads then attempt to push the serpents back under the sun shields, but the snakes resist. The action and the roaring increase in intensity as the

Hopi katsinas can represent the spirits of forces of nature, plants, animals, other tribes, and geographic places. Not all names have English translations, and not all English translations are accurate. From left are a Koyemsi/Mudhead, Tasaf, Hu, and the Anak'tsina or Long Hair katsina. William Quotskuyva

Mudheads wrestle with the Palolokon. The serpent figures give the impression of having tremendous strength, sending the Koyemsi tumbling. Finally, the serpents are forced back and the shields are closed—the kiva is darkened momentarily while the screen is dismantled and the performers depart.

The purpose of the Water Serpent Ceremony is to honor the giant reptiles who control the waters of the earth. If the unpredictable creatures can be placated the people will receive the moisture they need for their crops, and the springs, upon which the villages depend, will not fail.

NIMAN

Niman, or Home Dance, is a 16-day ceremonial that begins shortly before the summer solstice and ends in mid-July. The dance held then marks the final religious observance of the katsina ceremonial year, and the katsinas return to their homes on *Nuva'tukya'ovi*, Snow Mountain (the San Francisco Peaks near Flagstaff, Arizona), until the next Soyal.

Almost any katsina may be impersonated at the Niman, but the *Hemis*, with its elaborate tablita, is usually the preferred one. The dance follows the usual form, but between each round the katsinas distribute gifts to those present.

Clowns (*Koyemsi, Koshare,* or *Tsuku*) appear to entertain the spectators with skits and games, often ribald in nature. Always the source of great amusement, they sometimes mimic the antics of non-Hopi or villagers whose behavior has not been proper.

Since the Niman coincides with the early harvest, corn and melons are distributed to the villagers and spectators. Bread, piki, and native foods are also tossed to the crowd. Children receive gifts of rattles, baskets, dolls, and bows and arrows, as well as cattails, which are chewed like gum. Captive eagles, kept on rooftops, also receive similar gifts.

The day after the Niman Dance the kivas are ritually closed and the eagles, which have been held captive since early spring, are "sent home"—smothered in sacred cornmeal. (Most tribes believe that the spirit of an animal killed and treated with respect will return in animal form again.) The feathers are removed for a variety of religious uses, and the bodies are buried with the same attention and ceremony that is given to deceased members of the tribe.

FLUTE CEREMONY

The Flute Ceremony is performed biennially by the Gray Flute and Blue Flute societies. The usual explanation for the ritual is that it brings the late summer rains that are needed for the crops to reach full maturity. The ceremony is much more complex than this, however, for in addition to the rain-bringing function (which is a part of almost every ceremonial performed by the Pueblo Indians), the Flute ritual is a reenactment of the emergence and migration myths.

During the 16-day ceremonial, elaborate Flute altars are set up in the clan houses (rather than the kivas) and initiation rites for new society members are held. An important part of the ritual

Koshares, *black-and-white-striped Tewa clowns, help in a ceremony performed by male and female* Anak'tsina *or Long Hair katsinas, who are associated with the gentler summer rains that are vital to maturing crops in the arid Hopi homeland. A. A. Naha*

is a commemoration of the creation of the sun, and the participants in the public performance wear sun shields on their backs. On the sixteenth day, spectators may attend the final rites, which begin with the blessing of the village spring. Then the Gray Flute Society, followed by the Blue Flute Society, proceed to the village. Each is led by a priest and two Flute Maidens who carry small reed rings on slender rods.

On the way to the plaza the leader uses cornmeal to draw a cloud symbol on the ground, and the Flute Maidens, using the rods, toss the rings onto them—an act symbolic of the migrations (and stops along the way) of the Hopis. In some villages this rite is performed in the plaza.

When both societies are assembled in the plaza, the Gray Flute leader and his water carrier enter the *kisi* (a temporary shelter of cottonwood branches) to pray while the songs of the Emergence are sung by the chorus to the sound of reed flutes. At the end of the prayers, water from the water carrier's gourd is poured into the symbolic sipapu in the plaza. The Blue Flute leader and his assistant then enter the kisi and offer more prayers, and the ceremony ends after they emerge.

The flute is used in this ceremony to imitate the sound of cicadas, an insect associated with summer, since warm days and rain are needed to mature the crops. It is an attempt to prolong the summer growing season.

SNAKE DANCE

Alternating with the biennial Flute Ceremony is the *Tsuh Tikive* or Snake Dance, the most widely known of all Hopi ceremonies. Although it is one of the Hopi rituals of lesser importance, it has historically drawn huge, ever-increasing crowds made up largely of curiosity seekers who are fascinated by the idea of seeing the dancers handle live, often poisonous snakes. The overwhelming number of spectators has forced the Hopis to close this ceremony to outsiders.

A 16-day ceremonial like the Flute Ceremony, the Snake Dance is believed to be one of the more ancient of Pueblo rituals. There is evidence that this ceremony was once performed in most of the Rio Grande pueblos in pre-Spanish times. Today it survives only in the Hopi villages.

The ceremony itself is based on a legend concerning a young Hopi man who attempted to find the source of all waters by following the Colorado River to its source. In a journey fraught with dangers he was assisted by Spiderwoman.

Eventually he met the Great Snake who controlled the waters of the world from his kiva. The young man was initiated into the Snake Tribe and was taught their ceremonies. Before he returned to his own people he married a young girl who had been transformed into a snake. (All reptiles are believed to be descended from the offspring of this couple.)

During a serious drought Spiderwoman gave the young man the power to bring rain and designated him Antelope Chief, charged with the responsibility of teaching the wisdom and ceremonies of the Snake People to the Hopis.

The gathering of the snakes by the Snake men begins 8 days before the public performance. Four days are spent in hunting—1 day in each of the cardinal directions. All snakes encountered, poisonous and non-poisonous, are blessed and gathered. Special altars are set up and sandpaintings are made in the kivas where the Snake and Antelope societies conduct secret rites during the entire 16 days. Each day the snakes are taken to the Snake kiva where they are carefully tended. All of the reptiles are washed and purified while the priests smoke and pray over them.

At sunrise of the eighth day the Antelope Race is held. Runners of all ages race from far below the mesa to the village top. The winner receives prayer plumes and a gourd of sacred water to place in his cornfield.

Later in the day a *kisi* is constructed of cottonwood boughs in the plaza. A symbolic sipapu is dug in front of the kisi and then covered with a board.

In the later afternoon the Antelope Dancers with blue-gray painted bodies appear followed by the Snake Dancers who are red-brown in color.

The two groups form lines facing each other—the Antelope men singing and the Snake men dancing—both lines moving forward and back.

The kisi is circled four times with each dancer stamping on the board over the sipapu to establish communication with beings in the Underworld. The Antelope and Snake men pair off for the dancing. The Antelope member reaches into the kisi and brings out a cornstalk that he carries in his mouth while making a circuit of the plaza. Each pair completes a circuit with the Antelope man handling the cornstalk as though it were a reptile. Both groups then separate and circle the kisi four more times before departing.

The next morning the Snake Race is held, following the same course as the previous day. The Pueblo men pride themselves on their running ability, and the uphill race proves their stamina be-

The Snake Dance of the Hopi, a ritual that concerns itself with snakes as messengers and prayers for rain, holds a fascination for non-Hopi that is all out of proportion to its role in Hopi religion. More has been written about it than any other native ceremony performed in North or South America. Its immense attraction brought such crowds—consisting largely of curiosity-seekers—that the Hopi have been forced to close it to outsiders in recent years. The snake-handling ceremony happens on only one day of the 16-day ritual.
D. Pentewa

The Basket Dance is held at all villages. This particular form is held at the Hopi-Tewa village of Hano, which has kept many of the customs—as well as the language—they brought with them from their Rio Grande homeland over three centuries ago. Ray Naha

yond any doubt. Late in the afternoon, after the customary four circuits of the kisi, the two societies gather again to form two facing lines in the plaza. The lines dance back and forth—the Antelope men, with arms linked, sing and shake their flat, cylindrical leather rattles.

This time the Snake men pair off—one dancer reaches into the kisi and brings forth a snake. His partner, or "hugger," dances close behind and distracts the serpent with his eagle-feather snake whip. One circuit is made with each snake until all have been danced with. A circle of cornmeal is then inscribed on the ground, and the snake gatherers throw their armfuls of reptiles into it. Before they can escape, the Snake men grab them and race down the mesa to return them to their homes where, it is hoped, they will act as messengers and carry the Hopis' prayers for rain to the Spirits of the Underworld.

The performers then drink an emetic that causes vomiting—an act of purification that also has an association with rain.

Occasionally snake handlers are bitten by a poisonous snake, but the Hopi have a snake medicine that they use to protect them against the effects of the poison.

WOMEN'S DANCES

The *Marau*, *Lakon*, and *Oaqol* societies hold their rituals in the fall, after the Snake or Flute ceremonies but before the Wuwutsim. The cere-

monies closely duplicate those given by the men's societies, with weather control, fertility, and curing being the primary purposes.

The Lakon ritual is often called a Basket Dance. The performers form a semicircle to sing and dance. At the end of each song they throw gifts to the men who engage in a noisy free-for-all to grab the prizes. Baskets are the most sought-after gifts, but just as much enthusiasm goes into obtaining an ear of corn or a box of matches. Occasionally the gift is rendered totally unusable by the time a winner emerges.

Besides being given away at the Basket Dance, baskets are awarded Hopi runners in ceremonial races.

Apache

Mask worn by the Gaan *or Mountain Spirit Dancers of the Apache people.*

The Apache, who share a common linguistic and cultural background with the Navajo, also share similar religious beliefs and ceremonies (some of which are adapted from the Pueblo tribes). Curing rituals and blessing rites that include, among other things, the use of sandpaintings, make up the bulk of Apache ceremonialism. As a general rule, however, the Apache have fewer ceremonies and these tend to be less complex than those of the Navajo.

DEITIES

Ysun, a supernatural force identified neither by sex nor location, is the Creator of the Universe and looked upon as the Supreme Being. Referred to as "The Giver of Life," Ysun is the source of all power and has great influence over the affairs of people.

Everything on the earth, animate or inanimate, and in the sky is believed to have a spirit—the sun, moon, thunder, wind, and lightning are especially powerful. Thunder Beings once lived with the people and served as hunters by killing game with flint-tipped shafts of lightning. The earth itself is often referred to as Earth Woman but it is not personified.

Changing Woman existed "from the beginning" and is the most important female deity. Born-of-Water and Monster Slayer, whose mythological exploits are similar to those of the Navajo Twin War Gods, are also important supernatural figures. They are the children of White Shell Woman.

White Shell Woman (or White Painted Woman, as she is sometimes called) and Changing Woman are closely associated with one another, but the exact relationship is not consistent among various Apache bands. Similarly, Born-of-Water and Monster Slayer may be identified as sons, husbands, or brothers of White Shell Woman. In one version of the creation myth, Born-of-Water is described as creating humans of mud or clouds, but generally Monster Slayer is regarded as the most important figure after Ysun.

A lesser but still important category of supernatural beings includes the Mountain People and Water People. The latter is made up of He Who Controls Water, a being who is dressed in a shirt of colored clouds and is responsible for the rains, and Water Monster, an unpleasant creature in serpent or human form which inhabits lakes and springs and causes the drowning of people and animals.

The Mountain People are the more important beings in this grouping. Called *Gaan* (and similar to the Navajo *Yei* or Hopi *Katsina*) these supernaturals are identified with the specific mountaintops and caves that they inhabit. Like the Thunder Beings they too once lived with ordinary people but, wishing to avoid the death that humans must eventually face, they left to seek a world of eternal life.

Coyote, in his usual role as troublemaker, is held responsible for bringing to man such undesirable things as death, gluttony, thievery, adultery, and lying. Among a few Apache bands, however, Coyote was credited with teaching people how to weave baskets, tan hides, and prepare various foods—but then had to be banished from the camps for his thievery.

MOUNTAIN SPIRIT DANCE

Today the most important and elaborate ceremony given by the Apache is the girls' puberty rite. It is the only one they still have in common

The Gaan *traditionally appeared during times of impending disaster among the Apache people. They appear now only during the* Nah'ih'es *or coming-of-age ceremonies of Apache young women. They prevent any evil from disrupting the proceedings and possess power to cure by blowing away sickness. Ray Naha*

In Apache religion, one gains religious power through visions or dreams. The test of that power or the truth of the dream comes in the success (or failure) of the shaman—who may be a man or a woman. Delmar Boni

with their Athabascan-speaking relatives in Canada. According to their mythology it was White Shell Woman who taught this important ritual to the Apaches, and it is she with whom the young women identify during this annual summer ceremony.

Coming-of-age ceremonies are expensive affairs anywhere, and Apache society is no exception. The family of the young woman must hire a shaman (either male or female) to conduct the ceremony, provide payment for the Gaan dancers, and furnish huge quantities of food for the large number of friends, family, and visitors who will gather to attend the rituals and take part in the related social events.

On the first day a tipi frame is constructed of four spruce saplings to house the young girl and her older female attendant. The girl is dressed in ceremonial garments made of buckskin that have been painted yellow, the color of sacred pollen. The costume is a duplicate of the one worn by White Shell Woman, decorated with symbols of the moon, sun, and stars. The long fringe represents sunbeams.

The girl is believed to possess special curative powers at this time of her life, and may treat the sick and afflicted by touching or massaging.

Between the lengthy chants sung by the shaman (during which the girl dances on a buckskin) she attends all who come to her for aid.

Many taboos must be observed by the young lady, for her future depends on her disposition and deportment during the four-day ritual. She is cautioned against smiling or laughing because this would result in premature wrinkling. The ceremonial is symbolic of the life journey the girl will take. If all goes well she will enjoy a long, happy, and healthful life on the "pollen path."

On each of the four nights, impersonators of the Gaan—Mountain Spirits—will perform to bless the encampment and drive away any evil that may disrupt the proceedings. During this time the Mountain Spirit Dancers (often incorrectly referred to as Crown or Devil Dancers) also possess powers to cure and may treat patients by blowing away the sickness. The Gaan are popular with the Apache, and there is much rivalry among dance groups. In early times the Gaan

Central to the Apache creation story, depicted here by Yavapai-Apache artist Duke Sine, is Changing Woman, believed by many to represent the Earth itself. Her child, Born-of-Water (below) joined with Monster Slayer (right) to rid the earth of monsters, making it safe for the humans who would follow. To the left are the Gaan or Mountain Spirits—guardians of the Apache people. The game animals are at right, while animals not meant to be hunted for food are at left—including Coyote, who stole fire for the humans. The hummingbirds at each corner are messengers carrying the news that the Apache people have emerged.

dancers often appeared to protect the bands from impending disasters such as epidemics. Now their appearances are limited to puberty rites and public exhibitions.

The dancers, who may number anywhere from 4 to 16 plus 1 or more clowns, are painted under the direction of the shaman. At dusk they enter the dance ground, first approaching both the central fire and ceremonial tipi four times as a blessing.

A chorus, which carries the refrain to the verses sung by the medicine man, and a drummer accompany the dancers. The song determines which dance step will be used—short, high, or free. Aside from the basic step restriction, each dancer performs as an individual. The dance itself is characterized by short, jerky, angular movements, and much posturing and gesturing with painted swordlike wands of yucca.

The dancers perform at intervals throughout each night. In between times the crowd participates in Round Dances—a form of social dancing identical with the Round Dance of the Navajo.

At the end of four days the tipi is ceremonially dismantled and the visitors depart. The family remains at the campground until the ninth day, on which the girl is purified by a bath in yucca suds. She then assumes the role of a marriageable woman.

Tohono O'odham

While there is considerable doubt—among both tribal elders and archaeologists—as to how closely related the ancient Hohokam and the Tohono O'odham are, Hohokam motifs are sometimes utilized by tribal artists.

ORIGIN MYTH

The origin myth, which takes an experienced storyteller four nights to complete, varies considerably in detail among the four dialect divisions of the Tohono O'odham. The version given here, which shares some similarities with Pueblo emergence legends, is a mere outline of the full story.

In the beginning there was only a darkness in which Earthmaker and Buzzard drifted.

Earthmaker rubbed dirt from his skin and held it in his hand—out of it grew a greasewood (creosote) bush. From a ball of gum taken from the creosote Earthmaker then created the world. As the earth was being joined to the sky, *I'itoi*, another supernatural, came into being. *Coyote*, who served as a messenger for the deities, also appeared about the same time.

The newly formed universe was a wobbly affair until the Spider People sewed the earth and sky together. Buzzard formed the water courses with his wing tips, and Earthmaker created the stars, sun, and moon.

The first attempt to create human life resulted in imperfect beings, so the supernaturals brought about a flood to destroy them. Before the flood Earthmaker, I'itoi, and Coyote agreed among themselves that the first of them to appear afterwards would be known as Elder Brother. I'itoi emerged first and assumed the title.

Elder Brother then formed new human beings from clay, but this led to a conflict with Earthmaker who angrily disappeared underground where he lives today.

I'itoi dwelt with his creations (identified as the ancient Hohokam), and taught them how to live in the desert and gave them ceremonies necessary to bring rain. Hostility between I'itoi and the people broke out, and they decided to kill him. In four years I'itoi revived with the help of the winds, and then went underground to secure aid from the people there. These were the Pima and Tohono O'odham and they agreed to help I'itoi.

In this extremely dry land, "life-giving water" is more than an idle phrase. As evidenced by these large, well-formed water jars, the O'odham treat it preciously.

Gopher burrowed through the ground to lead the people out of the four Underworlds. With I'itoi's assistance they drove out the Hohokam. I'itoi then helped the Pima and Tohono O'odham establish themselves in the desert. In one version he explained that he was giving the Tohono O'odham the arid desert because only they, of all peoples, could survive there. The boundaries for each group were marked by corn kernels carried by the winds. I'itoi then left and returned to live underground in the vicinity of Baboquivari Peak.

CURING RITES

Most human disease is believed to be caused by animals that have been injured or otherwise treated disrespectfully. Medicine men called *makahs* have the power to diagnose the cause, and the patient then goes to a singer who possesses the power and fetishes to effect a cure.

Rattlesnakes can cause stomach aches—sore feet might be caused by a horned lizard. Offending a turtle could result in a crippled leg, and a deer that had been left wounded could bring rheumatism. Each malady requires a series of songs to cure it. In case the disease is traced to an animal introduced by the Spaniards, it might be necessary to recite a rosary.

AFTERWORLD

Disposal of the corpse took place soon after death, as the ghosts of the deceased were greatly feared. Formerly burial was made in a rock crevice and covered with stones, or in a stone cairn roofed with wood. Food and possessions were placed with the body in the grave to accompany the spirit on its four-day journey to the Underworld in the East. The afterworld was believed to be a place of much rain and plenty of food.

In small villages scattered in the vastness of the Sonoran Desert can be found large ramadas in front of traditional Rain Houses where ceremonies like the Wi:gida *are held. While most ceremonies held in public were traditionally open to attendance by Indian and non-Indian alike, the desire of non-Indians to know every detail, down to the most secret (and therefore most powerful) aspect, combined with the problem of sheer numbers, has forced many tribes to become more protective of their traditions.*

Today, annual offerings of food and drink are made at graves of the deceased on All Souls Day, a practice borrowed from the Mexicans, but not unlike the native custom.

TOHONO O'ODHAM CEREMONIES

Although most Tohono O'odham have long been converted to various Christian sects, a number of the old ceremonials are still performed.

Tohono O'odham ceremonialism is a mixture of hunting and agricultural rituals. The most important aspect of each rite is the bringing of life-sustaining rain to the land. Any successfully conducted ritual (inter-village races and games, salt pilgrimages to the Sea of Cortez, dances, curing and puberty rites, as well as ceremonies performed at local shrines) can bring rain.

Though rarely seen by non-Tohono O'odham, the Wi:gida, *a harvest ceremony, is still held. The recent publication of a 50-year-old description of this ceremony caused a controversy because of the tribe's desire to protect its traditions. Mike Chiago*

SAGUARO WINE FESTIVAL

Late in June, when the fruit of the giant saguaro cactus ripens, the Tohono O'odham conduct a ceremony to celebrate what is essentially the beginning of the new year. The period just before the saguaro harvest was one of starvation, for neither cultivated nor wild crops were available yet and last year's provisions were usually gone. It was once the custom to take the first ripened saguaro fruit one found and hold it over one's heart and breathe a silent prayer of thanksgiving.

This particular ceremony, called the *Nawait*, was taught them by I'itoi. According to one version, they had to hold the ceremony in order to convince Wind and Rain to return after an absence of several years. The saguaro, which produces fresh fruit, syrup, and a meal made from the seeds, can also produce a wine—from the fermented syrup.

The syrup-making process produces a juice that is allowed to ferment for three days in the Rain House, under the care of the Keeper of the Smoke, who is the village headman and ceremonial leader. Rain songs are sung while the liquid ferments, and the men and women—who once painted their torsos with butterfly designs—dance at night. As a part of the fertility ritual, sexual license was permitted at this time.

At noon on the third day, the headmen gathered to recite long poems over the baskets of wine. The men of the village sat in a circle and passed the baskets around until they were drained. The drinking of wine, like the smoking of tobacco, was considered a ceremonial duty and was not indulged in for mere pleasure.

The planting of crops takes place after the wine festival to make use of the rains that are bound to follow.

The Corso de Gallo *or Chicken Pull is a ritual that has rainmaking significance and is usually held on San Juan's Day (June 24), locally thought of as the first day of the summer rains. Leonard Chana*

Today, some families also prepare saguaro wine for their own use at this time, but the custom to "cover the wine with a song" continues and anyone who accepts a drink of the liquor must recite a poem relating to clouds and rains.

TCIRKWENA DANCE

It used to be customary for villages to challenge one another to games, contests, or dances. One such dance is the *Tcirkwena*, referred to variously as a Skipping Dance, Season Dance, or Winter Rain Dance.

The series of eight songs required for these dances were dreamed by a singer. This man would then train young boys and girls to perform the dance steps. During the dance they carry effigies of birds, clouds, or rainbows made of cotton.

Musical accompaniment is provided by basket drums, rasps, and a chorus of older men (or women, today) who had learned the song series.

The village that hosts the dancers considers the ceremony as a blessing which assures them of sufficient rainfall. The older women of the village might honor the visitors by dancing alongside them. After the performance, guests are given a feast and gifts in payment.

CHICKEN PULL

Corso de Gallo, or the Chicken Pull, is a game that was introduced into the Southwest along with the horse by the Spaniards. It is a contest of riding skill, traditionally performed on San Juan's Day (June 24), though it may be held at other times as a separate event or in connection with a native ceremonial.

The Tohono O'odham version of the Chicken Pull takes place on a sandy racetrack several hundred feet long. Halfway down the track a live rooster is buried up to its neck in the loose sand. Individual riders galloping past lean far out of their saddles and attempt to pull the rooster out of the ground. The rooster frantically tries to dodge the grasping fingers, and it usually takes many tries before a rider succeeds in wrenching the luckless fowl free.

A general free-for-all follows with all riders trying to grab the rooster and the successful contestant beating off the attackers by swinging the rooster at them.

Most tribes that adopted the Chicken Pull have given it some religious connotation. Among the Rio Grande pueblos it has an agricultural significance with the "planting" and subsequent removal of the rooster as symbolic of sowing and reaping. The blood and feathers of the fowl and the foam and sweat of the lathered horses represent rain and clouds, and are considered to be a blessing for the earth, promoting fertility.

Among the Tohono O'odham the rainmaking significance was probably the main consideration, for locally San Juan's Day is still traditionally thought of as a day of rain—often the first of summer.

Yaqui

The Yaqui world is called *Huiya Ania,* and within that world exists the *Seah Ania* or Flower World, which then contains the *Yo Ania* or Enchanted World where many of the spirits or spiritual forces reside. Then comes the *Tuka Ania* or Night World which includes all types of night phenomena and finally, within that, the *Tenka Ania* or Dream World, which is the source of dreams for the individual.

Yaqui legend tells of a time when there appeared a tree that spoke, but in a strange language none knew. Many came but no one could understand its words. Finally, two daughters of an old man came and listened and were able to translate. The Talking Tree prophesied the coming of Christianity, loss of lands, war and even, some say, drug abuse problems.

The Yaquis' native religion was greatly changed by the introduction of Catholicism by Jesuit missionaries in the early 1600s. As enthusiastic converts, they soon observed a full Roman Catholic ceremonial calendar. Church rituals were not led by ordained priests, but by Yaqui men known as *maestros* (from Spanish for "teacher") who conducted services in a combination of Spanish, Yaqui, and Latin. Even today the Yaqui churches are totally independent of the Roman Catholic Church.

ARIZONA STATE MUSEUM

The Yaqui Deer Dance is an ancient hunting ritual which has been incorporated into their observance of the Catholic Easter ceremony.

EASTER SEASON

The most elaborate ceremonies conducted in the Yaqui settlements of southern Arizona occur during Lent. These include the Yaqui version of the Catholic liturgy for the Lenten season and Easter, and a Passion play. The basic theme presented is the triumph of good over evil.

The *Fariseo* (Pharisees) and *Caballero* societies are in charge of the Easter ceremony. Their members impersonate the enemies of Christ who pursued and persecuted Him. *Chapayekas,* the common soldiers of the Fariseos, wear grotesque masks of painted hide or paper, and carry painted wooden swords and daggers. To prevent the evil he depicts from entering his heart, each Chapayeka must carry the cross of his rosary in his mouth while wearing the mask. The masks have no eyeholes, and can be taken off only when the mask is touching the ground.

The *Matachine* society is a men's dance group under vow to Mary, and is referred to as "soldiers of the Virgin." During the Easter ceremonies they are allied with the church group, led by the maestros, in opposition to the Fariseos. They wear headdresses decorated with paper flowers and ribbons, and carry wands decorated with brightly colored feathers. The young boys wear white dresses and act as guardians of the Virgin. The dances this group performs, including a maypole dance, all appear to be of European origin.

The Chapayekas *represent the soldiers of the* Fariseos *(Pharisees) in the Yaqui Easter ceremony. When they attack the church on Holy Saturday, the* Matachines *successfully defend it, "killing" the Chapayekas with flowers. Later, a figure of Judas is burned along with all the masks and equipment of the Chapayekas in order to purify the village of the evil they have absorbed.*

On Holy Saturday, the Matachines successfully defend the church against attack by the Fariseos and "kill" the Chapayekas with a barrage of flowers. (Flowers play an important part in Yaqui ceremonies—they represent divine blessings, a state of holiness, and a protection against evil.) The masks and equipment of the Chapayekas are later burned on a pyre along with a figure of Judas.

A feather wand and rattle are carried by each Matachine dancer during part of the Easter ceremonies. The Matachines are the "soldiers of the Virgin."

FIESTA DANCERS

The only remaining rituals of native origin are the performances of the *Pahkolas*, the *Maaso* or Deer Dancer, and the Coyote Society. Though the Pahkolas may appear at fiestas in their capacity as the hosts or "old men of the fiesta," they are best known and most often seen in connection with the Yaqui Deer Dance ceremony held at Easter. The Deer Dance itself is an ancient hunting ceremonial that dramatizes this once-important activity. Although these impersonators take part in the church processions, most of the dancing takes place in a small ramada at some distance from the chapel.

The Pahkolas *are generally thought of as the Old Men or hosts of the fiestas. During the Deer Dance they take the role of hunters. They may also take part in church processions.*

A chorus of three Deer Singers, who also play a water drum (a half gourd turned hollow side down in a bowl of water) and rasps, sing ancient hunting chants that poetically describe the world of the deer. A fourth musician simultaneously plays a two-piece bamboo flute and a flat, hide-covered drum.

The Pahkolas are aligned with the church when it is under attack by the Fariseos. During their own dances they act the part of clowns and entertain the spectators with jokes, pantomime, and horseplay.

The Pahkolas' dance has a shuffling step that emphasizes the soft rustling sound of their cocoon leg rattles. A jangling beat is provided by a wood rattle with metal disks, which is struck in the palm of one hand. When performing they wear a small wooden mask over the face—otherwise it is worn at the side of the head.

The Deer impersonator, the Maaso, wears a deer head when dancing. Red ribbons representing flowers are wound about the horns. The original purpose of this dance was to honor the deer so that it would allow itself to be caught by the hunters. The dance itself is a perfect pantomime of the deer's movements. More rapid and tense than the Pahkolas' dance, the Maaso maintains a steady "roll" with his gourd rattles, pausing occasionally to posture in imitation of a living deer.

THE COYOTE DANCERS

The *Go'i* or Coyote Society is a military society responsible for the defense of the village and discipline within the village. The Coyote Dancers may appear at any Yaqui fiesta or *wardia*, where they set their chairs, perform their dances, and honor their saint.

They dance to songs composed about various animals, and carry bows on which they tap a beat with a bamboo staff. The drummer uses a flat hide-covered drum that is slightly smaller and higher in tone than that used by the drummer who accompanies the Maaso.

The Maaso *or Deer Dancer is an important and powerful figure to the Yaqui. Though he appears during the Yaqui Easter ceremonies—a basically Catholic event—he has ties to the ancient beliefs and religion of the Yaqui as they existed before the coming of the Europeans. Ryan Huna Smith*

Peyote

Peyote (*Lophophora williamsii*) is a small turnip-shaped, spineless cactus that grows in the lower Rio Grande Valley from southern New Mexico and Texas southward to Nayarit, Mexico. It contains alkaloid substances that are hallucinogenic in nature—that is, they induce dreams or visions. Reactions to peyote seem to vary with the social situation under which it is used. In some it may merely cause nausea, while believers may experience optic, olfactory, and auditory sensations. They often report color visions, and say that the peyote may be "heard" singing or speaking. The effects wear off within 24 hours and leave no ill aftereffects. Peyote is non-addictive.

The use of peyote in rituals began in pre-Columbian times in Mexico. The Spaniards recorded its use by the Aztecs. It is still used today by the Tarahumara, Huichol, and Cora. Its purpose varies considerably, from use as a charm in footraces and hunting to a medicine in curing rites. It may also be employed to predict the weather or to locate lost objects (revelations appear in peyote-induced visions). Peyote also appears in elaborate rain-making ceremonies.

Peyote was introduced into the southern Plains in the 1840s. The Lipan Apache, Comanche, and Kiowa were the first tribes to adopt it. The first usage was primarily medicinal in nature—in the vision induced by peyote the patient made contact with supernatural powers that restored his health. Vomiting caused by nausea was believed to rid the body of the illness and spiritually purify it.

Occasionally peyote was used in connection with warfare—it revealed the location of the enemy by means of a vision or by speaking to the user.

From the southern Plains the use of peyote spread eastward to the Great Lakes regions and northward into parts of Canada. As it spread to other tribes, each group adapted peyote to fit their own cultural background. Following suppression of the Ghost Dance religion during the early reservation era, the peyote cult gained many followers. The drastic and demoralizing changes caused by reservation life made the Indian people receptive to a new religious philosophy that gave them a sense of well-being and pride, and stressed the importance of the "Indianness" of the participants. It was a religion of hope for a defeated people and its followers benefited spiritually, physically, and mentally.

It was at this time that the Native American Church had its beginnings. Drawing much from Christian teachings, it made use of peyote as a sacrament. The peyotists claim the white man had the Bible so he could learn about God—the Indian was given peyote for the same purpose. Biblical passages (all references to herbs are

K. C. DEN DOOVEN

Shown here with a mescal bean necklace worn by some practitioners, are the peyote "buttons" which contain a hallucinogenic used to create the visions or dreams that are a part of the religious services of the Native American Church.

construed to include peyote) were often quoted to justify its use.

The Native American Church stresses a high moral code, which includes brotherly love, care of the family, self-reliance, and the avoidance of alcohol.

Incorporated in 1918, the N.A.C., whose membership is restricted to American Indians, is estimated to have 500,000 followers. Not all peyote users, however, are members of the church.

There has been much opposition to the peyote cults. Tribal members who follow their traditional religion are naturally upset over the introduction of a new religion, and oppose it on the grounds that it is "foreign." Many Christian sects working among Indians oppose peyote because it "misinterprets" Christian beliefs to accommodate the use of peyote. Despite this opposition—and often because of it—the peyote cults continue to grow.

Tribes, states, and the federal government have had differing, evolving, and generally con-

The peyote box of a Road Chief includes rattles, fans, and a two-part staff, designed to fit in the box. They are frequently heavily beaded. A buckskin-covered metal drum, wooden beater, and eagle-bone whistle are also part of his belongings. The fan is used in blessing and purifying rites.

flicting legislation regarding the use of peyote. In 1994, federal legislation was finally passed that allows for the sacramental use of peyote by American Indians.

NAVAJO PEYOTISM

Despite its early appearance in the Southwest, the use of peyote among Navajos was unknown until the 1920s. Southern Ute medicine men who used peyote to treat Navajo patients were the first contacts they had with either the cactus or the cult. The success of peyote as a medicine in the treatment of their illnesses led many of them to follow the "Peyote Road." Through the closely knit extended family and clan system, knowledge of peyotism spread.

Then, as now, many cult members continued to make use of traditional Navajo curing rites and, as with other tribal groups, modified the rituals to fit their own cultural traditions.

The rapid spread of peyotism on the Navajo reservation in the late 1930s is attributed to the economic stresses caused by the government's stock reduction program. As their way of life appeared to be threatened, some Navajos found a sense of security in the peyote religion.

The sudden increase in peyote users alarmed many traditionalists, government officials, and missionaries, and resulted in official action by the Navajo tribal council. In 1940 the sale, use, or possession of peyote on the Navajo reservation was declared an offense punishable by fine and/or imprisonment. Despite this prohibition the cult continued to grow. By 1950 an estimated 9,000 to 10,000 Navajos were peyotists. In 1965 the number had grown to between 25,000 and 35,000 and is still increasing, with current estimates ranging up to 80,000. In 1967, the Navajo tribal council voted to allow use of peyote by N.A.C. members.

PEYOTE CEREMONY

There is no strict service that must be followed in conducting peyote ceremonies either by members of the Native American Church or non-affiliated users.

Among the Navajo peyote users, ceremonies may be given to bless a new house, celebrate a birthday or special holiday, solemnize a wedding, ensure good health, cure an illness, or treat substance abuse problems.

The meeting is usually sponsored by a family who arranges for a Road Chief to conduct the ceremony and provides food and peyote buttons for guests.

The meeting, usually held in a hogan, though occasionally in a tipi, begins at sundown with preparation of a crescent-shaped altar by the Road Chief, and kindling of a ritually laid fire by the Fire Chief. The altar represents the universe to some, and the moon to others. A line drawn through the length of the crescent is symbolic of the Peyote Road. In the middle of the altar, on a bed of sage, is placed Chief (or Father) Peyote, a button of unusual size.

Other opening rites include the blessing and purifying—in cedar smoke—of the peyote paraphernalia. Sage is also smudged and passed around to be rubbed on the hands and body as a medicine.

Cigarettes are ritually smoked by all present,

In this Navajo painting, a Road Chief is beginning the rapid drumbeat that accompanies the singing and chanting that goes on during much of the evening. He is also responsible for building the crescent-shaped altar which will have a "tail" of ash added to it, transforming it into a bird image.
Beatian Yazz

four puffs each to the Road Chief, Mother Earth, and the participant as a blessing and prayer. Peyote buttons are then passed around for the members to eat.

The Road Chief begins the singing with four opening songs, followed by solo performances by the drummer and Cedar Chief and later by other members.

During the evening the fire is constantly tended by the Fire Chief whose duty it is to keep the fire and altar in order. During the course of the night he adds a "tail" of ash to the crescent altar, transforming it into an eagle or thunderbird.

At midnight the Road Chief sings another set of songs, and water is brought in to be drunk. More cigarettes are smoked as prayers, started by members and finished by the Road Chief, to assure that the prayers will be heard. The Road Chief then goes outside to blow an eagle bone whistle to call the spirits. Occasionally confessions or testimonials to the power of peyote may be given by those present.

If the ceremony is being conducted as a curing rite, the Road Chief chews a peyote button and gives it to the patient to swallow. He also purifies

him by fanning him with cedar smoke.

At first morning light water is again served by the Water Woman (sometimes called Peyote Woman), and the Road Chief sings his special morning water songs.

After the closing ceremony, which includes four more songs by the Road Chief, the ritual disposal of cigarette stubs, and final prayers, the people gather outdoors for a feast.

During the course of the evening an average of four buttons is consumed by each person present and participating. The successful worshipper may see visions, or hear peyote talk to him and instruct him on how to solve his problems or improve his life. If he is sick or depressed peyote may cure him. The evening is spent in contemplation and communion with God, with peyote serving as the sacrament. Occasionally cult members will eat a bit of peyote at other times as a prayer, but generally the belief is that peyote is not effective outside of meetings. The companionship of fellow peyote members also enhances the sense of well-being resulting from the use of peyote itself.

Calendar of Southwestern Indian Ceremonials

Dates given here are approximate—ceremonies may be scheduled to fall on the nearest weekend to permit participation by tribal members who live or work in town. Many dances are scheduled a few weeks in advance or are announced annually.

Inquire locally for exact date and village if not given here. Also, due to the large numbers of visitors and periodic outrageous violations by non-Indians of tribal prohibitions against recording religious observances, not all of these ceremonials are still open to the public, and those that are may not be open every year.

NOTE: Taping, photographing, sketching, or note-taking at Indian ceremonials is generally strictly forbidden. In some cases photography anywhere on the reservation may be subject to paying a fee and receiving written permission. Even where photographs are being allowed, it is best to inquire first and receive formal permission. Please do not create unpleasant incidents by ignoring tribal regulations. For general conduct, a good rule of thumb is simply this: anything you would not hesitate to do (or wear) in your place of worship or community is probably also permissible at an Indian ceremonial or reservation.

ARIZONA

Date	Event	Tribe and Location
Feb.—usually last three weekends	Powamu (Bean Dance).	Hopi—all villages.
February through April	Night Katsina Dances.	Hopi—all villages.
Easter—from Ash Wednesday through Easter	Easter Ceremonies.	Yaqui. Villages of Pascua, New Pascua, and Barrio Libre (Tucson) and Guadalupe (Tempe).
April through July	Daytime Katsina Dances.	Hopi—all villages.
June 24	San Juan's Day—Chicken Pull.	Tohono O'odham, Santa Rosa, and other villages.
Late June or early July	Saguaro Wine Festival.	Tohono O'odham. Various villages.
Middle to late July	Niman (Home Dance).	Hopi—all villages.
July 30-31	San Ignacio's Day. Fiesta and dances.	Yaqui—Pascua.
Middle to late August	Flute Dance.	Hopi. Odd years at Shipaulovi, Shungopavy, and Hotevilla. Even years at Mishongnovi and Walpi.
August, third weekend	Peach Festival.	Havasupai at Supai village.
October 4 and prior week	Fiesta of Saint Francis.	Yaqui and Tohono O'odham pilgrimage to Magdalena, Sonora.

NEW MEXICO

Date	Event	Tribe and Location
January 1	Tablita and Turtle Dances.	Cochiti, San Juan, Taos, and Zia.
January 6	King's Day. Animal or Eagle dances in most Rio Grande pueblos.	Cochiti, Jemez, Sandia, San Juan, San Ildefonso, Tesuque, Taos, and Zia.
January 23	Buffalo and Comanche Dances	San Ildefonso.
February—entire month	Frequent dances in most Rio Grande pueblos.	Inquire locally for time and place.
February 2	Buffalo Dance.	San Felipe.
February 15	Buffalo Dance.	San Juan.
March 19	Fiesta and dances.	Laguna.
April 1	Spring Corn or Tablita Dances.	Most pueblos.
Easter	Tablita Dances. Races.	Most pueblos.
May 1	Tablita Dance.	San Felipe.
May 3	Santa Cruz Day. Tablita Dance.	Taos.
May 3	Tablita Dance and Coming of the River Men.	Cochiti.
June—first week	Corn Dance.	Tesuque.
June	Katsina Dances.	Zuni.
June 8	Buffalo Dance.	Santa Clara.
June 13	San Antonio's Day. Tablita or Buffalo Dances.	Cochiti, Sandia, San Juan, Santa Clara, San Ildefonso, Taos, and Ysleta del Sur.
June 24	San Juan's Day. Dances, races, and Chicken Pulls.	Acoma, Cochiti, Santa Ana, Santo Domingo, and Isleta.
July 4	Nambe Ceremonial.	Nambe Falls.

July 4	Mescalero Apache Gaan Dancers and Rodeo.	Mescalero.
July 14	San Buenaventura's Day. Tablita Dance.	Cochiti.
July 25 and 26	Santiago's and Santa Ana's Day. Corn Dances and Rabbit Hunt.	Acoma, Cochiti, Laguna, Santa Ana, and Taos.
Late July	Santa Clara Ceremonial at Puyé Cliff Dwellings.	Puyé.
August 2	Old Pecos Bull Dance.	Jemez.
August 4	Corn Dance.	Santo Domingo.
August 10	San Lorenzo's Day. Fiesta and Corn Dances.	Picuris, Acomita, and Laguna.
August 12	Santa Clara's Day Dances.	Santa Clara.
August 15	Corn Dance.	Zia.
August 15	Harvest Dance.	Laguna (Mesita).
August 28	Fiesta.	Isleta.
September 2	Harvest Dance and Fiesta.	Acoma.
September 4	San Augustin's Day. Harvest Dance.	Isleta.
September 8	Harvest Dance.	Laguna (Encinal Village).
September 8	Corn Dance.	San Ildefonso.
September 19	Harvest Dance.	Laguna.
September 25	St. Elizabeth's Day. Corn Dances.	Laguna.
September 29	Various dances.	Taos.
September 30	San Geronimo's Day. Pole climbing by Koshares. Races, dances.	Taos.
September—last week	Evergreen Dances.	Isleta (date announced annually).
	Harvest Dances.	San Juan (date announced annually).
October 4	Elk Dance and Fiesta.	Nambe.
October 17	Corn Dance.	Laguna (Paraje Village).
November 12	Corn Dance and Fiesta.	Jemez.
November 12	San Diego's Day. Animal Dances.	Tesuque.
Late November or early December	Shalako.	Zuni.
December 12	Matachine Dance.	Jemez.
December 24	Ceremonial dances in mission churches. Processions.	Most pueblos.
December 25	Various dances.	Most pueblos.
December 26	Turtle Dance.	San Juan.
December 26	Matachine Dance.	Taos.
December 31	Deer Dance.	Sandia.
Late December	Animal and other dances.	Most pueblos.

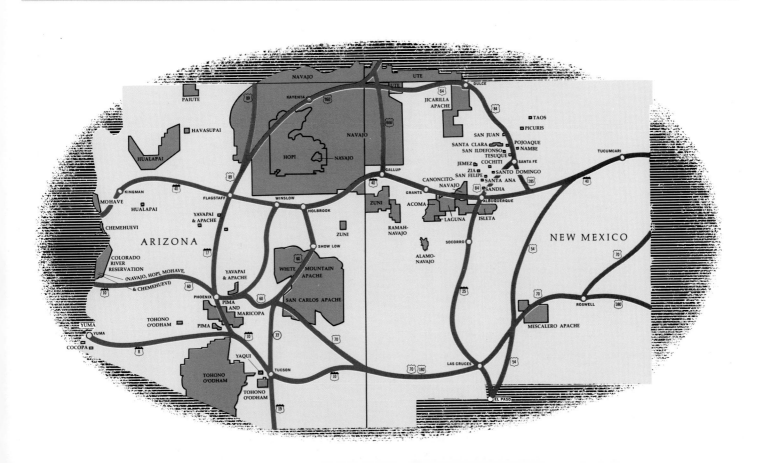

*T*he artwork of youth reflects the values and traditions
of their culture. Santa Clara Pueblo artist,
Heather Dashono, age 12, titled her painting
"Symbols of My Culture." The work of these new artists
indicates the artistic future of the Indians
will be as rich as the past.

Glossary

Anasazi. A Pueblo culture which occupied the Four Corners region beginning about 500 B.C. The Anasazi period is recognized as ending by A.D. 1540—when the Spanish entered the Southwest. Anasazi is from a Navajo word meaning "ancient enemies." Increasingly today, these people are referred to as Ancestral Puebloans.

Art. The tribes of the Southwest have no word for art as we do in English. Art is thoroughly integrated into their traditional way of life and so did not require a separate word.

Bezel. A thin strip of silver that holds a stone in place.

Bureau of Indian Affairs. Originally under the War Department in 1824, placed under the Department of the Interior in 1849. It is responsible for carrying out the trust obligations, created by treaty, of the federal government for the sovereign Indian nations. Since a 1991 act of Congress, more than 30 tribes have begun to assume control of their programs and services. The BIA is currently Indian-run, and the majority of its employees are Indian.

Cacique. A Spanish term, it is used in a confusing number of ways. Early on, many pueblos regarded the position as one created or imposed by the Spanish. Now it is often used to designate a traditional pueblo religious leader.

Ceremony. A religious observance which can include prayers, chants, songs, and dance, among other elements. Its focus can be as specific as curing, hunting, planting, or the bringing of rain—or as general (and important) as the renewal of the cycle of life.

Clan. A division within a tribe into which one is born. Depending upon the tribe, there may be special religious obligations or even different migration legends.

Clusterwork. A type of jewelry where a number of stones are arranged in a geometric pattern, each in its own silver bezel. It is usually associated with the Zuni and includes petitpoint and needlepoint work.

Coiled basketry. This technique involves a coil which spirals out from the center or beginning of the basket. Each row (turn) of the coil is stitched to the one below until the desired size and shape is reached.

Dance. The word commonly used by Indian and non-Indian alike to describe a religious observance that includes rhythmic movement and music as part of an involved and complex prayer ritual.

Fetish. An object—carved or in its natural state—which is believed to contain a spirit that, if treated properly and respectfully, will provide some form of supernatural assistance to the owner(s).

Gaan. The Mountain Spirits who dwell in the mountains of Apacheland and protect the Apache people. Also, the name for the Mountain Spirit Dancers who represent the actual Gaan.

Hatathli. Often translated as "medicine man," it is the Navajo name for the individual responsible for providing healing rituals.

Heishe. From a Keresan word for shell that is the generally accepted word for stone or shell beads.

Hogan. The Navajo name for their traditional style of home.

Hohokam. From a Pima Indian expression meaning "those who have gone," it was a cultural complex that occupied the Sonoran Desert region, including its fertile river valleys, from around A.D. 200 until about A.D. 1350. They were best-known for developing an extensive irrigation system.

Katsina. A Hopi term that refers to: a) spirit beings which mediate between the Hopi and the deities, b) dancers which represent the spirits, and c) cottonwood carvings that represent the dancers.

209

Kiva. A building in which many Pueblo religious observances are held. It may be round or rectangular and above or partially below ground, but it invariably has an entrance through an opening in the roof and down a ladder. Also has a hole in the floor symbolizing the place of emergence.

Koko. The Zuni name for the equivalent of the Hopi *katsina.*

Koshare. Striped sacred clowns that appear in pueblos from the Rio Grande to the Hopi. Their significance and role varies tremendously from group to group.

Medicine man. Usually refers to those responsible for healing rituals, but also used at times to refer to a religious leader. In general it is, at best, an inaccurate term.

Needlepoint. A Zuni clusterwork jewelry technique that uses long narrow stones set in individual bezels—often confused with petitpoint work.

Overlay. Traditionally thought of as a Hopi technique, it involves cutting the design out of one sheet of silver and overlaying it on a second, solid sheet and then chemically darkening the background to heighten the contrast.

Pawn jewelry. Once used to refer to fine old jewelry. The practice of pawning jewelry was discontinued on the Navajo Reservation in 1976. The term, now over-used, is no longer significant.

Petitpoint. A style of Zuni clusterwork that uses very tiny round stones, each set in its own bezel—often confused with needlepoint work.

Plaited baskets. A technique that involves weaving flat strips (usually yucca) over and under each other, with both creating the pattern or design.

Pueblo. A Spanish term signifying a village or small town, applied to the dwellings of groups like the Hopi and Zuni. It is also used to refer to the culture of the groups who live in pueblos.

Religion. There is no native word in the languages of the tribes of the Southwest for "religion." In the Hopi language, for example, there is simply the word *Hopitu* which is best translated as "the Hopi way" and includes all aspects of life. Each tribe has its own religion, but religion is such an integral part of their way of life that there was no need for a separate word.

Reservation. First introduced by the English in the 17th century, the concept was used to create borders between Indian land and land where English law was the rule. Later it was used by the Americans to define land open to settlers by confining the Indians. Reservation lands shrank from 138 million acres in 1887 to 48 million in 1934. Most reservations represent only a small fraction of Indian traditional lands and, in some cases, are located hundred of miles from their homeland. The reservation land is held in trust by the federal government for the Indians.

Sandcasting. A silverworking technique, first developed by the Navajo, in which a design is carved into a flat, heat-resistant stone. A second flat stone with a funnel carved into it completes the mold. Molten silver is poured in the top to create a piece of jewelry.

Sandpaintings. The English translation of the Navajo *ikaah,* images created in sand on the ground as part of their healing ceremonies. Also used to refer to the permanent sandpainting art on boards made by the Navajo.

Sgraffito. A surface carving technique applied after a pot is fired. It was first introduced in the 1960s.

Storyteller. Used to refer to the figurines created that honor the role of the storyteller who maintains oral traditions that embody all the values and traditions of the culture and who passes them on to the next generation.

Trading posts. Once an economic mainstay of Navajo life, the old trading posts were part store, part bank, part post office, and part livestock dealer—and often mediated between American laws and Navajo traditions. In the late 1900s their numbers have greatly diminished and their roles have changed tremendously.

Twining. A basketry technique in which the warp or foundation strips are laid radiating out from the center, and the weft strips (which form the pattern) cross over and under as they spiral out.

Yei. A category of spirit beings with supernatural abilities that are often depicted in sandpaintings and occasionally in rugs.

Yeibichai. Literally "yei grandfather"; used most frequently to refer to the masked dancers who represent or impersonate the yei.

Suggested Reading

ADAIR, JOHN. *The Navajo and Pueblo Silversmiths.* Norman: University of Oklahoma Press, 1944. (Still the best overall survey of the history of Indian silversmithing in the Southwest.)

BABCOCK, BARBARA AND GUY AND DORIS MONTHAN. *The Pueblo Storyteller.* Tucson: University of Arizona Press, 1986. (Documents the development of the creation of storyteller figurines and provides an extensive listing of the makers by Pueblo.)

BAHTI, MARK AND EUGENE BAATSOSLANII JOE. *Navajo Sandpainting Art.* Tucson, Arizona: Treasure Chest Publications, 1978. (An overview of Navajo sandpainting from the traditional to sandpainting art with detailed explanations.)

BRANSON, OSCAR T. *Turquoise: Gem of the Centuries.* Tucson, Arizona: Treasure Chest Publications, 1975. (Shows the locations of many of the mines and a range of the types of turquoise from each along with a variety of jewelry styles.)

CUSHING, FRANK H. *Zuni Fetishes.* Introduction by Tom Bahti. Facsimile edition. Las Vegas, Nevada: KC Publications, 1966. (With an updated introduction, it is still the most accurate source of information on the subject.)

DOCKSTADER, FREDERICK J. *The Kachina and the White Man.* Albuquerque: University of New Mexico Press, 1985. (A fine review of non-Indian perspectives on Hopi religion—ranging from observation to interference.)

DOZIER, EDWARD. *The Pueblo Indian of North America.* New York, New York: Holt, Rinehart and Winston, 1968. (A Tewa Indian and anthropologist, Dozier provides a superb introduction to Tewa Indian life.)

DUNN, DOROTHY. *American Indian Painting of the Southwest and Plains Areas.* Albuquerque: University of New Mexico Press, 1968. (An overview of the subject by one of the people most involved with it from the early years of its formal development in the schools.)

EVERS, LARRY, ed. *Between Sacred Mountains.* Tucson: Sun Tracks and the University of Arizona Press, 1982. (This book is part of a series that was one of the first to allow native peoples to speak for themselves.)

GONZALES, CLARA. *The Shalakos Are Coming.* Santa Fe: Museum of New Mexico Press, 1969. (A clear explanation of the Zuni Shalako ceremony.)

HAYES, ALLAN AND JOHN BLUM. *Southwestern Pottery: Anasazi to Zuni.* Flagstaff, Arizona: Northland Press, 1996. (A readable survey of Indian pottery with extensive photos showing the full range of styles, techniques, and expertise.)

HEDLUND, ANN LANE. *Contemporary Navajo Weaving— Thoughts That Count.* Flagstaff: Museum of Northern Arizona, 1994. (A fine updating of recent trends and developments in Navajo textile arts.)

HUCKO, BRUCE. *Where There Is No Name for Art.* Santa Fe, New Mexico: School of American Research Press, 1996. (Along with his other book, *A Rainbow at Night,* a wonderful look at contemporary Indian life through the artwork of Indian children.)

JERNIGAN, WESLEY. *Jewelry of the Prehistoric Southwest.* Albuquerque: University of New Mexico Press, 1976. (Many contemporary jewelry styles owe their roots to prehistoric jewelry traditions which this book covers admirably.)

KAWANO, KENJI. *Warriors: Navajo Code Talkers.* Flagstaff, Arizona: Northland Press, 1990. (A beautiful and moving photo essay of the Navajo men who contributed so much to the success of our Pacific forces in World War II.)

LABARRE, WESTON. *The Peyote Cult.* Hamden, Connecticut: Shoe String Press, 1959. (A good introduction to Peyotism from its origins.)

LOCKE, RAYMOND F. *The Book of the Navajo.* Los Angeles, California: Mankind Publishing, 1976. (An accurate, authoritative volume. Even the Navajo tribe has used this book in classes.)

MAXWELL, GILBERT. *Navajo Rugs: Past, Present and Future.* Santa Fe, New Mexico: Southwest Images [Revised Edition], 1984. (Revised many times, this is still the best overall introduction to Navajo weaving.)

ORTIZ, ALFONSO. *The Tewa World—Time, Being and Becoming in a Pueblo Society.* Chicago, Illinois: University of Chicago Press, 1969. (Provides an insightful view of Tewa Pueblo Indian philosophy and life as explained by a Tewa anthropologist.)

PAINTER, MURIEL T. *With Good Heart.* Tucson: University of Arizona Press, 1986. (The best comprehensive look at the religious beliefs and practices of the Yaqui.)

PARSONS, ELSIE C. *Pueblo Indian Religion.* (2 vols.) Lincoln: University of Nebraska, 1996. (The most comprehensive and accurate book on the subject—meant for people who want to learn, not mimic.)

REICHARD, GLADYS A. *Navajo Religion.* Tucson: University of Arizona Press, 1983. (The best reference on Navajo religion.)

REID, JEFFERSON and STEPHANIE WHITTLESEY. *The Archaeology of Ancient Arizona.* Tucson: University of Arizona Press, 1997. (An excellent overview of the prehistory of many of the major prehistoric cultural groups.)

SECAKUKU, ALPH. *Following the Sun and Moon.* Phoenix, Arizona: Heard Museum, 1995. (A Hopi speaks about Hopi traditions, history, and religion.)

SHERIDAN, THOMAS E. and NANCY PAREZO, eds. *Paths of Life—American Indians of the Southwest and Northern Mexico.* Tucson: University of Arizona Press, 1996. (The tribes themselves had a hand in the exhibit from which this book is drawn, so it provides insights few other sources can.)

SPICER, EDWARD H. *Cycles of Conquest.* Tucson: University of Arizona Press, 1962. (The finest account of the history of the Greater Southwest from pre-contact to the colonial era.)

TANNER, CLARA LEE. *Southwest Indian Painting.* Tucson: University of Arizona Press, 1957. (An excellent survey of Southwest Indian paintings.)

TRIMBLE, STEVE. *The People—Indians of the American Southwest.* Santa Fe, New Mexico: SAR Press, 1993. (A readable narrative of Southwest Indian life that extensively quotes Indian people themselves.)

TRIMBLE, STEVEN. *Talking with the Clay.* Santa Fe, New Mexico: School of American Research Press, 1987. (Gives the reader an opportunity to hear the potter's voice.)

UNDERHILL, RUTH M. *Singing for Power—The Song Magic of the Papago Indians of Southern Arizona.* Tucson: University of Arizona Press, 1993. (The author gathered the information for this book in the 1930s, and it remains one of the best references.)

WHITEFORD, ANDREW HUNTER. *Southwestern Indian Baskets: Their History and Their Makers.* Santa Fe, New Mexico: School of American Research Press, 1988. (No other book covers the subject as well.)

WRIGHT, BARTON. *Hopi Kachinas: The Complete Guide to Collecting Kachina Dolls.* Flagstaff, Arizona: Northland Press, 1977. (A useful guide for both novice and collector—though the latter may find his other book on katsinas necessary as well.)

ZUNI PEOPLE. *The Zunis: Self Portrayals.* Albuquerque: University of New Mexico Press, 1972. (The title pretty much says it all. One of the first books about a tribe by that tribe.)

POETRY

ASTROV, MARGOT. *Winged Serpent.* Boston, Mass.: Beacon Press, 1992.

DAY, A. GROVE. *The Sky Clears.* Lincoln: University of Nebraska Press, 1964.

ROTHENBERG, JEROME, ed. *Shaking the Pumpkin.* Garden City, N.Y.: Doubleday and Co., 1972.

(These three volumes provide examples of poetry and poetic prose from a range of tribes. To miss reading at least one of these is to miss much in all the other arts.)

MUSIC

CANYON RECORDS—Phoenix, Arizona. (They carry music from all the Indian music labels and all styles—from rap to concerto to traditional. Note: Traditional Indian music doesn't sound much like what you usually hear in the movies.)

Index

214